Caribbean Sea

Bay Islands

Roatan · Helena Barbarata

Utila · Bonacca Is.

Puerto Castilla

Cordillera · Trujillo · Brewers Lagoon

uras · Carbon

Juticalpa · Patuca river · C. Gracias á Dios

Wanky bila

Wanks river

Nicaragua

N

0 — 100 mil

## ALSO BY DOUGLAS PRESTON

### Nonfiction Books

*The Monster of Florence* (with Mario Spezi)
*Ribbons of Time*
*The Royal Road*
*Talking to the Ground*
*Cities of Gold*
*Dinosaurs in the Attic*

### Novels

*Impact*
*Blasphemy*
*Tyrannosaur Canyon*
*The Codex*
*Jennie*

### Novels (with Lincoln Child)

#### Agent Pendergast Novels

*The Obsidian Chamber*
*Crimson Shore*
*Blue Labyrinth*
*White Fire*
*Two Graves**
*Cold Vengeance**
*Fever Dream**
*Cemetery Dance*
*The Wheel of Darkness*
*The Book of the Dead***
*Dance of Death***
*Brimstone***
*Still Life with Crows*

*The Cabinet of Curiosities*
*Reliquary*†
*Relic*†

#### Gideon Crew Novels

*Beyond the Ice Limit*
*The Lost Island*
*Gideon's Corpse*
*Gideon's Sword*

#### Other Novels

*The Ice Limit*
*Thunderhead*
*Riptide*
*Mount Dragon*

* The Helen Trilogy
** The Diogenes Trilogy
† *Relic* and *Reliquary* are ideally read in sequence

# THE LOST CITY OF THE MONKEY GOD

 **A TRUE STORY**

## DOUGLAS PRESTON

**GRAND CENTRAL**
PUBLISHING

**LARGE PRINT**

Grand Central Publishing
Hachette Book Group
1290 Avenue of the Americas, New York, NY 10104
grandcentralpublishing.com
twitter.com/grandcentralpub

First edition: January 2017

Grand Central Publishing is a division of Hachette Book Group, Inc. The Grand Central Publishing name and logo are trademarks of Hachette Book Group, Inc.

Library of Congress Cataloging-in-Publication Data

Names: Preston, Douglas J., author.
Title: The Lost City of the Monkey God / Douglas Preston.
Description: First edition. | New York : Grand Central Publishing, 2017. |Includes bibliographical references and index.
Identifiers: LCCN 2016037247| ISBN 9781455540006 (hardback) | ISBN 9781455540020 (e-book) | ISBN 9781455569410 (large print) | ISBN 9781478964520 (audio CD) | ISBN 9781478964513 (audio download)
Subjects: LCSH: Mosquitia (Nicaragua and Honduras)—Description and travel. |Mosquitia (Nicaragua and Honduras)—Discovery and exploration. | Extinct cities—Mosquitia (Nicaragua and Honduras) | Cities and towns, Ancient—Mosquitia (Nicaragua and Honduras) | Indians of Central America—Mosquitia (Nicaragua and Honduras)—Antiquities. | Mosquitia (Nicaragua and Honduras)—Antiquities. | Preston, Douglas J.—Travel—Mosquitia (Nicaragua and Honduras) | BISAC: HISTORY / Americas (North, Central, South, West Indies). | HISTORY / Expeditions & Discoveries. | HISTORY / Latin America / Central America.
Classification: LCC F1509.M9 P74 2017 | DDC 972.85—dc23 LC record available at https://lccn.loc.gov/2016037247

ISBNs: 978-1-4555-4000-6 (hardcover), 978-1-4555-4002-0 (ebook), 978-1-4555-6941-0 (large print)

Printed in the United States of America

LSC-C

10   9   8   7   6   5   4   3   2   1

*To my mother*
*Dorothy McCann Preston*
*Who taught me to explore*

# Contents

## CHAPTER 1

## The Gates of Hell

Deep in Honduras, in a region called La Mosquitia, lie some of the last unexplored places on earth. Mosquitia is a vast, lawless area covering about thirty-two thousand square miles, a land of rainforests, swamps, lagoons, rivers, and mountains. Early maps labeled it the *Portal del Infierno*, or "Gates of Hell," because it was so forbidding. The area is one of the most dangerous in the world, for centuries frustrating efforts to penetrate and explore it. Even now, in the twenty-first century, hundreds of square miles of the Mosquitia rainforest remain scientifically uninvestigated.

In the heart of Mosquitia, the thickest jungle in the world carpets relentless mountain chains, some a mile high, cut by steep ravines, with lofty waterfalls and roaring torrents. Deluged with over ten feet of rain a year, the terrain is regularly swept by flash floods and landslides. It has pools of quickmud that can swallow a person alive. The understory is infested with deadly snakes, jaguars, and thickets of catclaw vines with hooked thorns that tear at flesh and clothing. In Mosquitia an experienced group of explorers, well equipped with machetes and saws, can expect to journey two to three miles in a brutal ten-hour day.

The dangers of exploring Mosquitia go beyond the natural deterrents. Honduras has one of the highest murder rates in the world. Eighty percent of the cocaine from South America destined for the United States is shipped through Honduras, most of it via Mosquitia. Drug cartels rule much of the surrounding countryside and towns. The State Department currently forbids US government personnel from traveling into Mosquitia and the surrounding state of Gracias a Dios "due to credible threat information against U.S. citizens."

This fearful isolation has wrought a curious result: For centuries, Mosquitia has been home to one of the world's most persistent and tantalizing legends. Somewhere in this impassable wilderness, it is said, lies a "lost city" built of white stone. It is called *Ciudad Blanca*, the "White City," also referred to as the "Lost City of the Monkey God." Some have claimed the city is Maya, while others have said an unknown and now vanished people built it thousands of years ago.

\*     \*     \*

On February 15, 2015, I was in a conference room in the Hotel Papa Beto in Catacamas, Honduras, taking part in a briefing. In the following days, our team was scheduled to helicopter into an unexplored valley, known only as Target One, deep in the interior mountains of Mosquitia. The helicopter would drop us off on the banks of an unnamed river, and we would be left on our own to hack out a primitive camp in the rainforest. This would become our base as we explored what we believed to be the ruins of an unknown city. We would be the first researchers to enter that part of Mosquitia. None of us had any idea what we would actually see on the ground, shrouded in dense jungle, in a pristine wilderness that had not seen human beings in living memory.

Night had fallen over Catacamas. The expedition's logistics chief, standing at the head of the briefing room, was an ex-soldier named Andrew Wood, who went by the name of Woody. Formerly a sergeant major in the British SAS and a soldier in the Coldstream Guards, Woody was an expert in jungle warfare and survival. He opened the briefing by telling us his job was simple: to keep us alive. He had called this session to make sure we were aware of the various threats we might encounter in exploring the valley.

He wanted all of us—even the expedition's nominal leaders—to understand and agree that his ex-SAS team was in charge for the days we would be in the wilderness: This was going to be a quasi-military command structure, and we would follow their orders without cavil.

It was the first time our expedition had come together in one room, a rather motley crew of scientists, photographers, film producers, and archaeologists, plus me, a writer. We all had widely varying experience in wilderness skills.

Woody went over security, speaking in his clipped, British style. We had to be careful even before we entered the jungle. Catacamas was a dangerous city, controlled by a violent drug cartel; no one was to leave the hotel without an armed military escort. We were to keep our mouths shut about what we were doing here. We were not to engage in conversation about the project within hearing of hotel staff, or leave papers lying around our rooms referring to the work, or conduct cell phone calls in public. There was a large safe available in the hotel's storage room for papers, money, maps, computers, and passports.

As for the hazards we would face in the jungle, venomous snakes were at the top of the list. The fer-de-lance, he said, is known in these parts as the *barba amarilla* ("yellow beard"). Herpetologists consider it the ultimate pit viper. It kills more people in the New World than any other snake. It comes out at night and is attracted to people and activity. It is aggressive, irritable, and fast. Its fangs have been observed to squirt venom for more than six feet, and they can penetrate even the thickest leather boot. Sometimes it will strike and then pursue and strike again. It often leaps upward as it strikes, hitting above the knee. The venom is deadly; if it doesn't kill you outright through a brain hemorrhage, it may very well kill you later through sepsis. If you survive, the limb that was struck often has to be amputated, due to the necrotizing nature of the poison. We were, Woody said, going into an area where choppers cannot fly at night or in weather; evacuation of a snakebite victim might be delayed for days. He told us to wear our Kevlar snake gaiters at all times, including—especially—when we got up to pee at night. He warned us always to step on top of a log, and then down; we should never put our foot down on the blind side. This was how his friend Steve Rankin, Bear Grylls's producer, was bitten when they were in Costa Rica scouting a location for a show. Even though Rankin was wearing snake gaiters, the fer-de-lance, which was hiding under the far side of the log, hit him on his boot below the protection; the fangs went through the leather like butter. "And here's what happened," Woody said, taking out his iPhone. He passed it around. It displayed a terrifying picture of Rankin's foot afterward, as it was being operated on. Even with antivenin treatment, the foot necrotized and the dead flesh had to be debrided down to tendons and bone. Rankin's foot was saved, but a piece of his thigh had to be transplanted to cover up the gaping wound.* The valley, Woody continued, appeared to be an ideal habitat for the fer-de-lance.

I snuck a glance at my compatriots: The convivial atmosphere of the group earlier in the day, beers in hand around the hotel pool, had evaporated.

Next came a lecture on the disease-bearing insects we might encounter, including mosquitoes** and sand flies, chiggers, ticks, kissing bugs (so called because they like to bite your face), scorpions, and bullet ants, whose bite equals the pain of being shot with a bullet. Perhaps the ghastliest disease endemic to Mosquitia is mucocutaneous leishmaniasis, sometimes called white leprosy, caused by the bite of an infected sand fly. The *Leishmania* parasite migrates to the mucous

---

* The picture is easily found on the web, for those readers with a strong stomach.

** The name Mosquitia does not derive from the insect; rather, it comes from a nearby coastal people of mixed Indian, European, and African ancestry who, centuries ago, acquired muskets (*mosquetes* in Spanish) and became known as the Miskito, Mosquito, or "Musket" people. Some, however, say the name is of indigenous language origin.

membranes of the victim's nose and lips and eats them away, eventually creating a giant weeping sore where the face used to be. He emphasized that it was important to apply DEET from head to toe on a regular basis, spray our clothing with it, and thoroughly cover up after dusk.

We heard about scorpions and spiders climbing into our boots at night, which we were to store upside down on stakes driven into the ground and shake out every morning. He spoke of vicious red ants that swarmed in the understory, and which, at the slightest tremble of a branch, would shower down like rain, getting into our hair, going down our necks, and biting like mad, injecting a toxin that would require an immediate evacuation. Look carefully, he warned, before placing your hand on any branch, stem, or tree trunk. Don't push willy-nilly through dense vegetation. In addition to hiding insects and tree-climbing snakes, many plants sport thorns and spikes that can draw blood. We should wear gloves while in the jungle, preferably the scuba kind, which do a better job preventing the entry of spines. He warned us how easy it was to get lost in the jungle, often a matter of wandering a mere ten or fifteen feet from the group. Under no circumstances would anyone, ever, be allowed to leave camp on his or her own or detach from the group while in the bush. On every trip we took from the base camp, he said, we would be required to carry a backpack with a kit of emergency supplies—food, water, clothing, DEET, flashlight, knife, matches, rain gear—under the assumption that we would get lost and be forced to spend the night sheltering under some dripping log. We were issued whistles, and as soon as we thought we might be lost, we were to stop, blow a distress signal, and wait to be fetched.

I paid attention. I really did. From the safety of the conference room it seemed clear that Woody was simply trying to scare us into line, offering an excess of caution for those expedition members inexperienced in wilderness conditions. I was one of only three people in the room who had actually flown over Target One, the exceedingly remote valley we were headed into. From the air it looked like a sun-dappled tropical paradise, not the dangerous, dank, disease- and snake-infested jungle Woody was picturing. We would be fine.

## CHAPTER 2

**I can tell you only that it is somewhere in the Americas.**

I first heard the legend of the White City in 1996, when I was on assignment from *National Geographic* to write a story about the ancient temples of Cambodia. NASA had recently flown a DC-10 carrying an advanced radar system over various jungle areas of the world, to determine if the radar could penetrate the foliage to reveal what lay hidden beneath. The results were analyzed at NASA's Jet Propulsion Laboratory in Pasadena, California, by a team of experts in remote sensing—that is, analyzing images of the earth taken from space. After crunching the data, the team found the ruins of a previously unknown, twelfth-century temple hidden in the Cambodian jungle. I met with the team's leader, Ron Blom, to find out more.

Blom was not your stereotypical scientist: He was bearded, rugged, and fit, with aviator glasses and an

Indiana Jones hat. He had gained international fame for discovering the lost city of Ubar in the Arabian Desert. When I asked Blom what other projects he was working on, he rattled off a number of missions: mapping the frankincense trade routes across the Arabian Desert, tracking the old Silk Road, and mapping Civil War sites in Virginia. He explained that by combining digitized images in different wavelengths of infrared light and radar, and then "beating up on the data" with computers, they were now able to see fifteen feet beneath desert sands, peer through jungle canopies, and even cancel out modern tracks and roads, revealing ancient trails.

Ancient trails were interesting, but I was particularly enthralled by the idea that this technology might be able to discover other lost cities like Ubar. When I asked him about that, Blom suddenly became evasive. "Let me just say we are looking at other sites."

Scientists are terrible at deception: I knew immediately he was covering up something big. I pressed further, and finally he admitted that it "could be a very major site, but I can't talk about it. I'm working for a private party. I've signed a nondisclosure agreement. It's based on legends of a lost city. I can tell you only that it's somewhere in the Americas. The legends suggested a general area, and we're using satellite data to locate targets."

"Have you found it?"

"I can't say more than that."

"Who are you working with?"

"I can't reveal that information."

Blom agreed to pass on my interest to his mysterious employer and ask him or her to call me. He couldn't promise that the person would be in touch.

Inflamed with curiosity about the possible identity of this "lost city," I called up several Central American archaeologists I knew, who offered their own speculations. David Stuart, then assistant director of the Corpus of Maya Hieroglyphic Inscriptions Program at Harvard's Peabody Museum and one of those who contributed to the decipherment of Mayan glyphs, told me: "I know that area pretty well. Some of it is almost unexplored by archaeologists. Local people were always telling me about sites they'd see while hunting out in the forest—big ruins with sculptures. Most of these stories are true; these people have no reason to lie." In Mayan texts themselves, he added, there are also tantalizing references to major cities and temples that are not correlated with any known sites. It is one of the last areas on earth where an actual pre-Columbian city could be hidden, untouched for centuries.

The Harvard Mayanist Gordon Willey (now deceased) immediately brought up the legend of the

White City. "I remember when I was down in Honduras in 1970, there was talk of a place called Ciudad Blanca, the White City, back in there away from the coast. It was bar talk from the usual random bullshitters, and I thought it was probably some limestone cliffs." Nevertheless, Willey was intrigued enough to want to check it out. "But I never could get a permit to go in there." The Honduran government rarely issued archaeological permits to explore that backcountry jungle, because it is so perilous.

A week later, Blom's employer did call me. His name was Steve Elkins and he described himself as a "cinematographer, a curious man, an adventurer." He wanted to know why the hell I was interrogating Blom.

I said I wanted to do a short *New Yorker* piece about his search for this legendary lost city—whatever it was. He grudgingly agreed to talk, but only if I didn't identify the site or the country it was in. Off the record, he finally admitted that they were, indeed, looking for Ciudad Blanca, the White City, also known as the Lost City of the Monkey God. But he didn't want me to reveal any of this in my *New Yorker* piece until he'd had a chance to confirm it on the ground. "Just say it's a lost city somewhere in Central America. Don't say it's in Honduras or we're screwed."

Elkins had heard the legends, both indigenous

and European, about the White City that described an advanced and wealthy city with extensive trading networks, deep in the inaccessible mountains of Mosquitia, untouched for centuries, as pristine as the day it was abandoned; it would be an archaeological discovery of enormous significance. "We thought that by using space imagery we could locate a target area and identify promising sites" for later ground exploration, Elkins explained. Blom and his team had zeroed in on an area about a mile square, which he had labeled Target One or T1 for short, where there appeared to be large man-made structures. Elkins refused to elaborate.

"I can't tell you any more, because this space-imaging data can be purchased by anybody. Anybody could do what we did and grab the credit. It could also be looted. All we have left to do is go there, which we plan to do this spring. By then," he added, "we hope we'll have something to announce to the world."*

---

* The short piece I wrote for the *New Yorker* was published in the October 20 & 27, 1997, issue.

## CHAPTER 3

## The devil had killed him for daring to look upon this forbidden place.

Most Sacred Majesty:—...I have trustworthy reports of very extensive and rich provinces, and of powerful chiefs ruling over them... [I] ascertained that it lies eight or ten days' march from that town of Trujillo, or rather between fifty and sixty leagues. So wonderful are the reports about this particular province, that even allowing largely for exaggeration, it will exceed Mexico in riches, and equal it in the largeness of its towns and villages, the density of its population, and the policy of its inhabitants.

In the year 1526, Hernán Cortés penned this report, his famous "Fifth Letter" to the Emperor Charles V, while aboard his ship anchored in Trujillo Bay off the coast of

Honduras. Historians and anthropologists believe this account, written six years after Cortés's conquest of Mexico, planted the seeds for the myth of Ciudad Blanca, the City of the Monkey God. Given that "Mexico"—i.e., the Aztec Empire—had staggering wealth and a capital city of at least 300,000 inhabitants, his assertion that the new land was even greater is remarkable. The Indians called it the Old Land of Red Earth, he wrote, and his vague description placed it somewhere in the mountains of Mosquitia.

But at the time, Cortés was embroiled in intrigue and had to fight off rebellion by his subordinates, so he never did embark on a search for the Old Land of Red Earth. The jagged mountains clearly visible from the bay may have convinced him that such a journey would be daunting. Nevertheless, his story took on a life of its own, much as tales of El Dorado persisted in South America for centuries. Twenty years after the Fifth Letter, a missionary named Cristóbal de Pedraza, who would become the first Bishop of Honduras, claimed to have traveled deep into the jungles of Mosquitia on one of his arduous missionary journeys, where he came across an astonishing sight: From a high bluff, he found himself looking down on a large and prosperous city spread out in a river valley. His Indian guide told him the nobles in that land took their meals from plates and goblets of gold. Pedraza was not interested in gold, however, and he continued on and never entered the valley. But his subsequent report to Charles V fed the legend.

For the next three hundred years, geographers and travelers told stories about ruined cities in Central America. In the 1830s, a New Yorker named John Lloyd Stephens became obsessed with finding those cities deep in the Central American rainforest, if indeed they existed. He managed to wangle a diplomatic appointment as ambassador to the short-lived Federal Republic of Central America. He arrived in Honduras in 1839, just as the republic was falling apart into violence and civil war. Amid the chaos, he saw an opportunity (albeit a dangerous one) to strike out on his own to seek out these mysterious ruins.

He brought with him a superb British artist, Frederick Catherwood, who packed a camera lucida in order to project and copy every tiny detail of whatever they might find. The two trekked for weeks through Honduras with native guides, pursuing rumors of a great city. Deep in the interior, they finally arrived at a miserable, unfriendly, mosquito-ridden village called Copán on the banks of a river near the Guatemalan border. They learned from the locals that across the river there were indeed ancient temples, inhabited only by monkeys. As they reached the riverbank, they saw on the far shore a wall of cut stone. After fording the river on muleback, they climbed a staircase and entered the city.

"We ascended by large stone steps," Stephens wrote later, "in some places perfect, and in others thrown down by trees which had grown up between the crevices, and reached a terrace, the form of which it was impossible to make out, from the density of the forest in which it was enveloped. Our guide cleared a way with his machete...and working our way through the thick woods, we came upon a square stone column...The front was the figure of a man, curiously and richly dressed, and the face, evidently a portrait, solemn, stern, and well fitted to excite terror. The back was of a different design, unlike anything we had ever seen before, and the sides were covered with hieroglyphics."

Up to this moment of discovery, the image most North Americans carried of Indians came from the hunter-gatherer tribes they had read about or encountered along the frontier. Most viewed the aboriginal inhabitants of the New World as half-naked, savage Indians who had never achieved anything approaching what was termed "civilization."

Stephens's explorations changed all that. It was an important moment in history, when the world realized that stupendous civilizations had arisen independently in the Americas. He wrote: "The sight of this unexpected monument put at rest at once and for ever in our minds all uncertainty in regard to the character of American antiquities…proving, like newly discovered historical records, that the people who once occupied the continent of America were not savages." The people—named the Maya—who had built this sprawling city of pyramids and temples, and who had covered their monuments with hieroglyphic writing, had created a civilization as advanced as any in Old World antiquity.

Stephens, a fine enterprising American, promptly bought the ruins of Copán for fifty dollars from the local landowner and made plans (later abandoned) to have the buildings disassembled, loaded on barges, and floated to the United States for a tourist attraction. Over the next few years, Stephens and Catherwood explored, mapped, and recorded ancient Mayan cities from Mexico to Honduras. They never did venture into Mosquitia, however, perhaps deterred by mountains and jungles far more discouraging than anything they had experienced in the Maya realm.

They published a two-volume work about their discoveries, *Incidents of Travel in Central America, Chiapas, and Yucatan*, packed with exciting stories of ruins, bandits, and brutal jungle travel, and lavishly illustrated with Catherwood's splendid engravings. Their book went on to become one of the biggest nonfiction bestsellers of the entire nineteenth century. Americans were thrilled by the idea that the New

World had cities, temples, and colossal antiquities that rivaled those of the Old World, equal to the pyramids of Egypt and the glories of ancient Rome. The work of Stephens and Catherwood established the romance of lost cities in the American mind and introduced the notion that the jungles of Central America must hold many more secrets waiting to be revealed.

Before long, the Maya became one of the most intensively studied ancient cultures in the New World, and not just by secular scientists. The Church of Jesus Christ of Latter-day Saints identified the Maya as one of the lost tribes of Israel, the Lamanites, as chronicled in *The Book of Mormon*, published in 1830. The Lamanites left Israel and sailed to America around 600 BC; *The Book of Mormon* tells the story that Jesus appeared to the New World Lamanites and converted them to Christianity, and it describes many events that occurred before the coming of the Europeans.

In the twentieth century the Mormon Church sent a number of well-funded archaeologists to Mexico and Central America to try to confirm the stories through site excavations. Although this resulted in valuable, high-quality research, it also proved difficult for the scientists themselves; facing clear evidence that disproved the Mormon view of history, some of the archaeologists ended up losing their faith, and a few of those who voiced their doubts were excommunicated.

The Maya realm, which stretched from southern Mexico to Honduras, seemed to end at Copán. The vast jungled mountains east of Copán, especially in Mosquitia, were so inhospitable and dangerous that very little exploration and even less archaeology took place. Glimpses of other, non-Maya, pre-Columbian cultures were being uncovered eastward of Copán, but these vanished societies also remained elusive and poorly studied. Just how far east and south of Copán the Maya influence stretched was also difficult to ascertain. In the vacuum, tantalizing rumors grew of even greater, wealthier cities—perhaps Maya, perhaps not—hidden in those impenetrable thickets, stories that fascinated archaeologists and treasure hunters alike.

By the dawn of the twentieth century, these stories and rumors had coalesced into a single legend of a sacred and forbidden Ciudad Blanca, a rich cultural treasure yet to be found. The name probably originated with the Pech Indians (also known as the Paya) of Mosquitia; anthropologists collected stories from Pech informants of a *Kaha Kamasa*, a "White House" said to lie beyond a pass in the mountains at the headwaters of two rivers. Some Indians described it as a refuge where their shamans retreated to escape the invading Spaniards, never to be seen again. Others said that the Spanish did, in fact, enter the White City, but were cursed by the gods and died or vanished into the forest, lost forever. Yet other Indian stories described it as a tragic city that was struck down by a series of catastrophes; the inhabitants, seeing that the gods were angry with them, abandoned the city. Forever after, it became a forbidden place, and anyone who entered it would die of sickness or be killed by the devil. There were also American versions of the legend: Various explorers, prospectors, and early aviators spoke of glimpsing the limestone ramparts of a ruined city rising above the jungle foliage somewhere in central Mosquitia. It seems likely that all these stories—indigenous, Spanish, and American—became conflated to form the basis of the White City or Monkey God legend.

Although many explorers had traveled into the Central American rainforests in the wake of Stephens's discoveries, almost none had ventured into the daunting terrain of Mosquitia. In the 1920s, a Luxembourgian ethnologist, Eduard Conzemius, became one of the first Europeans to explore Mosquitia, traveling by dugout canoe up the Plátano River. On this trip he heard tell of "important ruins discovered by a rubber tapper 20 to 25 years ago, when he was lost in the bush between the Plátano and Paulaya rivers," Conzemius reported. "This man gave a fantastical description of what he saw there. They were the ruins of a most important city with white stone buildings similar to marble, surrounded by a large wall of the same material." But shortly after the rubber tapper reported his discovery, he disappeared. One Indian told Conzemius that "the devil had killed him for daring to look upon this forbidden place." When Conzemius tried to hire a guide to take him to the White City, the Indians feigned ignorance, fearful (he was told) that if they revealed the location they would die.

By the beginning of the 1930s, the growing legend attracted the attention of American archaeologists and major institutions, who considered it not only possible, but even likely, that the unexplored, mountainous jungles along the Maya frontier could be hiding a ruined city—or perhaps even a lost civilization.* It might be Maya or it might be something entirely new.

In the early 1930s, the Smithsonian's Bureau of American Ethnology sent a professional archaeologist to explore eastward of Copán, to see if Maya civilization extended into the rugged thickets of Mosquitia. William Duncan Strong was a scholar, a man ahead of his time: quiet, careful and meticulous in his work, averse to spectacle and publicity. He was among the first to establish that Mosquitia had been inhabited by an ancient,

---

* Archaeologists today don't like the word "civilization" because it implies superiority, preferring the term "culture." I will, however, continue to use the word "civilization" with the understanding that no such value judgment is meant; it is merely a term for a culture that is complex and widespread.

unknown people who were not Maya. Strong spent five months traversing Honduras in 1933, going by dugout canoe up the Río Patuca and several of its tributaries. He kept an illustrated journal, which is preserved in the Smithsonian's collections—packed with detail and many fine drawings of birds, artifacts, and landscapes.

Strong found major archaeological sites, which he carefully described and sketched in his journal, and conducted a few test excavations. Among these finds were the Floresta mounds, the ancient cities of Wankibila and Dos Quebradas, and the Brown Site. His journey was not without adventure; at one point his finger was shot off. (The exact circumstances are unclear; he may have accidentally shot it off himself.) He battled rain, insects, venomous snakes, and dense jungle.

What Strong realized right away was that these were not Maya cities: The Maya built with stone, while this region had been extensively settled by a separate, sophisticated culture that built great earthen mounds. This was an entirely new culture. Even as Strong's work showed definitively that Mosquitia was not part of the Maya realm, however, his discoveries raised more questions than they answered. Who were these people, where had they come from, and why had all record of them vanished until now? How in the world did they manage to live and farm in such a hostile jungle environment? What was their relationship to their powerful

Mayan neighbors? The earthworks posed another enigma: Did these mounds hide buried buildings or tombs, or were they constructed for some other reason?

Even as he uncovered many other ancient wonders, Strong continued to hear stories of the greatest ruin of them all, the White City, which he dismissed as a "lovely legend." While sitting on the banks of the Río Tinto in Mosquitia, an informant told Strong the following story, which he recorded in his journal, under an entry entitled "The Forbidden City."

The lost city, he wrote, lies on the shores of a lake deep in the mountains to the north, its white ramparts surrounded by groves of orange, lemon, and banana trees. But if one partakes of the forbidden fruit, he will be lost in the hills forever. "So goes the tale," Strong wrote, "but it would be better to do as an informant's father did, follow the river until it becomes a mere trickle among dark rocks and woods and then have to turn back. The city would still be there that way. Like the 'Ciudad Blanco'— the 'forbidden fruit' will probably long remain a lure to the curious."

All these rumors, legends, and stories set the stage for the next phase: on the one side, obsessive and ill-fated expeditions seeking the lost city, and on the other, the beginnings of serious archaeological research in the same region. Both would help begin to untangle the mystery of the White City.

## CHAPTER 4

## A land of cruel jungles within almost inaccessible mountain ranges

Enter George Gustav Heye. Heye's father had made a fortune selling his petroleum business to John D. Rockefeller, and his son would go on to increase that wealth as an investment banker in New York City. But Heye had interests other than money. In 1897, fresh out of college and working on a job in Arizona, Heye came across an Indian woman chewing on her husband's splendid buckskin shirt "to kill the lice." On a whim he bought the lice-ridden garment.

The buckskin shirt launched one of the most voracious collecting careers in American history. Heye became obsessed with all things Native American, and he would eventually amass a collection of a million pieces. In 1916, he established the Museum of the American Indian on upper Broadway in New York

City to house his collection. (In 1990, the museum moved to Washington, DC, and became part of the Smithsonian.)

Heye was a gigantic man, six feet four inches tall, almost three hundred pounds, with a billiard ball head and a baby face framed by heavy jowls; he wore a gold watch-chain draped across a stout chest and dressed in black suits with a straw boater's hat, cigar protruding from a tiny pursed mouth. He often took buying trips across the country in his limousine, consulting the obituary columns in local papers and inquiring if the dearly departed had left behind any unwanted collections of Indian artifacts. On these trips he would sometimes put his chauffeur in the backseat and take the wheel himself, driving like a fiend.

Heye's obsession expanded to Honduras when a doctor in New Orleans sold Heye a sculpture of an armadillo said to come from Mosquitia. This curious and appealing object was carved in basalt, with a funny-looking face, an arched back, and only three legs so it could stand without wobbling. (It is still in the museum's collection.) It captivated Heye, and he eventually financed an expedition to the treacherous region in search of more artifacts. He hired an explorer named Frederick Mitchell-Hedges, a British adventurer who claimed to have found the Maya city of Lubaantun in Belize, where his daughter allegedly discovered the famous crystal "Skull of Doom." Mitchell-Hedges was the very picture of a dashing British explorer, down to the plummy accent, briar pipe, sunburned visage, and hyphenated last name.

Mitchell-Hedges explored the fringes of Mosquitia in 1930 for Heye until he was laid low with an attack of malaria and dysentery so severe it left him temporarily blind in one eye. When he recovered, he brought out over a thousand artifacts, along with an amazing story of an abandoned city deep in the mountains, home to a gigantic, buried statue of a monkey. The natives, he said, called it the Lost City of the Monkey God. Heye quickly sent Mitchell-Hedges back on a new expedition to Mosquitia to track down the lost city, cofinanced by the British Museum.

Interest in the second expedition was high. Mitchell-Hedges declared to the *New York Times*: "Our expedition proposes to penetrate a certain region marked on the maps of today as unexplored...Within my knowledge the region contains immense ruins never yet visited." The location was somewhere in Mosquitia, but the exact position he declared a secret. "The region can be described as a land of cruel jungles within almost inaccessible mountain ranges." But on the new expedition, Mitchell-Hedges did not go into the interior, perhaps wary of repeating his earlier travails. Instead, he spent most of his time exploring the sand beaches and coastlines of the Bay Islands of Honduras, where he pulled some stone statues from under the water, likely deposited there by coastal erosion. He justified his failure to go back into Mosquitia by claiming an even greater discovery: He had found the remains of Atlantis, which, he suggested, had been "the cradle of the American races." He returned with more tales of the Lost City of the Monkey God, which he had heard on his journeys along the coast.

Heye immediately began planning another expedition to Honduras with a new leader, this time wisely bypassing Mitchell-Hedges, perhaps because he had begun to suspect, belatedly, that the man was a con artist. The truth was, Mitchell-Hedges was a fraud on a spectacular scale. He did not discover Lubaantun, and the crystal skull was (much later) revealed as a fake. Yet he succeeded in fooling many contemporaries; even his obituary in the *New York Times* would eventually repeat as truth a string of dubious facts that Mitchell-Hedges had been peddling for years: that he had "received eight bullet wounds and three knife scars," that he fought alongside Pancho Villa, was a secret agent for America during World War I, and searched for sea monsters in the Indian Ocean with Sir Arthur Conan Doyle's son. However, some skeptical archaeologists had dismissed Mitchell-Hedges as a charlatan even before his second voyage to Honduras, and afterward they heaped ridicule on his outlandish claims about having found Atlantis. Mitchell-Hedges published a book about his experiences, *Land of Wonder and Fear*, about which one archaeologist wrote: "To me the wonder was how he could write such nonsense and the fear how much taller the next yarn would be."

For his third expedition into Mosquitia, Heye partnered with the National Museum of Honduras and the country's president, who hoped the new venture would help open up the vast Mosquitia region to settlement by modern Hondurans. Knowing that such an expansion effort would, regrettably, involve the displacement or even destruction of the indigenous Indians who still lived there—not unlike what had happened in the American West—the government and the National Museum were eager to document the Indians' way of life before they vanished. An important goal of the expedition was, therefore, to do ethnographic as well as archaeological research.

Although his intention was to employ a serious professional, once again Heye betrayed a weakness for swashbuckling men of questionable integrity. The man Heye chose to find his "great ruin, overrun by dense jungle" was a Canadian journalist named R. Stuart Murray. Murray had given himself the title "Captain" fifteen years before, when he involved himself in a shabby revolution in Santo Domingo. In an interview before he departed for Honduras, Murray said, "There's supposedly a lost city I'm going to look for, which the Indians call the City of the Monkey God. They are afraid to go near it, for they believe that anyone who approaches it will, within the month, be killed by the bite of a poisonous snake."

Murray led two expeditions for Heye into Mosquitia, in 1934 and 1935, journeys that became known as the First and Second Honduran Expeditions. In pursuing various tales and descriptions of the Lost City of the Monkey God, Murray believed he came tantalizingly close to finding it. But again and again, just as he thought he was on the verge of success, he always seemed to be thwarted—by jungle, rivers, mountains, and the death of one of his guides. In the archives of the Museum of the American Indian is a photo of Murray on the banks of a river, kneeling next to a row of small metates, or grinding stones, beautifully carved with the heads of birds and animals. On the back of the photo Murray wrote a message to Heye:

These come from the "Lost City of the Monkey God"—the Indian who brought them out was bitten by a Fer de Lance in September and died. With him died the secret of the city's location—More when I return. R. S. Murray.

Among the many artifacts he brought back were two he believed contained clues to the lost city: a stone with "hieroglyphic" characters on it, and a small statue of a monkey covering its face with its paws.

After the 1935 expedition, Murray moved on to other projects. In 1939, he was invited to be the guest lecturer on the *Stella Polaris*, the most elegant cruise ship of its day. There he met a young man named Theodore A. Morde who had been hired to edit the ship's onboard newspaper. The two became friends. Murray regaled Morde with stories of his search for the Lost City of the Monkey God, while Morde told Murray of his adventures as a journalist covering the Spanish Civil War. When the ship docked in New York, Murray introduced Morde to Heye. "I hunted for that lost city for years," Murray said. Now it was someone else's turn.

Heye immediately engaged Morde to lead the third Honduran expedition into Mosquitia, the trip that would finally—he hoped—reveal to the world the Lost City of the Monkey God. Morde was only twenty-nine years old, but his expedition and its monumental discovery would ring down through history. The American public, already captivated by the story of the Lost City of the Monkey God, followed it with enormous interest, and the expedition would give future historians and adventurers enigmatic clues to be endlessly debated and argued. If it weren't for Morde and his fateful expedition, the many bizarre and misguided quests for the lost city that littered the decades of the 1950s to the '80s would not have taken place. Without Morde, Steve Elkins would probably not have heard the legend and would never have embarked on his own eccentric search for the Lost City of the Monkey God.

## CHAPTER 5

**I'm going back to the City of the Monkey God, to try to solve one of the few remaining mysteries of the Western World.**

A handsome man with a pencil mustache, a smooth, high forehead, and slicked-back hair, Theodore Morde was born in 1911 in New Bedford, Massachusetts, into a family of old whaling stock. He was a sharp dresser, favoring Palm Beach suits, crisp shirts, and white shoes. He started his journalism career in high school as a sports reporter for the local paper, and then he moved into broadcast journalism as a writer and news commentator for radio. He attended Brown University for a couple of years, and then took a job editing newspapers aboard various cruise ships in the mid-1930s. In 1938, he covered the Spanish Civil War as a correspondent and photographer. At one point, he claimed to have swum a river to cross the front lines between the Fascist and Republican camps, so that he could cover both sides.

Heye was eager for Morde to set off on his expedition as soon as possible, and Morde wasted no time in organizing it. He asked his former university classmate, Laurence C. Brown, a geologist, to accompany him. In March of 1940, as war was breaking out across Europe, Morde and Brown departed New York for Honduras with a thousand pounds of equipment and supplies, in what Heye officially called the Third Honduran Expedition. Four months of silence followed. When the two explorers finally emerged from Mosquitia, Morde fired off a letter to Heye about the astounding discovery they had made—they had accomplished what no other expedition had been able to do. The news was published in the *New York Times* on July 12, 1940:

## 'CITY OF MONKEY GOD' IS BELIEVED LOCATED

---

### Expedition Reports Success in Honduras Exploration

"According to the communication received by the foundation," the *Times* article read, "the party has established the approximate location of the rumored 'Lost City of the Monkey God' in an almost inaccessible area between the Paulaya and Platano Rivers." The American public devoured the story.

Morde and Brown arrived back in New York in August to great fanfare. On September 10, 1940, Morde gave a radio interview for CBS. The script still survives, annotated in Morde's hand, and it appears to be the most complete surviving account of their find. "I have just returned from the discovery of a lost city," he told his audience. "We went to a region of Honduras that had never been explored...We spent weeks poling tediously up tangled jungle streams. When we could go no further we started hacking a path through the jungle...after weeks of that life, we were starved, weak and discouraged. Then, just as we were about to give up, I saw from the top of a small cliff, something that made me stop in my tracks...It was the wall of a city—the Lost City of the Monkey God!...I couldn't tell how large the city was, but I know it extended far into the jungle and probably thirty thousand people once lived there. But that was two thousand years ago. All that was left were those mounds of earth covering crumbled walls where houses once stood, and stone foundations of what may have been majestic temples. I remembered an ancient legend told by the Indians. It said that in the Lost City a gigantic statue of a monkey was worshipped as a god. I saw a great jungle-covered mound which, when someday we can excavate it, I believe may reveal this monkey deity. Today the Indians near that region fear the very thought of the City of the Monkey God. They think it is inhabited by great ape-like hairy men, called Ulaks...In creeks near the city we found rich deposits of gold, silver, and platinum. I found a facial mask...it looked like the face of a monkey...On nearly everything was carved the likeness of the monkey—the monkey god...I'm going back to the City of the Monkey God, to try to solve one of the few remaining mysteries of the Western World."

Morde declined to reveal the location of the city, for fear of looting. It seems he kept this information even from Heye himself.

In another account, written for a magazine, Morde described the ruins in detail: "The City of the Monkey God was walled," he wrote. "We found some of those walls upon which the green magic of the jungle had worked small damages and which had resisted the flood of vegetation. We traced one wall until it vanished under mounds that have all the evidence of once being great buildings. There are, indeed, still buildings beneath the age-old shroudings.

"It was the ideal spot," he continued. "The towering mountains provided the perfect backdrop. Nearby, a rushing waterfall, beautiful as a sequined evening gown, spilled down into the green valley of ruins. Birds themselves, as brilliant as jewels, flitted from tree to tree, and little monkey faces peered inquisitively at us from the surrounding screen of dense foliage."

He questioned the older Indians closely, learning much about the city, "handed down to them by their ancestors who had seen it."

"We would uncover, they said, a long staired approach to it which would be built and paved after the manner of the ruined Mayan cities to the north. Stone effigies of monkeys would line this approach.

"The heart of the Temple was a high stone dais on which was the statue of the Monkey God himself. Before it was the place of sacrifice."

Morde brought back a number of artifacts—figures of monkeys in stone and clay, his canoe, pots, and stone tools. Many of these are still in the collections of the Smithsonian. He vowed that he would return the following year "to commence excavation."

But World War II intervened. Morde went on to become an OSS spy and war correspondent, and his obituary alleges he was involved in a plot to kill Hitler. He never returned to Honduras. In 1954, Morde— sunken into alcoholism, his marriage failing—hanged himself in a shower stall at his parents' summer house in Dartmouth, Massachusetts. He never did reveal the location of the lost city.

Morde's account of finding the Lost City of the Monkey God received wide press and fired the imagination of both Americans and Hondurans. Since his death, the location of his city has been the subject of intense speculation and debate. Dozens have searched for it without success, parsing his writings and accounts for possible clues. One object became the Holy Grail of searchers: Morde's beloved walking stick, still in the possession of his family. Carved into the stick are four enigmatic columns of numbers that seem to be directions or coordinates—for example, "NE 300; E 100; N 250; SE 300." A Canadian cartographer named Derek Parent became obsessed with the markings on the stick and spent years exploring and mapping Mosquitia, trying to use them as directions to the lost city. In the process, Parent created some of the most detailed and accurate maps of Mosquitia ever made.

The most recent search for Morde's lost city took place in 2009. A Pulitzer Prize–winning journalist for the *Wall Street Journal*, Christopher S. Stewart, undertook an arduous journey into the heart of Mosquitia in an attempt to retrace Morde's route. Stewart was accompanied by archaeologist Christopher Begley, who had written his PhD dissertation on Mosquitia's archaeological sites and had visited over a hundred of them. Begley and Stewart went upriver and made their way through the jungle to a large ruin called Lancetil-lal, in the upper reaches of the Río Plátano, which had been built by the same ancient people Strong and other archaeologists had identified as once occupying Mosquitia. This previously known city, which had been cleared and mapped by Peace Corps volunteers in 1988, was in the approximate area Morde claimed to be, at least as far as Begley and Stewart could ascertain. It consisted of twenty-one earthen mounds defining four plazas and a possible Mesoamerican ball court. In the jungle some distance behind the ruin, they discovered a white cliff, which Stewart believed might have been mistaken for a broken wall from a distance. He published a well-received book about his search, called *Jungleland: A Mysterious Lost City, a WWII Spy, and a True Story of Deadly Adventure.* It is a fascinating read, yet despite Begley and Stewart's best efforts, there simply wasn't enough evidence to settle the question of whether the Lancetillal ruins were indeed Morde's Lost City of the Monkey God.

As it turns out, all these researchers have spent almost three-quarters of a century looking for answers in the wrong place. Morde and Brown's journals have been preserved and passed down in Morde's family. While the artifacts were deposited with the Museum of the

American Indian, the journals were not; this in itself is a remarkable departure from standard practice, because such journals normally contain vital scientific information and belong to the financing institution, not the explorer. The keeper of the journals until recently was Theodore's nephew, David Morde. I was able to get copies of the journals, which the Morde family had loaned to the National Geographic Society for a few months in 2016. Nobody at National Geographic had read them, but a staff archaeologist kindly scanned them for me because I was writing a story for the magazine. I knew that Christopher Stewart had seen at least parts of them but had been disappointed to find no clues as to the location of the Lost City of the Monkey God. He had assumed that Morde, for reasons of security, had withheld that information even from his journals. So when I began flipping through them, I didn't expect to find much worthy of note.

There are three journals: Two are hardcover books with dirty canvas covers stamped "Third Honduran Expedition," and a third is a smaller spiral book with a black cover labeled "Field Notebook." They run to over three hundred handwritten pages and give a comprehensive account of the expedition from start to finish. No dates or pages are missing; every single day was recorded in detail. The journals were the combined work of Brown and Morde, who each made their own entries in the same books as they journeyed into the heart of darkness. Brown's easy-to-read, rounded handwriting alternates with Morde's spiky, forward-slanted style.

I'll not soon forget the experience of reading those journals—first with puzzlement, then disbelief, and finally shock.

Heye and the Museum of the American Indian, it seems, were conned, along with the American public. According to their own writings, Morde and Brown had a secret agenda. From the beginning, neither man had any intention of looking for a lost city. The only entry in the journal mentioning the lost city is a random note jotted on a back page, almost as an afterthought, clearly a reference to Conzemius. It reads, in its entirety:

White City
1898—Paulaya, Plantain,* Wampu—heads of these streams should be near location of city.

Timoteteo, Rosales—one-eyed rubber cutter, crossing from Paulaya to Plantain—saw columns still standing in 1905.

---

* The "Plantain" was Morde's name for the Río Plátano, *plátano* being Spanish for plantain.

In hundreds of pages of entries, this is the entire sum of information touching on the lost city they were supposedly trying to find, the city they had described so vividly to the American media. They were not looking for archaeological sites. They made only cursory inquiries. The journals reveal they found in Mosquitia no ruins, no artifacts, no sites, no "Lost City of the Monkey God." So what were Morde and Brown doing in Mosquitia, during those four months of silence, while Heye and the world held their breath? What were they after?

Gold.

Their search for gold was not a spur-of-the-moment decision. Among their hundreds of pounds of gear, Morde and Brown had packed sophisticated gold-mining equipment, including gold pans, shovels, picks, equipment for building sluice boxes, and mercury for amalgamation. Note that Morde, who could have chosen any partner for his expedition, selected a geologist, not an archaeologist. Brown and Morde went into the jungle with detailed information on possible gold deposits along the creeks and tributaries of the Río Blanco and planned their route accordingly. This area was long rumored to be rich in placer gold deposited in gravel bars and holes along streambeds. The Río Blanco is many miles south of where they claimed to have found the lost city. When I mapped the journal entries, day by day, I found that Brown and Morde never went up the Paulaya or Plátano Rivers. While going up the Patuca, they bypassed the mouth of the Wampu and continued far south, to where the Río Cuyamel joins the Patuca, and then went up that to the Río Blanco. They never came within forty miles of that area encompassing the headwaters of the Paulaya, Plátano, and Wampu Rivers, which was the general region in which they later claimed to have found the Lost City of the Monkey God.

They were looking for another California, another Yukon. Everywhere they went they dug into gravel bars and panned for "color"—bits of gold—totting up in fanatical detail each fleck they spied. Finally, at a creek running into the Blanco River, called Ulak-Was, they did indeed strike gold. An American named Perl or Pearl (all this is noted in the journal) had set up a gold sluicing operation here in 1907. But Perl, the wastrel son of a wealthy New Yorker, frittered away his time drinking and whoring instead of mining, and his father shut him down; the operation was abandoned in 1908. He left a dam, water pipes, gate valves, an anvil, and other useful equipment behind, which Morde and Brown fixed up and reused.

At the mouth of Ulak-Was, Morde and Brown dismissed all their Indian guides and went up the creek, setting up "Camp Ulak" in the same place Perl had worked. They then spent the next three weeks—the heart of their expedition—in the backbreaking daily work of mining gold.

They repaired Perl's old dam to divert the creek into sluice boxes, where the flow of water over riffles and burlap was used to separate and concentrate the heavier gold particles from gravel, and recorded their daily take in the journal. They worked like dogs, drenched by downpours, eaten alive by swarms of sand flies and mosquitoes, picking thirty to fifty ticks a day off their bodies. They were in perpetual terror of poisonous snakes, which were ubiquitous. They ran out of coffee and tobacco and began to starve. They spent most of their free time playing cards. "We thrash out our gold prospects again and again," Morde wrote, and "ponder the probable progress of the war, wondering if America has already become involved."

They also dreamed big: "We have located a fine spot for an airport," Brown wrote, "just across the river. We will probably build our permanent camp on this same plateau if our plans go through."

But the rainy season fell upon them with a fury: torrential downpours that started as a roar in the treetops, dumping inches on them daily. Ulak-Was creek swelled with every new downpour, and they struggled to manage the rising water. On June 12, disaster struck. A massive cloudburst triggered a flash flood, which tore down the creek, bursting their dam and carrying off their gold-mining operation. "Obviously, we no longer can work gold," Morde lamented in the journal. "Our dam is completely gone—so are our planks. The best course of events we feel, is to wind up our affairs here as hastily as possible, and head down the river again."

They abandoned their mine, loaded the pitpan with their supplies and gold, and set off down the swollen rivers at breakneck speed. They careened down the Ulak-Was to the Blanco, to the Cuyamel, and into the Patuca. In one day they covered a stretch of the Patuca that had taken them two weeks to motor up. When they finally reached the edge of civilization, in a settlement along the Patuca where the residents had a radio, Morde heard about the fall of France. He was told that America "was practically *in* the war and *would* be *officially* in a day or so." They panicked at the thought of being marooned in Honduras. "We decided to haste completion of the entire expedition's aims." What they meant by this enigmatic sentence is debatable, but it appears they might have realized they had to get busy fabricating a cover story—and get their hands on some ancient artifacts allegedly from the "lost city" to bring back to Heye. (There is no mention in the journals up to this point of finding or carrying any artifacts out of the Mosquitia interior.)

They continued on, ripping down the swollen Patuca by day and sometimes at night. On June 25 they reached Brewer's Lagoon (now Brus Laguna) and the sea. They spent a week there, no longer in a rush as they had learned America was far from joining the war. On July 10 they finally arrived in the capital city, Tegucigalpa. At some point between these two dates Morde wrote the fabricated report to his patron, George Heye, which generated the *New York Times* article.

On their return to New York, Morde told the story of their discovery of the Lost City of the Monkey God again and again, and each time it got more detailed. The public loved it. Their rather modest collection of artifacts was put on display at the museum, along with a pitpan, or dugout canoe. The journals indicate that the two men hastily acquired these artifacts after they left the jungle, in a place west of Brewer's Lagoon near the coast; a Spaniard showed them a site with pottery scattered about, where they did some digging. It seems likely they also purchased artifacts from locals at the same time, but the journal is silent on that question.

Morde and Brown made no effort in the journals to conceal or dissemble their actions. Why they wrote down such a frank record of deception is hard to understand. Clearly, they had no intention of ever sharing the contents of these journals with their patron, Heye, or the public. Perhaps they were filled with hubris and dreamed that a fabulous gold strike would be part of their legacy, and they wanted to record it for posterity. Their announcement of the lost city discovery might have been a last-minute impulse, but it seems more likely it was planned all along as a cover for their real agenda.

We do know this: For decades, many have wondered if Morde found a city. The general consensus up until now has been that he probably did find an archaeological site, perhaps even an important one. The journals, however, are proof that Morde found nothing, and his "discovery" was an out-and-out fraud.

But what about the walking stick and its enigmatic directions? I recently corresponded with Derek Parent, who had spent decades exploring La Mosquitia, studying Morde's route, and trying to decipher the stick. He probably knows more about Morde than anyone alive, and he had been in close contact with Morde's family for decades.

Over the years, David Morde had sent Parent photocopies of various bits of the journals, a few pages at a time. At one point in our correspondence, Parent told me that Morde's discovery of the city was in the missing parts of the journals.

What missing parts? I asked.

That was when David Morde's apparent ploy unraveled.

David Morde had claimed to Parent that most of Journal 2 was missing. All that remained, he said, was the journal's first page, which he photocopied and sent to Parent. The rest of Journal 2 was gone, and he said he felt sure that the missing section was the part that recorded Morde's journey up the Paulaya River to the City of the Monkey God. And why was that part missing? Morde explained to Parent that British military intelligence had ordered the family to burn Morde's papers after his death, and it might have been lost that way; or it may have been destroyed during a period when the journals were being stored in a damp warehouse in Massachusetts that was infested with rats.

I was surprised when Parent told me this, because those pages David Morde claimed were gone are not missing from the original journal at all. I had the entirety of Journal 2—every single numbered page, firmly bound into the hardcover book—with no gaps in dates or missing text. The allegedly lost part of Journal 2 records nothing more than the time Morde spent relaxing in Brewer's Lagoon, "getting chummy" with local expats, sailing, and fishing—and taking a day trip to dig for artifacts.

Why the deception? One might speculate that

David Morde may have been protecting the memory of his uncle or the honor of his family, but unfortunately he is unavailable to explain; he is serving a prison term for a serious crime. After his incarceration, his wife, perhaps unwittingly, loaned the complete journals to the National Geographic Society.

When I shared these findings with Derek Parent, and sent him a copy of the rest of Journal 2, he e-mailed me back: "I'm in utter shock."

Despite the skullduggery, the mystery of the walking stick persists. In the wake of this news, Parent told me his latest theories. He thinks the stick may have recorded directions from Camp Ulak or its environs to "some locale of interest." Morde, he believes, found something and carved the directions to it on his walking stick instead of putting them in his journal—something so important he wanted to keep it even more secret than the journal he was sharing with Brown.

Parent took the directions from the walking stick and mapped them. The compass bearings and distances, he says, corresponded with the twists and turns of the Río Blanco going upstream from the mouth of Ulak-Was creek. He believes the stick logged a journey "recording steps along the river bank to a now well-defined end point." That end point, Parent identified, was a narrow, 300-acre valley through which the Río Blanco flowed. This valley has never been investigated. It might have been another promising deposit of placer gold, which Morde hoped to return to later, perhaps without Brown, or it might have marked some other discovery of interest. The mystery of the walking stick remains unsolved.

We now know, however, that it does not contain coded directions to the lost city. In a journal entry on June 17, 1940, on the very last day of the expedition before his reemergence from the wilderness and arrival in a civilized town, Morde wrote: "We are convinced no great civilization ever existed up there. And there are no archaeological discoveries of importance to be made."

## CHAPTER 6

**We took canoes into the heart of darkness.**

For three-quarters of a century, Morde's tall tale, so rich in romance and adventure, has given impetus to the fable of the lost city. The White City or Monkey God legend became a part of the Honduran national psyche, a tale familiar even to schoolchildren. In 1960, the Honduran government drew a line around two thousand square miles of the largely unexplored interior of Mosquitia and called it the Ciudad Blanca Archaeological Reserve. In 1980, UNESCO named the area the Río Plátano Biosphere Reserve and, two years later, declared this unique rainforest a World Heritage Site. Meanwhile, ambitious explorers continued to make dubious and unverified claims of having found the lost city, while many archaeologists suspected a city of that nature might exist, in some form, deep in the jungle, either near Morde's claimed area or somewhere else. In

1994, the chief of archaeology for the Honduran government, George Hasemann, said in an interview that he believed all the large sites in Mosquitia may have been part of a single political system whose center, the White City, had not yet been found.

Steve Elkins first heard of the White City from an adventurer named Steve Morgan, who was a professional collector of legends and stories. Morgan had compiled a list of what he considered to be the world's greatest unsolved mysteries, and he had boxes of files of research into various lost cities, pirate treasures, ancient tombs, and shipwrecks loaded with gold. Morgan engaged in marine salvage for a living and had actually found a number of shipwrecks. His house was full of stacks of Chinese porcelain and chests heaped with silver Spanish reals and pieces of eight. Elkins, who owned a business in LA renting camera equipment to television production crews, decided he wanted to go into television production himself, since he had the gear. He consulted Morgan and pored over his list of unsolved mysteries with fascination. Two mysteries attracted Elkins's special attention: the legend of Ciudad Blanca and the Loot of Lima, also known as the Cocos Island treasure.

Elkins and Morgan teamed up, did some research into Ciudad Blanca, and identified an area in Mosquitia they thought might contain it. They organized an expedition, led by Morgan. Elkins sold the idea of a television show about the search to Spiegel TV in Germany.

Elkins, his German coproducer and correspondent, along with his California film crew, arrived in Honduras in 1994. They hired a local fixer, a man named Bruce Heinicke, to handle logistics. A childhood friend of Morgan's, Heinicke was an American married to a Honduran. He'd been doing business in Honduras for many years as a gold prospector, drug smuggler, treasure hunter, and archaeological looter. While the choice of a man like Heinicke might have seemed eccentric, the expedition required someone who not only knew his way around Honduras but also had a keen understanding of when and how to bribe people (a delicate art), how to manage Honduran bureaucracy, how to intimidate and threaten, and how to deal with dangerous criminals without getting killed. Elkins recalled seeing Heinicke for the first time in the airport parking lot after their arrival. He was a big fat guy dressed in a pineapple shirt, pinky ring and gold watch, cigarette dangling from his mouth, with a wad of bills in his fist. He was barking orders in Spanish and passing out money. "We got a video of him," said Elkins. "It's hilarious."

It would be the beginning of a long and complicated relationship.

The crew filmed in Copán and then took a bush flight to a little town called Palacios on the Mosquito Coast. From there they set off into the interior, with indigenous guides and a rough idea of where the lost city might be, based on their research and interviews.

"We took canoes into the heart of darkness," Elkins remembered. Morgan led the expedition, hiring local informants who claimed to know of an area deep in the mountains where there were ruins. "To be honest," Elkins said, "I just tagged along. I really didn't know where the fuck we were going."

The canoes were forty-foot dugouts, hollowed out of a single mahogany tree trunk, equipped with small outboard Evinrudes. Each could fit six people and a bunch of gear. "We went up some little river. I don't even know the name of it." Upstream the water became so shallow and full of sunken logs and mud bars that they had to raise the engines and propel themselves along by poling. They went miles and miles through endless swamps and up unknown tributaries, following wavering, uncertain maps. "We were constantly in and out of the canoes, in the muck. It got denser and denser and denser, until we were up high in the mountains."

There was no sign of any lost cities, but they did make a discovery. "All of a sudden there was this big boulder in a stream," Elkins said, "with a carving on it showing a guy with a fancy headdress planting seeds." He had what he called an "epiphany"—here was proof, if more were needed, that a sophisticated and mysterious people had once lived and farmed in a land that today was deep, uninhabited jungle. Led by local Indian guides, Elkins and the group pushed on, forced to abandon their canoes and continue on foot, slashing their way through the jungle with machetes. On a hard day's travel they were lucky to make one or two miles. Steve and his crew ate MREs, while the Indian guides ate iguanas. At one point the guides became agitated; taking out their weapons, they confided that the group was being tracked by jaguars. They frequently ran into venomous snakes and were assaulted day and night by insects. "After I came out," Elkins recalled, "I had bites for six months." He was grateful not to have been stricken with one of the many frightful tropical diseases common to the area.

One night, he exited his tent to go to the bathroom. The entire forest was glowing with millions of points of bioluminescence, caused by fungi that glow when the temperature and humidity are right. "It was like looking down at LA from thirty thousand feet," he said. "The most beautiful thing I've ever seen."

Somewhere in the rainforest, they did find a scattering of broken stone sculptures, pottery, and tools. If there were mounds, it was impossible to tell, because the jungle was so thick. But either way, it was a small site and clearly not the White City. They finally gave up, exhausted and out of money.

Elkins was repeatedly shocked at Heinicke's methods of getting things done in Honduras. After they reemerged from the jungle and were filming on Roatán Island in the Bay of Honduras, Elkins's German producer got an emergency call on his satellite phone requiring his return to Hamburg immediately on business. They rushed to the airport to catch a flight out, but when they arrived they learned the plane was already full and on the runway. The next flight out wasn't for several days. Heinicke huffed and puffed his way out on the tarmac, boarded the plane, pulled out a Colt .45 pistol, and inquired who was the last to board. He waved his pistol at the unfortunate passenger. "I need your fucking seat," he said. "Get off." The man stumbled off the plane in terror; Heinicke shoved the gun back into his waistband and said to the German producer, "Okay, you got your seat."

Many years later, when Heinicke told me this story, he explained how he saw his role in the partnership: "See, Steve, he's kind of dangerous to be with. He'll tell me the good points he sees in someone, and I'll say, 'Fuck him, I don't like him, I don't trust him.' That's probably why we make a good partnership."

Elkins, for his part, said, "Bruce is definitely the

kind of guy you want to have on your side. And not the other way around." He added, lowering his voice: "In order to make this happen, I had to dance with the devil at times."

That first attempt to find the White City changed Elkins. He went in curious about the White City legend and returned having found his life's mission. "I call it the 'lost city virus,'" he told me later. "I became an addict. I was obsessed with the idea of trying to prove whether the lost city really existed."

Elkins has an appealing streak of persistence and an indefatigable nature, which may very well come from his unconventional family. Originally from England and Russia, his great-grandparents arrived in the States through Ellis Island in the 1890s. His grandfather Jack Elkins was a jazz piano player who toured with Dixieland bands in the 1920s. Elkins's father, Bud, went in an entirely different direction: into the army. He lied about his age to sign up at fifteen, but was caught during basic training and his mother had to come get him and drag him back home to finish high school. During World War II, Bud flew against the Japanese in the Aleutian Tigers squadron; after the war he went into the garment business, landing a contract to manufacture bunny outfits for Playboy clubs. He then went back into the army and took part in combat and intelligence-gathering missions in Vietnam, reaching the rank of colonel. His ultimate retirement dream was to own a Chicago-style kosher hot dog business; so after leaving the military he built a giant truck in the shape of a hot dog and drove it around LA selling dogs and Polish sausages before the business failed. Bud was a charmer and a ladies' man, restless, with a yearning for adventure. Because of his philandering, Steve's mother divorced him when Steve was eleven, and Steve grew up more or less fatherless in Chicago. "My mother was the salt of the earth and steady as a rock," he said.

Elkins seems to have inherited his father's wanderlust along with his mother's pragmatic steadfastness, a mixture of traits that would serve him well in the search for the lost city.

Elkins attended Southern Illinois University. An avid hiker, he roamed the nearby Shawnee National Forest with friends who called him Over-the-Next-Ridge Elkins because he was always urging them on "to see what was over the next ridge." On one of these jaunts he found a rock shelter on some bluffs overlooking the Mississippi River. He camped out there with friends, and they began scratching around in the dirt, turning up arrowheads, spearpoints, bones, and broken pottery. He brought them back to the university. His archaeology professor arranged an excavation of the cave as a special studies program for the semester. In test excavations Elkins and the group uncovered human bones, carvings in shell, stone tools, and remains of food. Radiocarbon dating indicated the bottom layers were thousands of years old.

"That was the moment I became hooked on ancient history," he told me. He spent many hours sitting in the shelter, looking out over the Mississippi River Valley and imagining what it would have been like to be born in the cave, grow up, raise children, get old, and die there—in the America of five thousand years ago.

Elkins's first expedition into Mosquitia had impressed on him one brutally simple fact: "Walking aimlessly through the jungle is crazy. This is no way to find anything."

He needed to address the problem in a more systematic way. He accomplished this with a two-pronged attack: historical research and space-age technology.

He delved deeply into the many stories of people who had looked for the White City, some of whom actually claimed to have found it. Most of these people were obvious cranks or otherwise untrustworthy, but there was one person who stood out. Steve Morgan had introduced Elkins to a man named Sam Glassmire, who said he had located and explored the White City. When Elkins met Glassmire, he found him to be a solid, respectable scientist with a surprisingly credible story—and in his living room were impressive stone sculptures he had allegedly carried out of the ruins. In 1997, Elkins and his video team interviewed Glassmire at his home in Santa Fe, and they captured his story on tape. (I first met Steve on this trip, as I lived in Santa Fe myself.)

In a twist on the Morde expedition, Glassmire, a geologist, had been hired to prospect for gold in Mosquitia and went looking for the lost city instead. He led three prospecting expeditions into Mosquitia in the late 1950s. A tough, weather-beaten man with a gravelly, slow-talking, New Mexico drawl, Glassmire had built a career as a respected scientist who had worked as an engineer for Los Alamos National Laboratory in the mid-fifties, when Los Alamos was still a closed city. He grew disenchanted with making nuclear bombs, so he moved to Santa Fe and set up a geological consulting firm.

In 1959, he had been hired by American mining interests to determine if there was placer gold along the gravel bars of the upper Patuca River and its tributaries. His employers had a lot of money: The budget for the first expedition alone was $40,000, and they would send Glassmire back twice more.

On that first expedition, Glassmire heard many rumors of the White City. "You hear about it as soon as you get in Honduras," he recalled to Elkins.

As he explored the rivers looking for gold, he pestered his guides with questions. "I frequently heard natives mention the mysterious Ciudad Blanca," he wrote in a 1960 article about his discovery in the *Denver Post*. "I asked my guide about it. He finally told me the men were afraid I planned to send the expedition up the Río Guampu [Wampu], toward Ciudad Blanca. If I did, he said, the men would desert." When Glassmire asked why, the guide said that when the conquistadors arrived, Ciudad Blanca was a magnificent city. "Then came an unforeseen series of catastrophes. The people decided the gods were angry," and so they abandoned the city, leaving all their belongings behind, and thereafter shunned it as a forbidden place.

On his third prospecting expedition into Honduras, Glassmire found placer beds along the Río Blanco and the Río Cuyamel—"gold beyond all my expectations"—in approximately the same area where Morde had struck gold. But Glassmire couldn't get the lost city out of his mind. "When I got all through with my work," he told Elkins, "I went off looking for it." He selected ten men, including an old Sumu (Mayangna) Indian who said he had been to Ciudad Blanca as a boy and remembered where it was. "I had to bribe them pretty heavy with money to get them to go with me. We went far up a jungle river, what they call the Río Wampu, and then went off on a tributary called the Pao. We were in dugout canoes all this time. We ran out of stream and we had to take off on foot." They slashed their way overland. "It's one of the most terrific jungles in the world," he recalled. "The area is very mountainous, very rough, and very steep...I don't know of any more remote place in the world."

After six days of brutal overland travel, on March 10, 1960, he saw an unusual mound "like a giant ice cream cone, overturned and covered with greenery." In a small meadow they came across artifacts strewn over the ground, including what appeared to be a ceremonial seat or throne, decorated with an animal's head. As they pushed forward, "Other mounds bulged out of the boundless jungle carpet...I also discerned elusive ash-gray specks sprinkled throughout the shimmering greenness. My nine-power binoculars exposed them for what they were—ruins of stone buildings!"

"I found it!" he cried out to his Indian guides. "I've found Ciudad Blanca!"

They hacked their way through and around the city for three days, but he estimated that their movement through the jungle was so slow that the entire exploration of the city amounted to no more than "a walk around the park." He brought out a collection of beautiful stone carvings and other artifacts, saying he had to leave "tons" behind.

Glassmire tried to interest a foundation or a

university in the discovery. The University of Pennsylvania expressed a desire to have his collection, he told Elkins, so he shipped off the majority of his artifacts, photographs, and maps, but still retained many sculptured heads and stone bowls. His daughter, Bonnie, still has the collection, which I have seen. It contains stone vessels, metates, and stone heads of fine workmanship, including a fabulous carving of Quetzalcoatl, the Plumed Serpent, identical to one in the Michael Rockefeller collection at the Metropolitan Museum in New York. The artifacts alone suggest he found a major site, and a photograph taken of a cache of objects at the ruins shows a tremendous collection of sculptures that he had to leave behind. His hand-drawn map delineates previously unknown details of streams in the upper watershed of the Pao River, proving he did indeed penetrate that unexplored region. According to Glassmire's interview, the university mounted an expedition, but instead of coming in from the sea and going up the rivers by canoe, it started in the town of Catacamas and they tried to take a "shortcut" over the mountains. "Three or four of them were killed," he said, "two by snakes" and the others by disease. The expedition had to turn back.

I have been unable to confirm that this expedition ever took place, and the University of Pennsylvania insists they have no such collection. (I also checked with Penn State, in case he was confused.) But Glassmire's daughter, Bonnie, is equally certain her father sent some of his materials to the University of Pennsylvania Museum of Archaeology and Anthropology.

Glassmire gave a copy of his map to Steve Elkins. It was not quite detailed enough to nail down the precise location, but it was accurate enough for Elkins to later identify a valley that probably contained Glassmire's ruin. Elkins would name it "Target 4" in his aerial survey as we were looking for the White City many years later. Glassmire's discovery was a major step forward: It gave Elkins a convincing report of at least one important, unknown ruin deep in the Mosquitia interior. He took it as strong evidence that the legends of lost cities were not fantasy.

The second prong of Elkins's attack on the problem involved bringing the latest space-age technology to the search. For this, Elkins turned to Ron Blom at the Jet Propulsion Laboratory. Elkins knew of Ron Blom's successful quest to find the lost city of Ubar in the Rub' al Khali Desert—the Empty Quarter—on the Arabian Peninsula. Ubar, also called Iram of the Pillars, had been mentioned in the Koran, which said the "Lord poured upon them a scourge of punishment" for corruption, smiting the city and driving it into the sands. By scrutinizing images of the Empty Quarter desert from space, Blom and his team discovered a radiating pattern of ancient caravan trails, not visible on the ground, that converged at what was already known to be an ancient watering hole and caravanserai, a place where ancient camel caravans bedded down for the night. The satellite data indicated far more was there than a mere campsite. When the team excavated, they uncovered the shattered ruins of a fortress, over fifteen centuries old, with massive walls and eight towers, matching the description in the Koran. They also figured out what had happened: The constant removal of water from the watering hole undermined the fortress, which one day collapsed into a sinkhole and was buried by drifting sands. The legend recorded in the Koran was based on a real event.

Elkins called Blom and asked if he was interested in looking for another lost city. Blom said yes.

The problem, however, was that Mosquitia offered a far greater challenge than the Arabian Desert. The desert is an open book; synthetic aperture radar can peer fifteen feet or more into dry desert sands. The key is "dry": Water molecules strongly absorb radar. For this reason, jungle foliage is far more difficult to see through with radar—a big leaf will block a radar beam that can penetrate several feet of dry sand. Undeterred by the challenge, Blom and his team started by analyzing scores of satellite images of Mosquitia taken in infrared and visual wavelengths of light. They looked at synthetic aperture radar images taken from the Space Shuttle. Blom combined images, crunched data, massaged and enhanced it. It took months of effort, but finally it seemed Blom hit the jackpot. He and his team identified an area that seemed to contain rectilinear and curvilinear shapes that were not natural. They termed both the valley and the unknown feature Target One, or T1.

On May 12, 1997, Elkins faxed one of his partners, Tom Weinberg, with the news:

THIS VALLEY IS COMPLETELY SURROUNDED BY VERY STEEP MOUNTAINS WITH THE EXCEPTION OF ONE SMALL "CUT" THROUGH THE MOUNTAINS THAT ALLOWS ACCESS. THERE ARE TWO SMALL STREAMS THAT FLOW THROUGH THE VALLEY. IT IS A PERFECT SPOT FOR A SETTLEMENT... KIND OF REMINDS ME OF THE MOVIE, "SHANGRA LA"!

Excitedly, he noted at the end of the fax that Blom had identified a "RATHER LARGE (1800 FT. ACCORDING TO RON'S MEASUREMENT) L-SHAPED OBJECT."

The valley itself was striking: a mysterious geological formation that looked like a crater or bowl, walled in by steep, encircling ridges, creating a natural fortress. It did indeed look very much like the descriptions of Shangri-la or, even more apposite, Sir Arthur Conan Doyle's "lost world." The terrain inside the valley, watered by the two rivers, was gentle and friendly, consisting of hills, terraces, and floodplains, well suited for ancient farming and settlement. The satellite images showed no sign of human entry, occupation, or indigenous Indian use; it appeared to be pristine, untouched rainforest. Absolutely uninhabited areas of tropical rainforest are very rare in the world today; even the remotest reaches of the Amazon, for example, or the highlands of New Guinea, are used seasonally by indigenous people and have been at least minimally explored by scientists.

It was an exciting idea, but for now it was just an idea, a hypothesis. Even with intensive image processing, the immense, 150-foot, triple-canopy rainforest did not yield its secrets. Most of the unclassified satellite imagery at the end of the twentieth century had a coarse, ninety-foot ground resolution—in other words, the smallest thing that could be seen in the images was at least ninety feet on a side. The images showed blurred outlines that, if one stared at them long enough, looked unnatural, but it was far from definite proof. They were a bit like Rorschach blots—perhaps the mind was seeing things that weren't there.

Eager to learn more, Elkins wondered if the valley had ever been explored. He and his partner Tom Weinberg scoured the world for people who had spent time in Mosquitia, and interviewed them on camera. He collected the stories of archaeologists, gold prospectors, drug smugglers, geologists, looters, and adventurers. He hired researchers who combed the archives in Honduras and elsewhere, piecing together which areas of Mosquitia had been explored and which had not.

After much research, he determined that T1 was truly unexplored. Virtually all expeditions into Mosquitia had gone up the big rivers and their navigable tributaries. Rivers are the traditional highways of the jungle; expeditions that departed from those rivers never got very far in the fierce, impassable mountains. But T1 had no navigable rivers and it was completely walled off by mountains.

In the end it was a gut feeling Elkins had about T1: "I just thought that if I were a king, this would be the perfect place to hide my kingdom."

## CHAPTER 7

## The fish that swallowed the whale

Convinced he was on the verge of solving the mystery, Steve immediately began planning an expedition into T1. The logistics were a nightmare. The Honduran government bureaucracy that controlled the permits was erratic and dysfunctional. The factionalized political environment meant that if one politician agreed to help, the opposition blocked it. But with gentle persistence and cultivation of both sides, along with some well-placed funds, Elkins finally did get the permits to explore T1. During this entire time, he had carefully kept the location secret from the Honduran government, fearing the information might lead to possible looting—a high-level diplomatic balancing act. He successfully lined up six figures in financing. Hoping to avoid weeks of brutal overland travel, he planned to go in by helicopter.

But all his plans came to an abrupt end on October 29, 1998, when Honduras was struck by Hurricane Mitch. Mitch dumped as much as three feet of rain in some areas, causing catastrophic floods and mudslides, leaving seven thousand dead, spreading disease, and triggering looting and civil unrest. The storm inflicted damage equal to about 70 percent of Honduras's GDP, and it destroyed two-thirds of Honduras's roads and bridges. The expedition had to be cancelled. There was little sense of when, if ever, it could be restarted.

The president at the time said the storm had set back the Honduran economy by half a century. Many years of chaos and collapse followed, in which the murder rate soared while investment and the judicial system crumbled. One Honduran businessman told a reporter for the *Telegraph* in 2013: "This country is turning into the perfect zombie apocalypse."

There are two major reasons why Honduras had such a difficult time getting back on its feet after the storm. The first was the land-tenure system it inherited from Spain, in which a small number of extremely wealthy families ended up controlling most of the land. But even more debilitating was the country's unhealthy relationship with the United States, whose shortsighted policies and business interests had kept the country politically unstable for more than a century. From the time of its independence in 1821 to the present, Honduras has suffered through a tumultuous history that includes close to 300 civil wars, rebellions, coups, and unplanned changes in government.

One might say that modern Honduran history began in 1873, when Jules Verne introduced Americans to the banana in his novel *Around the World in 80 Days*, where he praised it as being "as healthy as bread and as succulent as cream." Originally from Asia, bananas had been grown in Central America for centuries since they had been brought there by the Spanish, but they were an exotic delicacy in the United States because of their scarcity and perishability. In 1885, Boston entrepreneur Andrew Preston* and a partner formed the Boston Fruit Company, with the idea of using fast steamships, rather than sail, to get bananas to market before they spoiled. It was a success: Inexpensive, delicious bananas took the country by storm. By the turn of the century Boston Fruit, which was later merged into the United Fruit Company, had carved out forty thousand acres of banana plantations along the northern coastline of Honduras,

---

* Since my family is from Boston, I asked my cousin Ellen Cutler, our resident family genealogist, if Andrew was a relation. She responded that he was indeed my fifth cousin, twice removed—"another imperialist capitalist on the family tree!"

becoming the largest employer in the country. This was the beginning of a long and destructive relationship between American banana companies and the country of Honduras, earning it the pejorative nickname "Banana Republic." United Fruit and the other fruit companies that soon followed became infamous for their political and tax machinations, engineered coups, bribery, and exploitation of workers. They strangled the country's evolution and cultivated a corrupt and extreme form of crony capitalism, in which they subverted the government to their own ends.

A central figure in this history was an American named Samuel Zemurray, a young Russian immigrant who started off as a pushcart peddler in Alabama. When he was eighteen, he noticed that the Boston Fruit cargo ships arriving in the port of Mobile were throwing away the bananas that had ripened during the voyage, because they would spoil before they could get to market. Zemurray bought a load of these ripe bananas for almost nothing, filled up a railroad car, and rolled it inland, telegraphing grocers along the way to meet the boxcar and buy his cheap bananas, quick. By the time he turned twenty-one he had made over $100,000 and had become known as Sam the Banana Man. Zemurray founded the Cuyamel Fruit Company, with two tramp steamers and five thousand acres of banana groves on the Honduran coast.

The American appetite for bananas was insatiable. (And it still is; the banana is consistently the number one–selling item in Walmart superstores.)

While the fruit companies were flourishing, the Honduran economy was in almost perpetual crisis. At this time, the British were still the bankers to the world, and they had unwisely loaned Honduras far more money than the country could repay. Honduran sovereign debt had grown so large that the British were threatening to go to war with Honduras to collect it. The possibility of the United Kingdom, or any European power, interfering in Central America was unacceptable to US President William Howard Taft. In 1910 his secretary of state, Philander Knox, recruited J. P. Morgan in a scheme to buy Honduran debt from the British—which he did at fifteen cents on the dollar—and restructure it. Under the deal Morgan struck with the Honduran government, Morgan's agents would physically occupy Honduran customs offices and shortstop all tax receipts to collect the debt.

This incensed Zemurray. Over the years, he had worked out a web of favorable tax-free deals with the Honduran government. Now Morgan was promising a banana tax so heavy, at a penny a pound, that Cuyamel Fruit would soon go out of business. Traveling to Washington to protest this new arrangement,

Zemurray had a meeting with Knox. The meeting did not go well. Knox lectured Zemurray with self-righteous zeal, insisting that Zemurray do his part to help the fine bankers at J. P. Morgan make money for the good of the country. Zemurray left furious, and Knox was worried enough about his reaction that he ordered a Secret Service detail to follow him.

Zemurray saw one simple solution to the problem: Overthrow the government of Honduras that had cut the deal with Morgan. Conveniently, a deposed former president of Honduras, Manuel Bonilla, was living penniless in New Orleans a few blocks from Zemurray's mansion. Easily avoiding Secret Service surveillance, Zemurray furtively recruited mercenaries to acquire arms, get a ship, and smuggle Bonilla back into Honduras. Meanwhile, he made sure the Honduran press railed against the "Morgan plan," emphasizing how it would subvert Honduran sovereignty. The Honduran people, already suspicious of the arrangement, were soon roused to revolutionary fervor. The "invasion" worked; Bonilla returned in triumph, the president of Honduras resigned, and Bonilla was elected in a landslide. He rewarded Zemurray with a twenty-five-year tax-free concession, a $500,000 loan, and a gift of 24,700 acres of excellent plantation land on the north coast.

Although the Honduran debt would mostly go

unpaid, Zemurray had achieved a remarkable personal victory. He had outmaneuvered Knox, successfully defied the US government, poked J. P. Morgan in the eye, and ended up a much wealthier man. In engineering the "invasion," he had covered his tracks so well that contemporary investigations into the scheme were never able to connect him to it or prove he broke any laws. But he had also intentionally overthrown a government to achieve his own financial ends.

Under the presidency of Andrew Preston, United Fruit had grown to be the largest fruit and sugar company in the world. But Zemurray's Cuyamel Fruit had also grown and was now powerful enough to engage it in debilitating price wars. In 1930, United Fruit solved the problem by buying Cuyamel Fruit, paying Zemurray $31 million in United Fruit stock and giving him a seat on the board. But the Great Depression hit United Fruit hard; after Preston's death in 1924, the company had become bloated, lazy, and mismanaged. Over the next few years, Zemurray watched United Fruit's stock decline by over 90 percent, shrinking his stake to $2 million. He tried to offer the board advice, but was rudely rebuffed. At that point the board was dominated by members of the Protestant elite of Boston, many—though not all—of whom were ugly anti-Semites; they did not like the Jewish immigrant they had been forced to admit to the board as part of the Cuyamel deal. In a fateful meeting in 1933, Zemurray tried once again to persuade the board to consider his ideas for saving the company; the chairman, an effete Boston Brahmin named Daniel Gould Wing, listened to Zemurray's heavy shtetl accent with open disdain and then, to the chuckles of other board members, said: "Unfortunately, Mr. Zemurray, I can't understand a word you say."

Zemurray was not a man to be ignored or insulted. He had come to that particular meeting with a weapon of mass destruction: a bagful of proxies from other United Fruit shareholders that gave him majority control of the company and the authority to act as he saw fit. He left the room, fetched the bag, came back in, and flung it on the table, saying: "You're fired. Can you understand *that*, Mr. Chairman?" He turned to the board and said: "You've been fucking up this business long enough. I'm going to straighten it out."

After ousting the chairman, president, and most of the board, Zemurray took over the gigantic, bumbling company, roused it from its stupor, and swiftly returned it to profitability. This dramatic move caused the *New York Times* to call Zemurray the "fish that swallowed the whale."

With full control of United Fruit, Zemurray continued to play a heavy hand in Honduran politics until he retreated from business in 1954 to pursue philanthropy full time. In the latter part of his life, perhaps to make up for his earlier questionable dealings, Zemurray donated lavishly to Central American causes, schools, and philanthropic ventures; he played a significant role in the founding of Israel; he endowed a female professorship at Harvard, which led to the appointment of the first woman full professor at that university; and he financed the progressive magazine the *Nation*. Zemurray was a remarkably brilliant, complex, and contradictory man.*

But, colorful as their history was, it must be said: Preston, Zemurray, and the fruit companies left a dark colonialist legacy that has hung like a miasma over Honduras ever since. The fruit companies' effect on Honduras's development was deeply pernicious. Though Honduras did eventually emerge from under their yoke, this legacy of instability and corporate bullying lives on in political dysfunction, underdeveloped national institutions, and cozy relationships among powerful families, business interests, government, and the military. This weakness magnified the disastrous effects of Hurricane Mitch. The country fell prey to narcotraffickers. Effective antidrug policies and raids

---

* His positive legacy lives on; his daughter, Doris Zemurray Stone, became a well-known archaeologist and ethnographer who did groundbreaking work in Honduras and Costa Rica. She and her husband founded the Stone Center for Latin American Studies at Tulane University.

in Colombia in the 1990s pushed much of the drug trade from that country into Honduras. Traffickers turned Honduras into the premier drug-smuggling transshipment point for cocaine between South America and the United States, and Mosquitia was at the heart of it. Crude airstrips were bulldozed out of the jungle and used for nighttime crash landings of drugs flown from Venezuela—the drugs being worth far more than the plane and the occasional death of a pilot. The murder rate soared while law enforcement and the judicial system crumbled. Violent gangs gained control of swaths of major cities, engaging in extortion and protection rackets and creating no-go zones for the military and police, except when the police themselves were involved in the activities, which was not uncommon. The unremitting gang violence caused thousands of desperate Honduran families to send their children northward, often alone, in search of safety in the United States.

There was no way Elkins could get permits or mount an expedition in this environment. The country looked hopeless. He gave up on the search for the White City, apparently for good. He told me then: "I've had enough. I'm done. Maybe this will be one mystery I can't solve."

## CHAPTER 8

## Lasers in the jungle

After giving up on the White City, Elkins turned his attention to the second item on Steve Morgan's list of mysteries: the Loot of Lima. He hoped, among other things, that the cutting-edge technology he had learned about in the search for the White City might also be applicable to a hunt for buried treasure. That search, into which he also drew me, would consume the next ten years of his life.

Also known as the Cocos Island treasure, the Loot of Lima was an alleged fortune in gold and gems—estimated to be worth around a billion dollars—that is believed to have been spirited out of Lima, Peru, in 1821, during the Peruvian War of Independence. The city of Lima was under siege, and the Spanish viceroy reportedly wanted to keep the city's vast treasure out of the hands of the revolutionaries, should the city fall to the rebels.

The revolutionaries had blockaded the harbor but were allowing noncombatant foreign ships free passage. The viceroy secretly entrusted the treasure to a British ship captained by an Englishman he knew well. Just in case, he placed on board a contingent of Spanish soldiers and priests to guard the treasure. The plan was for the ship to sail past the blockade and then either bring the treasure back if the city repelled the invaders, or take it to the Spanish treasury in Mexico for safekeeping.

But, as the story goes, the temptation of the treasure was too much. At the first opportunity past the blockade, the British crew murdered the soldiers and priests, threw their bodies into the sea, then took off with the treasure. Pursued by the Spanish, they landed on Cocos Island, a remote, uninhabited volcanic landmass in the Pacific Ocean. There they buried the treasure and sailed off. They were soon captured by a Spanish frigate. The Spanish hanged the officers and crew for piracy, sparing only the lives of the captain and first mate, on the condition that they lead them back to the treasure.

Once they arrived back on the island, the two men escaped into the island's mountainous interior. The Spanish hunted them for weeks until their supplies ran low and they had to give up and sail away. The captain and first mate were eventually rescued by a passing whaling ship that believed they had been shipwrecked. In secret, the British captain and first mate drew a map and prepared other documents recording the location of the buried treasure, intending to return for it at the earliest opportunity.

The captain died shortly thereafter. The first mate, a Scotsman named James Alexander Forbes, eventually settled in California, married the daughter of a prominent Spanish family, and became the patriarch of a wealthy, landowning California dynasty. He became so involved in his various business enterprises, and made so much money so fast, that he never did try to recover the treasure, but he allegedly gave his eldest son, Charles, the maps and documents indicating its location. Those materials were passed down in the Forbes family from father to son to the present day.

After Hurricane Mitch scuttled his White City dreams, Elkins and his partners teamed up with the Forbes family descendants who still had possession of the papers, and they began making plans to recover the treasure. Because the island, now a national park, had changed greatly over the years, many landmarks were gone. Elkins was keen to try out the latest technological advances in the remote sensing of metal buried under the ground. He and his partners spent years trying to raise money and obtain the necessary permits from the government of Costa Rica, which owns the island, but the project collapsed before reaching the point of an actual expedition. The treasure, if there, presumably remains undiscovered.

It was now 2010. Steve Elkins, at fifty-nine years old, had spent the last twenty years of his life and many thousands of dollars trying to solve two of the world's most enduring mysteries—and he had nothing to show for it.

And then, in that same discouraging year, Elkins read an article in *Archaeology* magazine entitled "Lasers in the Jungle." The article described a powerful technology called lidar, or Light Detection and Ranging, which had just been used to map the Maya city of Caracol, in Belize. The lidar mapping of Caracol was a watershed moment in archaeology. The article electrified him: He realized he might finally have the tool he needed to locate Ciudad Blanca.

Explorers had discovered Caracol in the 1930s and realized it was one of the largest cities in the Maya realm. The article told the story of how, in the 1980s, the husband and wife team of Arlen and Diane Chase had begun the daunting project of mapping Caracol and its environs. For twenty-five years, the Chases and teams of assistants and students tramped through the rainforest, recording and measuring every wall, rock, cave, terrace, road, tomb, and structure they could find. By 2009 they had created some of the most detailed maps ever made of a Maya city.

But over the years of work, the Chases felt continually frustrated. The city was enormous, and they always had the uneasy sense there was a great deal they weren't finding, due to the thickness of the jungle and the struggle and dangers of mapping in such an environment. "We cut paths with machetes," they wrote, "scramble through thick underbrush, and wonder what we might be missing." They longed for a better way to map the city without, they said, "spending another twenty-five years in the field."

And so they turned to a new tool: lidar. Although lidar had been used for mapping the moon's surface and doing large-scale terrestrial charting, only in the previous decade had it gained the resolution necessary to resolve fine-scale archaeological features. It had been used to map the ruins of Copán after the hurricane, but that was about the extent of its use in Central America. The Chases joined forces with NASA and the National Center for Airborne Laser Mapping (NCALM) at the University of Houston to map Caracol using airborne lidar, a technology many times more powerful than the radar and satellite data available to Blom. The best ground resolution Blom could obtain in the mid-nineties was about ninety feet; lidar promised a resolution of better than three feet even under the forest canopy.

NCALM owned a small Cessna Skymaster that had had its guts ripped out to carry a big green box containing the million-dollar lidar machine. A pilot trained in lidar missions flew the aircraft from Houston to Belize, where he was joined by three mapping engineers. The team flew five missions over Caracol and its environs, scanning the rainforest with lasers, a process that took a little over a week.

When the images came back, the Chases were floored. "Seemingly without effort," they wrote, "the system produced a detailed view of nearly eighty square miles—only 13 percent of which had previously been mapped—revealing topography, ancient structures, causeways, and agricultural terraces," as well as caves, terracing, buildings, tombs—tens of thousands of archaeological features that their ground-mapping had missed. In five days, lidar had accomplished seven times more than the Chases had achieved in twenty-five years.

Their paper declared lidar a "scientific revolution," and an "archaeological paradigm shift." It was, they said, the greatest archaeological advance since carbon-14 dating.

## CHAPTER 9

**It was something that nobody had done.**

The more Elkins studied lidar, the more he was convinced that, if the lost city existed and he had the fortitude to resume the search, lidar would find it. His excitement, however, was tempered by the thought of trying to get the permits from the Honduran government, which had been a nightmare the previous time around. The government had changed hands several times and undergone a military coup, and the permitting process looked more daunting than ever. "I wondered," Elkins told me, "if I wanted to go through all that bullshit again." Mosquitia in the dozen intervening years had become extremely dangerous, an outlaw region controlled by violent drug cartels and criminal gangs. Even to fly a plane in Mosquitia airspace was perilous, as it was the prime flight corridor of cocaine smugglers, where unidentified planes might be shot down by either the US or Honduran military.

Then came one of those crazy coincidences that a novelist wouldn't dare put in a book. As Steve Elkins was pondering what to do, he got a call from his old friend and fixer in Honduras, Bruce Heinicke.

Bruce and his Honduran wife, Mabel, had moved to St. Louis in 1996 after Mabel's sister had been murdered in Honduras. Bruce gave up his drug smuggling and looting career and settled down to more mundane pursuits. But he, like Elkins, couldn't shake his obsession with finding the White City.

At the end of 2009, Mabel returned to Tegucigalpa, without Bruce, to attend her father's funeral. At the time, the country was recovering from a military coup. The coup had taken place earlier in the year, when the current leftist president, José Manuel Zelaya, had launched a heavy-handed effort to hold a referendum to rewrite the Constitution so that he could try to gain a second term of office. The Supreme Court ruled the attempt illegal; Zelaya defied the court; and the Honduran Congress ordered his arrest. Early on a Sunday morning, the military disarmed the presidential guard, rousted Zelaya from bed, and put him on a plane to Costa Rica, where, in the airport, he gave a fiery speech of defiance still wearing his pajamas. The press reported that Zelaya had been forced out of the country so quickly he wasn't allowed to dress, but Honduran officials privately told me later that he had been allowed to dress and take some clothes with him; in a moment of wily stagecraft, he had changed back into his pajamas on the airplane in order to garner more sympathy and outrage.

The military turned power back over to the civilian sector, and elections were held five months later. Those bitterly contested elections brought into power Porfirio "Pepe" Lobo Sosa. While Mabel was in the church for the funeral, she heard that Pepe, the new president-elect, would be attending services in the same church the following Saturday with his cabinet, to get God's blessing for his upcoming four-year term.

She mentioned this in a phone call to Bruce, who urged her to seize the opportunity. Mabel told me in an interview: "Bruce kept bringing it up all week. 'You get close with this guy,' he said 'and explain to him about the White City. Just leave the rest up to me.'"

On the day of the president's visit, she went to the church with her brother, Mango, a Honduran soccer star, to try to buttonhole the president. The place was jammed. The president arrived late, with twenty bodyguards and a contingent of local police with rifles.

After the service, Mango told Mabel to stay in her seat and he would arrange everything. He went up to talk to the pastor, but as their conversation dragged on, it became clear to Mabel that he was getting nowhere. Meanwhile, the president and his entourage got up to leave, and Mabel realized she was about to lose the opportunity. She rose from her seat and barreled through the thronging crowds, shoving people aside. She drove toward the president, who was surrounded by a chain of bodyguards with arms linked. She called out his name—"Pepe! Pepe!"—but he ignored her. Finally she rammed her way to the ring of guards, reached over them, and grabbed the president's arm. "I said, 'Pepe, I need to speak to you!'"

"Okay," he replied, resignedly turning toward her, "you got my attention."

"I said to the bodyguards, 'Excuse me, let me through.' And they shook their heads no. The bodyguards put their hands on their guns. They were holding their hands very strong and I was trying to push them around. Pepe was laughing and I told him, 'Can you tell them to let me through?' They did, then they closed the circle around me holding hands again, very tight.

"I ask him if he had heard about Ciudad Blanca. He says yes. I say my husband tried to find this city twenty years ago. He says, 'This sounds kind of interesting, keep going.' I say he's been there.* He says,

---

* This is of course an exaggeration. As I heard more of Bruce's stories I realized he habitually referred to almost any large ruin in Mosquitia as the "White City."

'Can your husband go there again?' And I say, 'That's why we need your permission.'"

Lobo looked at her and finally answered: "Okay, you made it through here. You got to me, God only knows how. I've heard about this city but I've never heard of anyone who's been there physically. I trust you and I want you to trust me. I will introduce you to a member of my cabinet. He will speak for me, and he will be able to get all your permits and everything you need to get this done. His name is África Madrid."

So Mabel went to where the cabinet had gathered and found África. "I start talking with him about the project. He said, 'Wow, that does sound interesting.' He said, 'If the president told you we're going to do it, we're going to do it. I'm going to get you everything you need.'"

They exchanged e-mail addresses.

As Mabel was leaving, she saw the president getting into his car and rushed over to him, asking to have a selfie taken with him on her cell phone. He obliged and then asked for the phone, saying he wanted to speak to her husband. She gave it to him and he called Bruce Heinicke in the States.

"I'm sitting in St. Louis, and here comes this call," Heinicke said to me. "It's the president of Honduras on the phone. He asks me, 'You really know where it's at?' I said, 'Yes, sir.' He said, 'I want to do this. It will be good for the country.'"

The president hung up the phone and gave it back to Mabel, saying, "Now can I go?"

"Yes, Pepe," she said, "you can go." Mabel recalled: "He took off like I was going to chase him down and ask for something else!"

Elkins was astounded and skeptical when he heard this bizarre story, which happened to coincide with his reading the article on lidar. But when he followed up with Bruce and the new Honduran government, he discovered it was true. President Lobo was enthusiastic about the project, seeing the advantages such a discovery would offer his country as well as its potential to bolster his own shaky popularity.

With the president's blessing and his permits assured, Elkins flew to Houston to meet with the staff at the National Center for Airborne Laser Mapping, which had mapped Caracol, to try to persuade them to take on his scheme. NCALM is a joint project of the University of Houston and the University of California, Berkeley, funded by the National Science Foundation, and its mission is confined to academic and scientific research, not raw exploration for lost cities that probably don't exist. The co–principal investigator and chief scientist at NCALM is a man named William Carter, one of the fathers of lidar. As a graduate student, Carter had worked on the Apollo missions and helped design and operate one of the first lunar laser ranging stations, able to measure the earth–moon distance to an accuracy of a few centimeters.

Elkins spent the day trying to convince Carter and Ramesh Shrestha, director of NCALM, and their team to join in the search for the lost city. It was an eccentric proposal, unlike anything NCALM had done in the past. With Caracol, they were mapping a world-renowned site with guaranteed results; Elkins's project was a crapshoot that might be a waste of time and a scientific embarrassment. Lidar had never been used before as a tool of pure archaeological exploration—that is, to look for something nobody could be sure even existed.

"We don't really know if there's anything there," Shrestha said. "The question is: Can we find anything at all?" But Carter was impressed that Elkins had earlier enlisted NASA in the hunt for the city. He looked over Ron Blom's images of T1 and felt there was enough there to take a chance.

It was a risky project on many levels. Shrestha remembered their debate. "It was something that nobody had done. It had the potential to find something and have a significant impact in the archaeological field. I said explicitly to Steve: 'Look, this is an experimental project. We will do the best we can. We can't promise it will work—and we can't take the blame if it doesn't!'" Shrestha and Carter were both, however, attracted to the challenge of trying to map terrain under the densest rainforest on earth. If lidar worked in Mosquitia it would work anywhere. It would be the ultimate test of the technology.

A few members of the NCALM team were more skeptical. "There were some on my staff," said Shrestha, "who said we cannot do this" because the rainforest is too thick.

" 'Without trying it,' I said, 'you can't tell me it's not doable.' "

Others were troubled that no archaeologists were involved. "Steve Elkins is a *film* guy," Michael Sartori, the chief mapping scientist at NCALM, said to me later. "Many times, I told my coworkers that this was a bad idea, that this is not the kind of project we should be doing. This is not the normal mode of supplying quality data to academics in the field of archaeology."

Elkins first proposed to NCALM that they survey all of Mosquitia with lidar. But when he learned it would cost millions of dollars, he whittled down the search area to about fifty square miles. Mapping that would run to about a quarter million dollars in direct costs and a similar amount in supporting costs.

T1 was only twenty square miles. In case T1 came up empty, Steve chose three other unexplored areas to survey. He called these T2, T3, and T4. T2 was a deep valley surrounded by white limestone cliffs that had also been rumored to contain the White City. T3 was an area like T1—difficult to get to, scientifically unexplored, a gentler landscape with large open areas, locked in by mountains. T4 was the valley where Elkins believed Sam Glassmire had found his ruin.

Elkins did intensive research into the four target areas to see if any recent exploration had been done, archaeological or otherwise. He pulled together the latest maps of all the known archaeological sites in Mosquitia. He combed the archives of the Honduran Institute of Anthropology and History looking for unpublished reports, and he searched the official Honduran register of archaeological sites.

Over the course of the twentieth century, archaeologists had identified about two hundred archaeological sites in Mosquitia. This is almost nothing when compared to the many hundreds of thousands of sites recorded in the Maya region, or the 163,000 registered archaeological sites in my home state of New Mexico. These two hundred Mosquitia sites ranged from some large settlements with massive earthworks to many smaller sites, cave burials, rock art, and artifact scatters that all appeared to belong to the same widespread culture. Many of these sites, unlike in the Maya area, were simply dots on a map that had never been accurately surveyed, and virtually none had been fully excavated. A century of archaeology in Mosquitia had produced few answers, and much that had been done was limited, superficial, or of poor quality. Archaeologists so far had not been able to answer some of the most basic questions of this culture—who they were, where they came from, how they lived, and what happened to them. Without doubt, Mosquitia harbored many, many undiscovered sites that would yield essential secrets.

Elkins could find absolutely no archival evidence that anyone had ever explored T2, T3, or (aside from Glassmire) T4. With no record of human entry, they were blank, unknown to science. But were they also uninhabited? The archives wouldn't document indigenous use of the areas for hunting and gathering.

Elkins ordered the latest satellite imagery of the four target areas. When the imagery came in, he had a shock. The most recent satellite photography of T4, the valley containing Glassmire's White City, showed that it was pockmarked with several recent clear-cuts from illegal deforestation. Deforestation and archaeological looting go hand in hand; Glassmire's ruin, if it existed, would have been uncovered and quietly looted, its movable artifacts likely dispersed into the black market or hauled off by locals. But Elkins also knew that there were many big ruins in Mosquitia, known and unknown, any one of which might be the legendary White City, if it indeed existed in its described form, which was at the time an open question. Elkins eliminated T4 from the list.

Sadly, T4's fate was far from unusual. The Honduran rainforests are disappearing at a rate of at least 300,000 acres a year. Between 1990 and 2010, Honduras lost over 37 percent of its rainforest to clear-cutting. All of Elkins's targets of interest lie within or close to the nominally protected Tawahka Asangni Biosphere and Río Plátano Biosphere Reserves, but protection and law enforcement are weak. The remoteness, the rugged mountains, and the hostility of the jungle are no match for the profits to be gained from logging and cattle grazing. Archaeology is in a race against deforestation; by the time archaeologists can reach a rainforest site to survey it, it may well be gone, fallen prey first to the logger's ax and then the looter's shovel.

The permits to lidar the Mosquitia rainforest were granted in October of 2010. They came with the blessing of the president and the minister of the interior and population, Áfrico Madrid, along with the full support of the Instituto Hondureño de Antropología e Historia (IHAH) and its chief, Virgilio Paredes. The new government of Honduras was squarely behind the search.

President "Pepe" Lobo was taking office after a contested election at one of the lowest points in Honduran history. The Honduran economy was the second poorest in the Americas. Large swaths of the countryside, towns, and parts of some large cities had been taken over by narcotraffickers. Gangs had sprouted up and were running brutal extortion and kidnapping rackets. The murder rate, already the highest in the world, was skyrocketing. Corruption was rampant. The judicial system and law enforcement were in collapse. The people were impoverished, adrift, cynical, and restive. The 2009 coup had left the country, including the archaeological community, bitterly fractured. Honduras was a country desperately in need of good news. The discovery of the White City, President Lobo told me later, would be that good news.

## CHAPTER 10

**I would never go back up that river. That's the most dangerous place on the planet, that river.**

With permits in hand, Elkins went out to raise money. He asked a friend, filmmaker Bill Benenson, to help him find investors for a film project documenting the search. Benenson knew a lot of money people. But after thinking about it for a while, Benenson decided to look for the money in his own pocket. This was too good an opportunity: He would finance the expedition himself. Eventually, Benenson and Elkins divided their filmmaking roles into being codirectors of the documentary film, with Benenson being the sole producer, and Tom Weinberg and Steve credited as coproducers.

Seventy-two years old at the time of the project, Benenson is a fit, handsome man with a close-clipped beard. He speaks with deliberation, weighing every word, and he does not look like a man who takes risks. He admitted that the project was an "amazing insanity" but he felt driven to take a chance on it. "I'm *interested* in this story. And also in this lost city and all the adventurers, liars, and crazy people who've been looking for it. If you're going to be a gambler at all with a film project, I thought this was the one to put my money on. This was my number 17 on the roulette wheel."

Benenson's grandfather, Benjamin, came to America from Belarus in the late nineteenth century and settled in the Bronx, New York. He worked as a carpenter, initially building houses for other people, switched to building for himself, and today Benenson Capital Partners, of which Bill is a principal, is a major real estate company owning premier properties in Manhattan and elsewhere. But Benenson's real love is film and its intersection with anthropology and archaeology. Out of college, he joined the Peace Corps and spent two years in Brazil, where he made his first film, *Diamond Rivers*, which aired on PBS. Today he has more than twenty feature films and documentaries to his credit. He was an executive producer of the documentary *Beasts of No Nation*, and he directed and produced *The Hadza: Last of the First*, about the last true remaining hunter-gatherer people of East Africa.

Benenson had a keen eye for offbeat projects, and

he believed that even if nothing was found, the failure of yet another crazy search for the legendary city would actually make an engaging film. Elkins and Benenson, with other partners, created a company called UTL, LLC—"Under the Lidar"—to handle the details of the expedition and film.

With things finally turning a corner on his decades-old project, Elkins proceeded to put together a team. He and I had been in regular communication for years, and he asked if I'd write about the search for the *New Yorker*, for which I occasionally wrote archaeological pieces. I agreed, but only reluctantly. Truth be told, I was so skeptical about the outcome that I decided not to pitch the idea to the *New Yorker* at all until after the expedition was over—and only then if they found something. I didn't want to risk looking like a bloody fool if the lidar survey came up empty, which I thought was likely, given that every attempt to find the lost city in the past five hundred years had ended in fraud or failure. When I confessed this to Steve, he said, "Well, if we draw a blank, at least you'll get a vacation out of it."

On April 28, 2012, the ten members of the expedition rendezvoused in Houston and flew as a group to the island of Roatán, in the Gulf of Honduras. Roatán is a world apart from the Honduran mainland; thirty miles long and about two miles wide, it is a tropical paradise of pearlescent sand beaches, turquoise waters, dazzling coral reefs, fishing villages, and luxury resorts—a major cruise ship and scuba dive destination. Because of its history as a British colony, English is the primary language.

Lovely as it was for a vacation spot, Elkins and Benenson had chosen Roatán, above all, because the island's airport offered better security than the mainland for our plane and its classified payload. The State Department had issued a two-week permit for the plane to leave the country, but the permit required it to be kept in a high-security, nonpublic area with armed guards protecting it day and night. Elkins and Benenson hired the Honduran military to do the job.

Roatán, being in the northeastern part of the country, was also well situated with regard to Mosquitia: The three target areas were only about an hour's flying time away. It had one drawback, however: The Roatán airport was forbidden to stock aviation gas. Because of narcotrafficking, avgas was tightly controlled in Honduras. Fuel tankers were routinely hijacked, the drivers killed and the fuel diverted for drug smuggling. The Cessna would have to touch down at the airport in La Ceiba, on the mainland, to refuel after every lidar flight before returning to Roatán.

At our headquarters, the Parrot Tree Plantation on the island's south shore, the expedition team occupied a cluster of bungalows with red tile roofs, spreading along the shores of a turquoise lagoon, surrounded by white sand beaches, burbling fountains, and rustling palm trees. The suites sported marble bathrooms, kitchens with granite countertops, and bedrooms trimmed in polished tropical hardwoods. The complex was air-conditioned to frostbite levels. Behind the bungalows sprawled a huge freshwater pool, set among fake rocks, waterfalls, bridges, and dew-laden clusters of tropical flowers, with pergolas draped in snowy sheets, chiffon curtains billowing in the tropical breezes. At the adjacent marina, million-dollar yachts sat in their berths, lapped by Caribbean waters, their polished hulls blazing in the sun. The hills above were sprinkled with whitewashed villas.

"Why be uncomfortable?" Elkins said, as we gathered for a dinner of grilled lobster tails under a *palapa* on the beach, looking out over the lagoon, the night sky glittering with stars, the waves whispering along the strand.

These luxurious surroundings, however, only heightened the expedition's anxious mood. On its journey down from Houston, the tiny Cessna had gotten stuck in the Florida Keys, grounded by a series of storms over the Gulf. It could be days before the weather cleared.

Benenson and Elkins were paying thousands of dollars a day for everyone to sit around waiting. Nobody was happy.

NCALM had sent down three lidar engineers to run the mission: Dr. Juan Carlos Fernández Díaz, mission planner and chief lidar engineer; Michael Sartori, resident skeptic and data-mapping scientist; and Abhinav Singhania, lidar technician.

Fernández was, by happy coincidence, Honduran by birth. He had a PhD in Geosensing Systems Engineering from the University of Florida; he also held an MBA, summa cum laude, from the Catholic University of Honduras, and he was a Fulbright scholar. His familiarity with Honduran politics and culture, his fluency in Spanish, his knowledge of lidar, and his engaging personality would make him one of the most indispensable members of the expedition. The thirty-five-year-old engineer had a calm, matter-of-fact presence, behind which lay a brilliant scientific mind and a sly sense of humor. He was diplomatic, soft-spoken, and never ruffled when everything was going to hell around him, which happened frequently during the course of the expedition. Juan Carlos was delighted to be part of the project, and his involvement has since made him into a kind of national hero in Honduras. "It has to be the Monkey Gods," he said with a laugh, "an amazing combination of luck, chance, and fate that I was in a position to help. If you're from Honduras, you're a mix of so many different things, Spanish and Indian. Even though my name is Spanish, I know there is some Indian in there." He was hopeful about what the effort would mean for his country. "The people of Honduras don't have a clear cultural identity. We have to start learning more about our past in order to create a brighter future."

Sartori, by contrast, made no secret of his skepticism. "You're really going to go down there in this *huge* wilderness, and you're going to target these areas, but you don't know what's there? It just seems like such a crazy shot in the dark." The absurd poshness of the resort, so unlike the usual penurious academic field expedition, added to his misgivings.

The expedition team also included a film crew, a still photographer, and Tom Weinberg, the film's other coproducer and the expedition's official chronicler. Weinberg was a man with an infectious laugh and a sweet, gentle personality, seventy-two years old, with a fringe of unruly gray hair and a beard. He had been working with Elkins since 1994 on the White City project. In his long career in film and television, he had earned several Emmy Awards and had become a legend in the Chicago film world. He cofounded the TVTV video collective in 1972, which produced "guerilla video" documentaries on progressive subjects in American culture and politics; later, he created the Media Burn Independent Archive, which, long before the Internet, stored thousands of hours of important documentary footage that might have been lost otherwise, including most of Studs Terkel's interviews.

The most unforgettable member of the group was Bruce Heinicke, Elkins's longtime fixer par excellence. I had been curious to meet him for years, after hearing Steve's vivid descriptions of him and his adventures. I found him under the palapa bar before dinner, a morbidly obese man wearing a Panama hat, unbuttoned Hawaiian shirt displaying gold chains, a cigarette in one hand and a beer in the other. He had a terrific scowl on his face. He told me he had returned from the airport, "where I just handed out a fucking Kansas City roll" to get the expedition's equipment through Roatán's customs office—computers, video and film cameras, sound gear, tripods, and all the rest. Even with the blessing of the president, people needed to be taken care of. "They wanted a 'deposit' of a hundred eighty thousand dollars," he said, his jowls trembling at the outrage of it. "Said they would give it back when the equipment left the country. I told them, 'No, no, that's not fucking gonna happen.' But a lot of grease went to a lot of different people." When I started taking notes, he said, "You can't print a fucking word I tell you unless I say so specifically." He had a trove of tales, but at the end of almost every story, he turned his watery eyes on me, jabbed his finger, and said: "You can't write that down. It's off the record."

Finally, in frustration, I asked him: "Isn't there a way I can tell at least *some* of these stories?"

"Oh sure," he said, "absolutely. No problem. After I'm fucking *dead!*"* He snorted with laughter and almost choked on an eruption of phlegm.

I asked Bruce about his relationship with Steve Elkins and how their partnership worked.

"Lemme tell you a story. I was in a restaurant and some guys were mouthing off. I could see trouble coming. So I put a gun at this guy's head and said, 'Get the fuck out of here or you'll see all your fucking brains all over the fucking wall behind you.' That's the way I get things done. You gotta be that way down here. *Don't fuck with that gringo, he will fucking kill you.* When you're dealing with people like that, they got no respect for anybody, human life's not important, so you have to treat them that way or you will get walked all over. Steve thinks everybody is his friend. He wants to be their friend. And he doesn't

---

* Bruce Heinicke later allowed me to take extensive notes, from which these conversations have been taken, as long as I promised not to publish anything until after his death. He passed away on September 8, 2013.

understand that some people, they're just looking for a chance to rob you and maybe kill you. Steve trusts everybody and down here you just can't."

Heinicke had a bum knee from a gunshot wound, which he was happy to explain. Back before he met his wife, he'd dated a Colombian woman and become close to her father, who ran one of the major drug cartels in Colombia. Heinicke did some business for the father, transporting drugs and collecting money. He was caught by the DEA, who demanded he work for them as an undercover informant, to avoid prison. But he said he continued to work for the cartel boss and kept the DEA satisfied by giving up some low- and mid-level people from the cartel. "I was smuggling coke out of fucking Colombia," making a cocaine delivery from Colombia to Nicaragua for his boss, he said. He went to Cartagena to pick up the "product" in a small duffel bag, to carry to the contact, who was supposed to pay $75,000 for it. He went to a shuttered restaurant, where he was surprised to see not one man, but two. One man had a bag full of money. "I told him to show me the money. He started to walk over and I told him to stop and just open the bag and slide it over," which he did. As the man stepped back, both men pulled guns and started shooting at Heinicke. "They were only ten feet from me when I pulled my .45 and shot one in the right shoulder, the other in the face, and before the one I shot in the shoulder hit the ground I split his head like a watermelon. The whole gunfight took two to three seconds. I caught a round in the right knee." He collected all the guns, money, and drugs. He was in terrible pain, so he snorted some lines and packed cocaine powder into the bullet wound, which made him feel better.

"I had seventy-five thousand dollars cash in a fucking backpack, five kilos of cocaine, and two pistols," he said. "This friend in La Ceiba flew down. I said, 'Get me out of here, I got a bullet in me.' Later, X [I have removed here the name of a well-known American writer and ex-soldier] set me up with the US Embassy out of Honduras—they sent me to Nicaragua to take pictures of Sandinista encampments and get GPS locations."

After dinner, Elkins led the team in a planning meeting. The first item on the agenda was getting our cover story straight for the locals. Only a few people in the Honduran government knew what we were doing. There was to be no loose talk of Ciudad Blanca or the Lost City of the Monkey God. We were, Elkins explained, merely a bunch of nerdy scientists doing an aerial survey of Mosquitia using a new technology, to study the ecology, rainforest, flora, and fauna. The legend had grown to the point where many Hondurans were convinced the White City hid an immense treasure in gold; it would not be safe if our actual activities became known.

Before launching the plane, the lidar team had to find secure locations for three fixed GPS units to be erected on the ground. These units would communicate with the GPS unit in the plane during flight. Each unit had to have a power source and, ideally, an Internet connection to upload the data. Juan Carlos Fernández had worked out the geometry of the system, which was difficult to do since most of the ground area was either impassable or too dangerous. He finally mapped out an almost linear arrangement for placement of the units: one on Roatán Island, the second forty-five airline miles away in Trujillo (the coastal city near where Cortés wrote his letter to Emperor Charles V), and the third in a tiny village called Dulce Nombre de Culmi, at the edge of Mosquitia, a hundred miles distant. The first unit was erected at the end of the beach that formed the artificial lagoon at the Parrot Tree. The second went onto the roof of the Christopher Columbus Hotel in Trujillo.

Placing the third—and most crucial—receiver in Dulce Nombre de Culmi posed a greater challenge. Culmi was the closest you could reasonably get to the Mosquitia interior. The town lay a dangerous sixteen-hour drive from Trujillo, on roads infested with drug smugglers and bandits. The team decided to bring the GPS unit in by helicopter and set it up at a farm outside Culmi owned by a cousin of Mabel and Mango's.

But hours before the flight, the helicopter Elkins had reserved for the trip to Culmi was expropriated by the US DEA for an antidrug operation. Bruce was tasked with borrowing a helicopter and pilot on short notice from the Honduran government, which he was—astoundingly—able to do. ("Who else could get a fucking helicopter in fifteen minutes in a country like Honduras? These guys here don't appreciate what I do.") While flying in, Mango couldn't recognize his cousin's farm from the air so the chopper had to land in the village's soccer field to ask directions, causing a sensation. Fernández erected the GPS in a pasture on the farm, where its very remoteness would keep it secure, powered by a solar panel and deep-cycle battery. Because there was no Internet connection, Mango had to physically retrieve the data every day on a USB stick and drive it to Catacamas, the closest town with an Internet connection, several hours south on a dirt road, and upload it to NCALM in Houston. This was no simple task. The drive was risky, as Catacamas was ruled by a drug cartel and had one of the highest murder rates of any city in the world. But, as Mango explained, the narcotraffickers stuck to their own business as long as they weren't bothered. After he uploaded the data to Houston, Michael Sartori could then download it to his laptop on Roatán Island.

For three days we waited for the plane to complete its final leg from Key West to Roatán. We lounged around the resort, subjected to an enforced vacation, eating, drinking beer, and—luxury be damned—getting ever more irritable and impatient for the search to begin.

Every day, around noon, the peculiar figure of Bruce Heinicke would appear in the shade of the palapa, where he ensconced himself in a fanback wicker chair like Jabba the Hutt, beer and cigarettes at hand. He would remain parked there for most of the afternoon and evening, unless something happened that required his attention, in which case he could be heard swearing into his cell phone in Spanish or English. With nothing else to do, I got in the habit of buying him a beer and listening to his stories.

He talked openly about his days looting archaeological sites in Mosquitia. (I was surprised he'd be so forthcoming about these activities, given the nature of his employment with Steve, but he was never concerned by contradictions.) "In the early nineties," he said, "I had a friend, Dimas, we used to go out and dig up gravesites and steal artifacts, and I was smuggling those to the States."

Somewhere far up an unnamed river, while on one of these looting expeditions, Bruce shot a tapir for dinner. They had camped on a sandbar and built a fire. Bruce cut the meat into strips, but as he laid it on hot stones to cook, he "heard a loud screaming growl." He grabbed his M16 and turned just in time to see an animal charging them; he had the weapon on full-auto and sprayed it with "at least twenty rounds"; it dropped five feet from him: a huge, seven-foot jaguar. He and Dimas rolled it into the river. "I hated to kill the jaguar," Bruce said. "It was such a beautiful animal."

The next day, they reached a fork in the river and went up a small tributary, wading in the shallow, fast-running stream. After two days they reached the site. About forty feet up the steep embankment, sticking out, was the side of a huge, carved stone table. They climbed out of the river and, in the benchlands above, found piles "of what used to be stone structures all over the place." Bruce scrambled down the embankment to the table and cleared some dirt away, exposing a vivid, snarling, carved jaguar. The table was too large to remove whole, so they spent three days chiseling the jaguar from it. Then, poking among the piles of stones for an entrance into the underground structures or tombs, they exposed a hole. Bruce stuck his head in and spied pottery on the floor about five feet below. He squeezed through and dropped down, but landed awkwardly on the floor, twisting his leg and tearing the tendons in his knee, which was still weak from the shootout at the drug deal.

He tried to stand up but couldn't, and he called to Dimas to get him a stick to use as a crutch. While he was waiting, his eyes adjusted to the darkness, and that was when he saw that the "floor was alive with spiders, scorpions, and a few snakes for good measure." But the same survey revealed that the walls were pockmarked with niches, inside of which sat gorgeous painted pots and marble bowls. Hobbling gingerly around the creatures at his feet, he collected the treasures and handed them up to Dimas. As he worked his way farther into the underground room, he spied a bright yellow object on the floor. He picked it up, stunned: It was a solid gold statue, about two and a half inches wide and five inches tall, "the most beautiful gold art I'd ever seen." He said it "looked like some kind of king with a feather headdress and a shield on his chest. It was very thick." He found more items, including hundreds of polished jade beads. "Anything that wasn't perfect I didn't fuck with."

After clearing out the room, they made their way back downriver to civilization, and headed for the

States. They got the loot through customs in their carry-on bags by mixing the artifacts in with a lot of "tourist junk" bought at a gift shop, putting fake prices on everything, and wrapping them in newspaper.

The next day, Bruce was at the bar in the Metropolitan Club in New York City, drinking Chivas on the rocks. "I used to meet X there"—this was that same writer—who had previously helped him sell looted antiquities. "X had buyers." When X arrived, Bruce took him to his hotel room and showed him the loot. "He said, 'Son of a bitch, this is great. Bruce, old boy, you've topped it all!'"

But Bruce had no idea what he had, and neither did X. And so X contacted "a gal" he knew who worked at an auction house I will call Y. "She would take a look at stuff and tell us what we had." The woman met the two of them in Bruce's room, with all the artifacts spread out on the bed. When she saw them, her mouth fell open and she exclaimed, "You're fucking crazy!" She told them what the pieces were and what they were worth, although she couldn't positively identify the culture they came from, because they were so unusual. She also helped connect them with buyers. They sold the artifacts a few pieces at a time, so as not to flood the market. "We were making a ton of money, I'm not shitting you. That gold statue, it sold for two hundred forty thousand dollars back then—that was in the early nineties." The looted objects disappeared into the vast black market of the Central American antiquities trade, probably never to be seen again.

I continued to buy Bruce beers, and the stories continued to roll out. Despite his foul language and alarming appearance, he had a certain rough charm and charisma, conveyed by a pair of deep blue eyes. As he talked, I found myself again amazed that Steve would team up with a man with this history to locate what could be one of the most important archaeological sites in Central America. I recalled his aside to me earlier about having to "dance with the devil" at times to make things happen. It was undeniably true that Bruce's help was crucial to the success of the effort.

"There's two ways to get in there [into Mosquitia]," Bruce told me, "the Río Plátano and the Río Patuca. I had had some problems up the Río Patuca. I was buying gold from some Indians who panned for gold up in that area. I bought some gold, maybe eight ounces total. The guys who were taking me up there decided they were gonna rob me. I got up where the Wampu and the Patuca meet. The Wampu heads west toward the Río Plátano. As I got in the boat, they hit me with an oar, knocked me into the water. I came out of the water with my .45. The other guy was coming at me with a machete. I shot him in the face, and shot the other guy. Tied them together and towed them to where the alligators are and cut them loose. I would never go back up that river. That's the most dangerous place on the planet, that river. When I got back to Brus Lagoon, I had to call in and get a private plane to pick me up. I had to hide in the bushes by the airstrip until the plane got there. After that I avoided that area up the Río Patuca like the plague. Life has no meaning up there."

## CHAPTER 11

**It's uncharted territory: You're out there on your own, out in the middle of nowhere.**

On May 1, the weather finally cleared on Key West. The plane carrying the lidar machine took off, refueled in Grand Cayman, and arrived in the Roatán airport at 2:00 p.m. Everyone rushed out to the airport to meet it, applauding and cheering when it finally touched down. Now our search for the lost city could begin.

The Skymaster is a twin-engine aircraft driven by what aviators call a push-pull configuration, with the two engines mounted in-line, one on the nose and the other at the rear of the fuselage. The plane's most distinctive features are two struts or booms that extend behind the wings. Once a cheerful red and white, the paint job on this plane was full of patches and strips that had peeled off, and an ugly streak of oil ran down the fuselage from the forward engine. A big green lidar box almost filled the interior of the plane. This sleek, advanced, and costly piece of technology, so top secret that it had to be guarded by soldiers, was being schlepped around in a shabby flying tin can—or so it seemed to my inexpert eye.

After it landed, seven Honduran soldiers with M16s escorted the plane to a far corner of the airport, away from the public areas, where it could be kept secure. Nobody seemed to be paying attention anyway; the airport was small and the military was ubiquitous. The six soldiers, most barely older than teenagers, and the commanding lieutenant had been hanging around the airport, bored, for three days. They were excited at the plane's arrival, and they marched around it, posing with their weapons while Elkins's film crew shot footage.

The pilot, Chuck Gross, was a large, soft-spoken man from Georgia who addressed everyone as "sir." He had recently returned from Iraq, where he had been flying classified lidar missions for the US military. He couldn't disclose much, but I gathered that they involved, among other things, lidaring areas along patrol routes multiple times to detect tiny changes in topography. A new heap of trash or a fresh dirt pile suddenly appearing next to a route would often indicate the placement of an IED.

Gross mentioned he had a Cuban overflight number, which allowed him to fly through Cuban airspace. I asked him what would have happened if he'd had engine or weather trouble and had been forced to land in Cuba. After all, the plane carried classified military hardware, and relations with Cuba were at that time still in a deep freeze.

"First, I would have torched the plane on the runway." This was, he explained, the standard protocol with airborne lidar. "In the desert, that's what we would have done too: immediately destroy the equipment." He added, "You should have seen the paperwork I had to do to get that Cessna out of the US."

The technology of lidar was developed soon after the discovery of lasers in the early 1960s. Put simply, lidar works like radar, by bouncing a laser beam off something, capturing the reflection, and measuring the round-trip time, thereby determining the distance. Scientists quickly realized its potential as a mapping tool. Both the Apollo 15 and 17 missions carried a lidar machine on the orbiter, which mapped swaths of the moon's surface. The Mars Global Surveyor, a satellite orbiting Mars, also carried a lidar machine, which bounced laser beams off the surface of Mars ten times per second. Over its ten-year mission, from

1996 to 2006, the Surveyor created a prodigiously accurate topographic map of the Martian surface, one of the supreme mapping projects of human history.

There are three types of lidar instruments: space-borne, aerial, and terrestrial. On earth, aerial lidar has been used in agriculture, geology, mining, tracking glaciers and ice fields for global warming, urban planning, and surveying. It had numerous classified uses in the wars in Iraq and Afghanistan. Terrestrial lidar is currently being tested in self-driving vehicles and "intelligent" cruise control, which use lidar to map the ever-shifting environment around a car moving down a roadway, as well as to make detailed three-dimensional maps of rooms, tombs, sculptures, and buildings; it can re-create digitally, in incredibly fine detail, any three-dimensional object.

The target sites of T1, T2, and T3 would be mapped with this Cessna, the same one used over Caracol. As the plane is flown in a lawnmower pattern over the jungle, the lidar device fires 125,000 infrared laser pulses a second into the jungle canopy below and records the reflections. (The laser pulses are harmless and invisible.) The time elapsed gives the exact distance from the plane to each reflection point.

The lidar beam does not actually penetrate foliage. It does not "see through" anything in fact: The beam will bounce off every tiny leaf or twig. But even in the heaviest jungle cover, there are small holes in the canopy that allow a laser pulse to reach the ground and reflect back. If you lie down in the jungle and look up, you will always see flecks of sky here and there; the vast number of laser pulses allow lidar to find and exploit those little openings.

The resulting data is what lidar engineers call a "point cloud." These are billions of points showing the location of every reflection, arranged in 3-D space. The mapping engineer uses software to eliminate the points from leaves and branches, leaving only bounce backs from the ground. Further data crunching turns those ground points into a hill-shade picture of the terrain—revealing any archaeological features that might be present.

The resolution of the lidar image is only as good as how well you keep track of the position of the plane flying through space. This is the greatest technological challenge: In order to achieve high resolution, you need to track the plane's position in three dimensions during every second of flight to *within an inch*. A standard GPS unit using satellite links can only locate the plane within about ten feet, useless for archaeological mapping. The resolution can be refined to about a foot by placing fixed GPS units on the ground underneath where the plane will be flying. But an airplane in flight is being bounced around by turbulence, subjected to roll, pitch, and yaw, which not even the finest GPS unit can track.

To solve this problem, the lidar machine contains within it a sealed instrument that looks like a coffee can. It contains a highly classified military device called an inertial measurement unit, or IMU. This is the same technology used in cruise missiles, allowing the missile to know where it is in space at all times as it heads toward its target. Because of the IMU, the lidar machine is listed as classified military hardware, which cannot leave the country without a special permit, and even then only under highly controlled conditions. (This is another reason why there was a long lag-time in the use of lidar at Third World archaeological sites; for years the government prevented the IMU from being used outside the country in civilian applications.)

Aerial lidar can achieve a resolution of about an inch, *if* there is no vegetative cover. But in the jungle, the canopy causes the resolution to drop precipitously, due to many fewer pulses reaching the ground. (The fewer the pulses, the lower the resolution.) The Belizean rainforest around Caracol, where the Chases had used it in 2010, is thick. But it doesn't come anywhere near the density of Mosquitia.

\*    \*    \*

The first lidar flight over T1 took off the next day, May 2, 2012, at 7:30 a.m., with Chuck Gross at the controls and Juan Carlos Fernández acting as navigator and running the lidar machine. We all went to the airport to see the plane off, watching it rise into the Caribbean skies and wink into the blue across the Gulf of Honduras, heading for the mainland. It would take three days to map the twenty square miles of T1. If all went well, we would know in four days if T1 held anything of interest. After that, the plane would shift to T2 and T3.

The plane returned from its first mission in late afternoon. By nine in the evening Sartori confirmed that the data was clean and good; the lidar machine was operating flawlessly and they were getting enough ground points through the forest canopy to map the underlying terrain. While he had no images yet, he saw no technical reason why we wouldn't get detailed terrain maps.

After the second day of flying, on May 3, Juan Carlos came back with intriguing news. He had seen something in T1 that didn't look natural and had tried to photograph it through the windows of the Skymaster. We gathered in his bungalow to look at the photos on his laptop.

It was my first glimpse of the valley. The photos, taken with a shaky telephoto through scratched

Plexiglas, were not clear; but they showed two squarish white objects that looked like the tops of carved limestone pillars, opening into an area of low vegetation that was square in shape. The feature was on a brushy floodplain in the upper end of the valley. Everyone crowded around the laptop, squinting, pointing, and talking excitedly, trying to make sense of the pixilated images that were so tantalizingly ambiguous—they could be pillars, but then again they could be trash dropped from a plane or even the tops of two dead tree stumps.

I pleaded to accompany the third and final flight over T1, despite the logistical issues it posed. There was no room in the plane, but after some discussion, Chuck Gross agreed that he might be able to clear out a tiny space for me to crouch in. He warned me it would be mighty uncomfortable over six to seven hours of flying time.

On May 4, we arrived at the airport as the sun was just rising above the curve of the ocean, the plane throwing an Edward Hopper shadow across the tarmac. The soldiers guarding the plane greeted us sleepily. Now that I was about to be a passenger I looked at the plane more attentively, and I did not like what I saw.

"What's with that oil streak?" I asked Chuck.

"Don't worry about that," he said. "I'm topping

it off every day. In one flight it won't lose enough to make a difference."

As I crawled on board, my dismay deepened. The interior of the Cessna, once a rich velvetized fabric in burgundy, was now worn, greasy, and faded; much of the inside appeared to be held together with duct tape. It smelled of Eau de Old Car. Parts of the plane had been sealed with acrylic caulk, now peeling out in strings. As I tried to maneuver around the giant lidar box into the micro-space provided, I bumped my elbow into a panel, which fell off.

"No worries, that always happens," said Gross, reseating it with a blow from his fist.

I marveled that a plane as unsafe and decrepit as this one looked would be used to carry a million-dollar scientific instrument. Chuck firmly disagreed. "No, sir," he said. "This plane's a perfect platform for the job." He assured me the 337 Skymaster was a "classic," and a "great little aircraft." Unlike a King Air or a Piper Navajo, he said, this craft was ideal, with a fuel efficiency that would allow us to spend "six hours on station." Even though it was forty years old, it was "totally dependable."

"What if we go down?"

"Wow," said Chuck, "what a question! First thing, I'd look for a clearing to set it down in. It's uncharted territory: You're out there on your own, out in the middle of nowhere, no two-way coms." He shook his head—unthinkable.

Despite my worry, I had a lot of confidence in Chuck because I had learned of his feats of flying; at the age of eighteen, he had soloed across the Atlantic, one of the youngest pilots to do so. I hoped the aircraft's deficiencies were mainly cosmetic. I told myself a world-class pilot like Chuck would never fly a plane that wasn't safe.

I jammed myself behind the lidar box: no seat, my knees in my mouth. Juan Carlos was right in front of me. He was concerned about how I would fare; I sensed he was worried I might get airsick and vomit down the back of his neck. He asked if I'd had anything to eat or drink that morning. I said no. He casually mentioned how grueling it was out there, flying low and slow over the jungle for six hours straight, banking steeply turn after turn, tossed around by thermals, sometimes dodging vultures. The A/C on the plane was broken, he said; we would be sealed in a metal tube flying in full sun. The plane had no bathroom. If you had to go, you went in your pants. I tried to assure him I would be an exemplary passenger.

Elkins gave me a GoPro video camera and a still camera with a telephoto lens and asked me to take more pictures of the mysterious white pillars and anything else of interest I spied down below.

Chuck Gross climbed into the pilot's seat and began running down the checklist, while Juan Carlos jacked his laptop into the lidar box. He showed me the flight plan he had programmed on his computer screen, dozens of parallel lines crisscrossing the valley, designed to maximize coverage while minimizing flight time. In addition to being a lidar engineer, Juan Carlos was also a licensed pilot, enabling him to work seamlessly with Chuck.

We took off from Roatán and were soon winging over the glittering Bay of Honduras, the mainland looming up ahead. It was a gorgeous day, the sky dotted with fluffy white cumulus. Far ahead, where the blue mountains of Mosquitia rose up, we could see the cloud cover was sparse and high. As we flew inland, the settlements along the coast gave way to scattered hamlets and agricultural fields alongside slow brown rivers. The land mounted into forested foothills, where hundreds of ragged patches of clear-cutting came into view. Plumes of smoke rose from the jungle in every direction.

The logging holes eventually disappeared and we were flying about four thousand feet over unbroken, precipitous forest. Chuck maneuvered his way through the mountains as we approached T1. An hour out of Roatán, Juan Carlos pointed out the rim of the valley in the distance, a wall of green mountains with a sharp

notch in them. Chuck eased the plane to a lower altitude and we cleared the rim at a thousand feet, which
gave a tremendous view of the landscape. As the land
dropped away beyond the rim, I was struck by the valley's picturesque topography, the ring of mountains
embracing a gentle, rolling landscape divided by two
rivers. It really did look like a tropical Shangri-la.

The plane leveled off at an altitude of about 2,500
feet above ground, and Juan Carlos booted up the
lidar machine, picking up where they had left off the
day before. As the lidar bombarded the canopy with
laser pulses, Chuck steered the Cessna in parallel lines
across the valley, each four to six miles long, in a pattern
that, on the computer screen, looked like a gigantic
weaving. The plane was buffeted by thermals, knocked
up and down, back and forth, and sometimes sliding
sideways in a gut-wrenching fashion. Juan Carlos had
been right; it was a brutal and scary ride. But Gross
worked the controls with constant finesse and a sure
hand.

"We were rocking and rolling pretty good," Gross
said later. "It's like flying a big spiderweb. It takes
incredible skill. You have to fly the middle of the line,
and you can't go sixty feet on either side of that line. You
have to slide that plane around, doing all rudders. To
stay on the line, in that wind, *that* was challenging.
And you have to hold the altitude and airspeed. I had

to climb with the terrain and maintain the same altitude. If the terrain starts coming up, I have to come up with it."

Through it all, I peered out the window, transfixed. I can scarcely find words to describe the opulence of the rainforest that unrolled below us. The tree crowns were packed together like puffballs, displaying every possible hue, tint, and shade of green. Chartreuse, emerald, lime, aquamarine, teal, bottle, glaucous, asparagus, olive, celadon, jade, malachite—mere words are inadequate to express the chromatic infinities. Here and there the canopy was disrupted by a treetop smothered in enormous purple blossoms. Along the central valley floor, the heavy jungle gave way to lush meadows. Two meandering streams glittered in the sunlight, where they joined before flowing out the notch.

We were flying above a primeval Eden, looking for a lost city using advanced technology to shoot billions of laser beams into a jungle that no human beings had entered for perhaps five hundred years: a twenty-first-century assault on an ancient mystery.

"It's coming up," Juan Carlos said. "Right there: two white things."

In an open area, I could see the two features that he had photographed the previous day, standing about thirty feet apart next to a large, rectangular area of darker-colored vegetation. The plane made several passes as I photographed. Again, they looked to me like two square, white pillars rising above the brush.

We got through the flight without mishap, other than the moment a few hours into the flight when I turned off the lidar machine with my knee as I tried to shift my aching legs. The machine and the pilot's navigational system were linked, so shutting off the lidar turned off Gross's navigation. He immediately went into a tight, stomach-sickening holding pattern while Juan Carlos booted the machine back up and I apologized profusely. "No worries," he said, far less perturbed than I thought he would be.

We finished mapping T1 with enough fuel left over to fly a few lines over T2, twenty miles distant. The route took us over the Patuca River, Heinicke's "most dangerous place on the planet," a brown snake of water winding through the jungle. T2 was magnificent and dramatic, a deep, hidden valley shut in by sheer, thousand-foot limestone cliffs, draped with vines and riddled with caves. But recent deforestation—only weeks old—had reached the mouth of the T2 valley. As we flew over, I could see the freshly cut trees lying on the ground to dry out so they could be burned, leaving a hideous brown scar.

At the end of the day, we flew to La Ceiba, on the mainland, to refuel. Chuck had pushed the envelope and we landed with less than twenty gallons of aviation fuel remaining, about forty minutes of flight. But the airport had no fuel and nobody could locate the tanker bringing the resupply. Airport officials feared the tanker had been hijacked by drug smugglers. Juan Carlos called Elkins in Roatán. Elkins put Bruce Heinicke on the problem. After calling around, Bruce learned the truck was still en route, delayed by a blowout.

We couldn't leave the Cessna unguarded, especially if the fuel didn't arrive and the plane had to stay overnight in La Ceiba. Juan Carlos and Chuck debated sleeping in the plane, but that wasn't ideal, since they were unarmed. They finally decided that, if fuel didn't arrive, they would go to the US Air Force base in La Ceiba and ask the soldiers to stand guard for the night. Meanwhile, Michael Sartori was desperate to get the data and finish mapping T1, so it was agreed I'd head back to the island on my own. Fernández gave me the two hard drives with the data, and I went to the airport desk to see if I could get a commercial flight from La Ceiba to Roatán. There was a flight to Roatán that afternoon but it was already full. For $37 I was able to hitch a ride in the copilot's seat. The plane looked even less reliable than the Cessna, and as I boarded, Juan Carlos joked about what a pity it would be to lose all that precious data in a plane crash after their hard work collecting it.

I landed in Roatán at sunset and gave the hard drives to Sartori, who snatched them up and disappeared into his bungalow, emerging only once to chow down a couple of lobster tails at dinner. He now had all the data he needed to map T1. Late that night Juan Carlos and Chuck Gross finally landed back in Roatán, exhausted but relieved. The fuel truck had arrived at the last minute.

Sartori had hours of work ahead of him. He had to merge data from several sources: the lidar machine, the GPS ground stations, the GPS data from the aircraft itself, and the data from the IMU. Together, all this would create the point cloud, forming a three-dimensional picture of the rainforest and the underlying terrain. First, he had to wait for Mango to retrieve the USB stick from the GPS unit in Culmi and bring it to Catacamas to upload to the server in Houston; Sartori then had to download the data from Houston. The lights in Sartori's bungalow were still burning at midnight when I went to bed. Ramesh Shrestha, back at NCALM in Houston, remained awake, pressing him for updates.

This was the moment of truth: The images would show what was in the valley—if anything. It was almost one in the morning when Sartori finished creating the raw images of T1; Shrestha had finally gone to bed and the Internet connection on Roatán was down. Exhausted, Sartori went to bed without even looking at the images he had just created.

The next day was Saturday, May 5. Rising early, Sartori uploaded the raw images to a server in Houston, again without examining them. Immediately on receiving them, Shrestha forwarded them to NCALM's chief scientist, William Carter, who was at his vacation home in West Virginia. Shrestha intended to review them soon, but Carter beat him to it.

At 8:30 a.m. on that quiet Saturday morning, the terrain images of T1 arrived in Carter's in-box just as he was about to leave the house to run errands. He needed to buy a refrigerator. He hesitated and then told his wife that he wanted to have a quick look. He downloaded the data and displayed the maps on his computer screen. He was thunderstruck. "I don't think it took me more than five minutes to see something that looked like a pyramid," he told me later. "I looked across the river at a plaza area with what looked like buildings—clearly man-made objects. As I looked at that river valley, I saw more, as well as alterations to the terrain. It was kind of surprising how easy it was to find them." He e-mailed the coordinates to Sartori and Shrestha.

Sartori pulled up the images and scanned them. In his excitement Carter had mistyped the coordinates, but it took Sartori only a moment to find the cluster of features on his own. He said, "My skepticism wasn't easily broken," but this was clear enough to convince the most resolute doubter. Sartori was chagrined. "I was mad at myself for not seeing it first, since I was the guy producing the images!" He rushed out the door to report it to Steve Elkins, but then had second thoughts. Was it real? Maybe it was just his imagination. "I was in and out the door about six different times," Sartori said.

I was walking back from breakfast with Steve and some others when Sartori appeared along the quay, running madly in his flip-flops, waving his arms and shouting: "There's something in the valley!" We were startled by this sudden behavioral change, the sober-minded skeptic transformed into a raving Christopher Lloyd.

When we asked what it was, he said, "I can't describe it. I *won't* describe it. You just have to see it yourself."

There was pandemonium. Steve started to run, and then remembered he was a filmmaker, so he began shouting for his film crew to get their gear together and record the moment—cinema verité. With the cameras rolling, everyone crowded into Sartori's room to look at the images on his laptop. The maps were in gray scale and a first iteration, but they were clear enough. In the valley of T1, above the confluence of the two streams, we could see rectangular features and long, pyramid-like mounds arranged in squares, which covered an area of hundreds of acres. Also visible, but impossible to interpret, were the two objects that looked like square pillars we had seen from the plane. As we examined the images, Sartori's in-box was pinging continuously with e-mails from Carter and Shrestha, who were poring over the same maps, shooting off an e-mail with coordinates every time they found another feature.

I was stunned. It sure as hell looked like a very large set of ruins, perhaps even a city. I had thought we would be fortunate to find any kind of site at all; I had not expected this. Was it possible that an entire lost city could still be found in the twenty-first century?

I could see Sartori's spiral-bound notebook lying open next to the laptop. In keeping with the methodical scientist he was, he had been jotting daily notes on his work. But underneath the entry for May 5, he had written two words only:

HOLY SHIT!

"When I saw those rectangles and squares," Steve told me later, "my first feeling was one of vindication." Benenson, who had been feverishly capturing the unfolding discovery on video, was happily stunned that the million-dollar spin of the roulette wheel had landed on his number. "I'm witnessing this," he said, "but I'm not processing this very well. I have chills."

Nobody dared wake up Bruce Heinicke to tell him the news. He finally emerged from his bungalow at 1:00 p.m. and listened with a frown on his face. He wondered why we were all so worked up—of course the White City was there. Who the fuck thought otherwise? He got on the phone to África Madrid, the minister of the interior. África said he would fly out to Roatán as soon as possible to review what we found and, if he was convinced it was real—and he had no reason to doubt it—he would convey the news to President Lobo, as well as to the president of the Honduran Congress, Juan Orlando Hernández. Meanwhile, the director of the Instituto Hondureño de Antropología e Historia, Virgilio Paredes, flew to Roatán to take a first look at our findings. Later, he recalled that moment: "I saw that and I said 'Wow!' We know Mosquitia is full of archaeological sites, but to see real *cities*, a big population of people living there—that is *amazing!*"

The valley of T1 had been mapped, but the project was only 40 percent complete: T2 and T3 remained to be explored. Chuck and Juan Carlos had headed off early that Saturday morning to continue mapping T2, unaware of the uproar of discovery occurring back at the Parrot Tree. Once in the air, however, Juan Carlos discovered the lidar machine was dead. They returned to Roatán and tried to get the machine working while the plane was on the ground, with no success. At around nine that morning all three lidar engineers examined it and confirmed the machine was kaput.

NCALM in Houston had a technical maintenance contract with a team in Toronto, Canada, where this lidar box had been designed and built. As it was a weekend, there was only a single tech-support person in Canada manning the phone. After he walked the lidar engineers through a plug-unplug sequence, trying to wake up the machine, they determined that a crucial part had failed. It was called a Position and Orientation System (POS) board, and it contained a GPS receiver and other components that "talked" to the IMU, exchanging data. There were only two POS boards in the world, both in Canada. The company would put a technician on a flight from Toronto to Roatán early Monday morning, transporting the $100,000 board in person in his carry-on bag. The part would have to clear customs twice, once in the United States and a second time in Honduras.

The engineer flying the part was Pakistani and, not having a US State Department export clearance for the POS board, he was worried about being stopped with it at Dulles Airport in Washington, DC, where he had an overnight connection. Before boarding the plane in Toronto, he panicked and stuck the part in his checked luggage, thinking that it would be less likely to prompt a security challenge in the United States.

The airlines (of course!) lost his bags. The two bags included not only the POS board but all the tools the technician needed to install it. The fact that the part was insured meant little to the expedition, which was spending many thousands of dollars a day and only had use of the plane for a strictly limited period of time. The flustered engineer arrived in Roatán on Tuesday morning with little more than the clothes on his back.

Desperate and futile phone calls to United and TACA airlines took up all of Tuesday. They learned the bags had arrived in Dulles Airport but had failed to be transferred onto the flight to San Salvador and then Roatán. They seemed to have vanished in Dulles. Then, as the frenzy of phone calls continued into Wednesday afternoon, the bags unexpectedly arrived at the Roatán airport. Virgilio Paredes went with Steve to the airport to speed them through Honduran customs. He did a masterful job of intimidation, waving about the president's official card, and the bags sailed through and were rushed to the Cessna at the far end of the airport tarmac. It took the technician and Juan Carlos two hours to install the part and get the lidar machine working again. As they arrived back at the Parrot Tree, elated that the expensive, five-day delay was over, United Airlines called to once again say that, despite a most diligent effort, they were terribly sorry but they had been unable to trace the lost bags.

The mission resumed the next morning, on Thursday, with overflights of T2 and T3. They went flawlessly. Once again we gathered in Michael Sartori's bungalow to look over the images on his laptop. And once again we were absolutely floored: *T3 contained an even larger set of ruins than T1*. T2 also revealed enigmatic, man-made features that were harder to interpret. Some guessed they might be quarries or fortifications.

In his quixotic search for the mythical White City, Elkins and his team had found not one large site but two, apparently built by the almost unknown civilization that once inhabited Mosquitia. But were they cities? And could one of these actually be *the* White City, *the* Lost City of the Monkey God? This, however, was the wrong question—it was clear to everyone by this point that the White City was a conflation of stories and probably did not exist in its described form. Like most legends, however, it was anchored in truth: The lidar discoveries had confirmed that Mosquitia had indeed been the territory of a great and mysterious civilization that built many large settlements before it disappeared. It was exactly as Cortés had written five centuries ago: This land had been home to "very extensive and rich provinces." But what had caused it to vanish so suddenly and completely?

## CHAPTER 12

**There is a big city here.**

On Friday, África Madrid arrived in Roatán along with a group of Honduran officials. They crowded into Sartori's room to examine the images on his screen. That evening, Madrid called President Lobo at home to report that he believed Ciudad Blanca had been found. When he heard the news, Lobo told me later, he was "completely speechless." He said, "This finding will contribute to all of humanity, not just Honduras." Just how important it was would have to await a ground expedition, but it was clearly one of the major archaeological discoveries of the new century.

Both men credited the hand of God; after all, Mabel Heinicke had approached them in church at the very moment when the new administration was being formally blessed. "There are no coincidences," Madrid said to me. "I think that God has extraordinary plans for our country, and Ciudad Blanca could be one of them." The discovery, he believed, was the beginning of a change in Honduras: "It will put Honduras on the map in terms of tourism, scientific research, history, and anthropology."

A celebratory dinner was held at a long table set up on the beach, with flaming torches, speeches, and toasts.

After the mapping of T3, the two-week lidar expedition ended and Chuck Gross departed for Houston in the sturdy little Skymaster packed with all its classified technology. Steve and Juan Carlos were summoned to the presidential palace in Tegucigalpa to present the discovery at a cabinet meeting, which was televised live to the nation. A press conference followed on the palace steps. A press release, issued jointly by Elkins's team and the Honduran government, announced the discovery of "what appears to be evidence of archaeological ruins in an area long rumored to contain the legendary lost city of Ciudad Blanca." The careful qualification in the statement was lost on the popular press, which announced with huge fanfare that the actual Ciudad Blanca had been found.

While Hondurans celebrated, a small number of American archaeologists greeted the news with criticism and anger. In two postings on the Berkeley Blog,

Professor Rosemary Joyce, a highly respected authority on Honduran prehistory at UC Berkeley, denounced the project as "big hype." She wrote: "The Honduran press began trumpeting, yet again, the discovery of Ciudad Blanca, the mythical White City supposedly located somewhere in eastern Honduras." She was also critical of lidar as an archaeological tool. "LiDAR can produce images of landscapes faster than people walking the same area, and with more detail. But that is not good archaeology, because all it produces is a *discovery*—not *knowledge*. If it's a competition, then I will bet my money on people doing ground survey... LiDAR is *expensive*. And I question the value you get for the money it costs... [Lidar] may be good science—but it is bad archaeology."

I called up Dr. Joyce a few days after my return to the States to hear her views in more detail. She told me that when she heard the news, she was furious. "This is at least the fifth time someone's announced they've found the White City," she said, apparently conflating the sensational Honduran press reports, which claimed we had found the White City, with the expedition's carefully hedged press release. "There *is* no White City. The White City is a myth, a modern myth, largely created by adventurers. I'm quite biased against this group of people because they are adventurers and not archaeologists. They're after spectacle.

Culture is not something you can see from the lidar plane or from thousands of feet up. There's this thing we call 'ground truthing.'"

I mentioned that the team did intend to ground-truth everything, and that they were looking for an archaeologist to help interpret the findings, but she seemed unmollified. I asked her if she would be willing to look at an image of T1 and give me her interpretation of it. At first she said no. But when I pressed her, she reluctantly agreed. "I'll look at it, but I may not call you back."

I e-mailed her a lidar image of a portion of T1. She called back immediately. Yes, she said, this was an archaeological site, and not a small one. (I had sent her only a tiny section of T1.) She could see "three major clusters of larger structures," as well as "a plaza, a public space par excellence, and a possible ball court, and many house mounds." She guessed that the site dated from the Late- or Post-Classic period, between AD 500 and 1000. Nevertheless, she closed the call with another blast at the expedition: "It's infuriating to see archaeology portrayed as a kind of treasure hunting."

Despite Professor Joyce's concerns, Elkins and Benenson were determined to establish the discovery's archaeological legitimacy. They looked for an archaeologist who could study the lidar images and figure out more precisely what they represented. They needed someone who was not only a Mesoamerican specialist but also an expert in lidar interpretation. They found the right combination in the person of Chris Fisher, a professor of anthropology at Colorado State University. Fisher had worked with the Chases on the Caracol lidar project, had coauthored the scientific paper with them, and had been the first archaeologist to use lidar in Mexico.

Fisher came sideways into archaeology. Growing up in Duluth and then Spokane, he became an accomplished drummer and marched in the Drum Corps International Salem Argonauts. He did a national tour from coast to coast with the drum corps in a decrepit passenger bus whose driver was an ex–Hells Angel who had lost a leg in a motorcycle accident; they slept on the bus, as they traveled at night and performed during the day.

With aspirations to be a jazz drummer, after high school, instead of going to college he drummed while working at "a bunch of crappy jobs." When he was offered the coveted position of manager of a 7-Eleven, he had an epiphany: "I said to myself, 'Holy shit, I've got to get to college. I can't do this for the rest of my life.'" He started as a music major, realized he didn't have the focus to be a successful jazz drummer, and switched to anthropology. At an archaeological field school, where he helped excavate an archaic site in the middle of a cornfield, he "just absolutely fell in love" with archaeology. He went on to get his PhD, with his dissertation focusing on a site in Michoacán, Mexico. While doing a survey in the area, he came across what looked like the remains of a small pre-Columbian village scattered about an ancient lava bed, called Angamuco, once a settlement of the fierce Purépecha (Tarascan) people, who rivaled the Aztecs in central Mexico from around AD 1000 until the arrival of the Spanish in the early 1500s.

"We thought we could knock out Angamuco in a week," he recalled. "We just kept going and going and going." It turned out to be a huge site. In 2010, Fisher used lidar to map Angamuco. The results were perhaps even more astounding than those at Caracol. The images gathered after flying over Angamuco for just forty-five minutes revealed *twenty thousand* previously unknown archaeological features, including a bizarre pyramid that, seen from above, is shaped like a keyhole.

"I almost started crying when I saw the lidar images" of Angamuco, Fisher told me. Not only were they spectacular to him as an archaeologist; he realized they had also changed his professional life. "I thought, 'Oh, my God, I've just got back ten or twelve years of my life.' It would have taken me that long to survey those nine square kilometers."

Since that time, he had expanded his lidar survey of Angamuco: "I'm scared to say we now know Angamuco covers twenty-six square kilometers [ten square miles]. We're looking at maybe a hundred or a hundred and twenty pyramids," along with dense settlements, roads, temples, and tombs. The "small site" turned out to be an immense and important pre-Columbian city.

Pleased to have Fisher on board, Elkins sent him the lidar maps. Fisher spent six months studying them. In December, in a meeting in San Francisco, he presented his findings to the expedition team. While T1 was imposing, Fisher believed T3 was even more impressive.

The two ruins were definitely not Maya. They belonged to an ancient culture all of its own that dominated Mosquitia many centuries ago. He concluded that the ceremonial architecture, the giant earthworks, and the multiple plazas revealed in the images suggested that both T1 and T3 were ancient "cities," as defined archaeologically. He cautioned that this was not necessarily how the average person might define a city. "A city," he explained, "is a complex social organization, multifunctional; it has a socially stratified population with clear divisions of space, intimately connected to the hinterlands. Cities have special functions, including ceremonial, and are associated with intensive agriculture. And they usually involve major, monumental reconstruction of the environment."

"There is a big city here [in T3]," Fisher said in the meeting. "It's comparable in geographic area to the core of Copán," the Maya city in western Honduras. He displayed a map of the central area of Copán, superimposed on the lidar map of the unknown city in T3; both covered about two square miles. "The scale of the site is amazing," he told the audience. "These are data that would have taken decades to gather in traditional archaeology." After further examination of the lidar images of T1, Fisher identified nineteen connected settlements strung along several miles of the river, which he believed were part of a chiefdom ruling the valley.

Later, Fisher told me the two cities appeared to be larger than anything previously found in Mosquitia. In the images he also identified several hundred smaller sites, from farming hamlets to monumental architecture, canals and roads, and signs of terraced hills. "Each of these areas was once a completely modified human environment," he said. T2 also presented many intriguing features that were harder to interpret.

These two cities were not unique. They were similar to other major sites found in Mosquitia, such as

Las Crucitas de Aner, the largest ruin in Mosquitia. T1, however, is at least four times bigger than Las Crucitas (based on published maps), and T3 is several times larger than that. (T1 is at least five times larger than Stewart's site of Lancetillal.) But that, he explained, wasn't saying much, since no site in Mosquitia had ever been mapped in its entirety. The lidar picks up details, such as terracing and ancient canals, that would be extremely difficult to see any other way, which naturally would make T1 and T3 appear bigger than Las Crucitas—a lidar image of Las Crucitas might show that the city extended over a much larger area than previously known. The lidar maps of T1 and T3 hinted that many Mosquitia sites, almost all of which had been poorly mapped if they had been mapped at all, could be far larger than previously thought: The lidar maps proved that the unnamed civilization that had built T1 and T3 had been widespread, powerful, and successful. Also of immense significance, he said, and extremely rare, was that T1 and T3 gave every appearance of being completely undisturbed and unlooted.

Fisher noted that, unlike ancient cities such as Copán and Caracol, which were built around a central core, the Mosquitia cities were spread out, "more like LA than New York." He added, "I hear myself saying this stuff, and I know, I just know, that there's going to be a firestorm of criticism. But I've taught myself how to analyze these data. There aren't yet a lot of archaeologists who have experience working with lidar." But in ten years, he predicted, "everyone will be using it."

I asked Fisher whether the White City had finally been found. He laughed. "I don't think there is a single Ciudad Blanca," he said. "I think there are many." The myth, he said, is real in the sense that it holds intense meaning for Hondurans, but for archaeologists it's mostly a "distraction."

Professor Joyce was right about one thing: A site is not really "found" until it is ground-truthed. Elkins and Benenson immediately began planning an expedition to explore either T1 or T3. Fisher lobbied hard for T3, but Elkins felt T1 offered a more compact, complex, and interesting site. The truth was, he had been trying to get into T1 for twenty years; he was not going to stop now.

Elkins and Benenson spent the next two years organizing the expedition to T1 and securing the exploration and filming permits. In 2014, when President Pepe Lobo's term was up, the former president of Congress, Juan Orlando Hernández, was chosen in fair and monitored elections. Luckily, he was on the same page as his predecessor about the importance of Elkins's project; if anything, he was even more enthusiastic and made the exploration of the ruins one of the top priorities of his new administration. The permitting process, while as crazy as ever, came to a successful conclusion. Once again Benenson put up his own money—another half million. Most of these funds were to pay for helicopters, the only feasible (and safe) way to travel into the valley of T1. The team then began planning a scientific expedition into one of the most dangerous and remote places on earth. I was fortunate to be invited to join the team, this time as a correspondent for *National Geographic* magazine.

## CHAPTER 13

**It has been observed to squirt venom
over six feet from its fangs.**

Our expedition to explore the valley of T1 assembled in Tegucigalpa, the capital of Honduras, on Valentine's Day, 2015. Tegucigalpa lies in the southern highlands of Honduras. It is a dense city of crooked little neighborhoods and slums clinging to steep hills, tin roofs glittering in the sun, surrounded by dramatic volcanic mountains. A smell of cooking fires hangs in the air, combined with diesel fumes and dust. Toncontín International Airport is infamous for its steep and tricky approach and its undersized runway, which pilots say make it one of the most difficult commercial aviation landings in the world.

In covering the expedition for *National Geographic*, I was partnering with the well-known photographer Dave Yoder. Yoder was a broad-shouldered, red-faced, gruff perfectionist who had come straight to Honduras from an assignment photographing Pope Francis in the Vatican. "I've never been so totally dislocated in my life," he said on arriving in the jungle. On that assignment he had taken a candid picture of Pope Francis standing alone in the Sistine Chapel, which he shared with us on his iPad, expressing his hope it might become the magazine's cover. It was an evocative and visually stunning photograph, and it did indeed make the cover of *National Geographic*'s August 2015 issue. He was bringing into the jungle three Canon cameras, two computers, and a suitcase of hard drives. Unlike many other photographers I'd worked with, he refused to set up a shot, ask someone to pose, or arrange a redo; he was a purist. As he worked, he never said a word; he remained a silent, scowling figure hovering in the background (or foreground, or in your face), his camera clicking almost continuously. In the rare times he did not have a camera, he became notorious for his dry, ironic quips. Over the course of the expedition he would take tens of thousands of photographs.

The team gathered at the Marriott Hotel in Tegucigalpa. Late in the afternoon, we convened with Honduran officials and military officers to discuss the expedition's logistics. In the intervening years, Bruce Heinicke had died; long gone were the days of bribes, under-the-table deals, and implied threats of violence.

The expedition had hired a team of less colorful but equally effective coordinators to make sure everything went as planned.

Chris Fisher had prepared huge lidar maps of both T1 and T3. These maps were a far cry from those first grayscale images we had seen on Sartori's computer. The data had been carefully massaged and tweaked, realistic color had been added, and the images were now printed on paper charts in unprecedented detail. Electronic versions were set up to match an online "data dictionary" that would allow Chris to immediately mark and record on the electronic maps any feature he found in the jungle.

Steve Elkins unrolled the maps on the conference table, one showing T1, and the other T3. T1 was the primary objective, but Elkins hoped a quick ground survey of T3 might also be possible.

The first step was getting into T1 by helicopter. This was not a simple matter. The expedition had brought down a small Airbus AStar helicopter, and the Honduran Air Force also agreed to furnish a Bell 412SP helicopter and the soldiers who would accompany it. We needed to identify potential helicopter landing zones in T1 and figure out how to clear them of trees and other vegetation.

The Honduran military contingent was commanded by Lt. Col. Willy Joe Oseguera Rodas, a quiet, low-keyed man in casual military fatigues. He was a well-known figure in recent Honduran history—the military officer to personally handcuff deposed president Zelaya during the 2009 coup.

Oseguera opened the discussion by explaining that the air force had closely examined the terrain and felt that the only safe landing zone for their Bell 412 was twenty kilometers away—outside the valley. Elkins disagreed. Twenty kilometers in the Mosquitia mountains might as well be a thousand miles; an overland journey of that length would take a week or more, even for seasoned jungle troops.

"This," Elkins said, gesturing at the huge map, "is the T1 valley. There's only one way in—through this gap. Where the two rivers split, there's an area of no trees. This would be an easy area to land, but it would require the clearing of two to three meters of brush." He pointed to an area a few miles to the north, just below the city. "And there's another possible landing place next to the ruins. But the trees might be too close together."

The military men wanted to know exactly how tight these two landing zones were.

Elkins brought out his laptop and booted up the three-dimensional point cloud of the landing zone, which, remarkably, can be rotated and sectioned in any way. Chris and Juan Carlos had already prepared for him digital cross sections of several potential landing zones, which showed the trees, the height of the brush, and the ground level, exactly as if the landscape had been sliced vertically with a knife. Steve had also hired a plane for Juan Carlos to fly over the potential landing zones late in the fall of 2014, to see if there were any noticeable terrain changes and to take good, visible-light photographs and video. All this preparation paid off. It appeared that the river junction LZ might be just large enough for the Bell, and that a smaller LZ might possibly be cleared on the bank of the stream below the ruins, broad enough to insert the AStar.

All this remained theoretical until it could be confirmed in a visual reconnaissance overflight of the valley, planned for February 16, in two days' time.

Lt. Col. Oseguera explained that once we had scouted out our location, the Honduran military would deploy sixteen soldiers in the valley, who would camp next to our base camp and provide security. These were Special Forces TESON soldiers, many of whom were indigenous Pech, Tawahka, Garifuna, and Miskito people from eastern Honduras. "The soldiers are self-sufficient," Oseguera said. "They camp on their own. They are very old-school and live like Indians." The soldiers, he said, would be providing security against possible narcotraffickers, criminals, or others who might be hiding in the forest, although that seemed unlikely, given the remoteness of the valley. They would, more importantly, be taking part in a military exercise called *Operación Bosque*, "Operation Forest," to train them on how to protect the rainforest and its archaeological treasures.

Here was yet another way in which the exploration of the valley of T1 meshed with the goals of the newly elected president. Hernández had expressed concern about deforestation, the looting of Honduras's archaeological treasures, and the acute need for Honduras to lower its crime rate, reduce drug smuggling, and—above all—increase tourism as a way to lift the economy. To combat crime, he called the army into the streets. Some Hondurans were outraged that the military was deployed in a civilian capacity, but the program was popular in neighborhoods plagued by gangs and crime. Operation Forest would do for the rainforest what Hernández's policy was doing in the streets: Soldiers trained to live self-sufficiently in the rainforest for rotations of duty would become a quasipermanent deterrent to illegal loggers, archaeological looters, and narcotraffickers, who count on the jungle's isolation to conduct their business.

As he reviewed our plans for the expedition, however, Oseguera felt obliged to register a serious objection to our logistics. He noted we were bringing only seven doses of snake antivenin: two for coral snake bites and five for crotalid (viper) bites. He did not believe these would be sufficient; at least twenty doses would be the minimum. (A single bite, depending on the size of the snake and the amount of poison it injects, usually requires multiple doses for treatment.) In the military's experience, poisonous snakes were everywhere and difficult to avoid in the heavy foliage. Especially problematic were the smaller ones that rested in low branches and, when disturbed, fell down on the unwary traveler.

Elkins balked: It had been almost impossible to get those seven doses to begin with, due in part to an antivenin shortage. They had cost thousands of dollars, and there was no way to obtain more on short notice. The discussion ended there, but as I glanced around I noted a number of people looking uneasy, me among them.

That evening the core group of us—Steve Elkins, Dave Yoder, Chris Fisher, and myself—met with James Nealon, US ambassador to Honduras, and his wife, Kristin, in the heavily fortified embassy and residence perched on a hill overlooking the twinkling lights of the city. Nealon was gripped by the story of the lost city and fascinated to hear about what we might find, and he gave us a detailed and insightful briefing on Honduras, which, he noted pointedly, was off the record. The phrase "cognitive dissonance" came up several times. We promised to report back on our discoveries when we emerged from the jungle in two weeks.

The following morning, our convoy left Tegucigalpa in vans, headed toward Catacamas, a four-and-a-half-hour drive. The expedition's AStar helicopter followed the convoy from above. Honduran soldiers in military vehicles before and behind the convoy provided security, a routine precaution against banditry and kidnapping, especially necessary because we were hauling a bowser of aviation fuel, highly coveted by drug smugglers. The convoy was in constant communication with us and the other soldiers by two-way radios.

It was a long, dusty drive over mountain roads, through a succession of impoverished villages with dilapidated houses, heaps of trash, open sewers, and sad-faced, droopy-eared dogs slinking about. We did pass through one strikingly different and pretty village, the neat houses painted in cheerful colors of turquoise, pink, yellow, and blue, adobe walls draped with purple bougainvillea, and flower boxes in the windows. Those streets were clean and well swept. But as we entered the town, the soldiers warned by radio that under no circumstances were we to stop, as this was a town run by a powerful drug cartel. We were assured that the narcos were engaged in their own business and wouldn't bother us as long as we didn't bother them. We drove on.

Eventually we reached the town of Catacamas, the expedition's base of operations. It, too, was an attractive city of whitewashed houses with red-tiled roofs, population 45,000, nestled against the mountains, overlooking a rich, broad plain dotted with beef cattle and fine-looking horses, watered by the Río Guayape.

Ranching is a proud and venerable tradition in Catacamas, but in recent years it had been eclipsed by the business of drug smuggling. The city had been taken over by narco lords, who came to be known as the Catacamas cartel. The Catacamas cartel was in competition with another cartel in the nearby city of Juticalpa, and the road between the two cities—which we had been driving over—had become a battle zone, plagued with robberies, murders, and carjackings, often committed by criminals posing as Honduran law enforcement. In 2011, it was the scene of one of the worst drug massacres in Honduras, in which a gunman opened fire on a minibus of civilians, killing eight women and children. In 2015, by the time we arrived, the drug smuggling had subsided somewhat, but the town was still dangerous. While there,

I learned from a local businessman that the cost of a contract murder in Catacamas was twenty-five dollars. However, we were assured that we were in no danger because of our guard of elite Honduran soldiers.

The Hotel Papa Beto was the finest in town, a whitewashed fortress located in the old city center, with a luxurious swimming pool and an enclosed courtyard with shady, arched portals. The building was surrounded by twenty-foot concrete walls topped by broken glass and concertina wire. As we checked in and got our keys, our escort soldiers with M16s and Israeli Galil automatic weapons stood guard in the lobby. The expedition had taken over the entire hotel, and we spread out our gear poolside in organized piles, ready to be packed and flown into the jungle.

.We would spend two nights in the hotel before jumping into the unknown, flying into the valley and establishing a base camp. Snake antivenin shortages aside, Elkins and his team had planned everything to the last detail, a remarkably thorough job, even though we had only a vague idea of the actual conditions we might encounter in the valley of T1 in terms of snakes, insects, diseases, weather, and the difficulty of travel. Only two people on the expedition had actually seen the valley of T1 up close: Juan Carlos and myself. (Tom Weinberg did a brief flyover of T1 in 1998 on a mercy mission with the US military, on their way to deliver supplies to stranded villagers after Hurricane Mitch. Although the storm had derailed their plans, Steve hoped Tom might spot something in the mysterious valley he was convinced held a lost city. So Tom persuaded the pilot to alter his flight plan to get a quick look-see en route, but there was nothing but dense tree cover.) No one had been in there on the ground in perhaps hundreds of years. There was nobody to ask, no guidebooks to consult, no maps beyond the lidar images, and no way of visualizing what we would find in the ruined city. It was both unnerving and exciting to know we would be the first.

Elkins and Benenson had hired three British ex–Special Air Services officers to handle the logistics of making camp and navigating through the jungle. Their leader was Andrew Wood. Woody had served in many roles in the SAS, including senior instructor in jungle warfare, explosives and demolition expert, and advanced-trauma combat medic; he spoke Arabic, Serbo-Croat, and German. He was a skilled tracker, sniper, and free fall parachutist. After leaving the military, Woody had founded a company called TAFFS, Television and Film Facilitation Services. The company specialized in bringing film and television crews into the world's most dangerous environments, keeping them alive so they could shoot their projects, and then getting them out safely. TAFFS handled the logistics for the extreme survival shows of Bear Grylls, and the company's numerous television credits include *Escape from Hell, Man vs. Wild, Extreme Worlds*, and *Naked and Marooned*. Woody, himself a trained survivalist of the highest rank, had been asked many times to star in his own show, but he had always refused.

Woody brought along two partners from TAFFS, Iain MacDonald Matheson ("Spud") and Steven James Sullivan ("Sully"). Despite their self-deprecating British manner, both were also ex-SAS and tough as nails. The three had very different personalities and each played a role: Woody the manager; Spud the friendly and laid-back doer; Sully the drill sergeant whose part was to intimidate, dragoon, and scare the shit out of everyone.

As we gathered for that first briefing, we had a chance to look around the room and meet our fellow expeditioners for the first time all in one place. A few of us had been involved in the original lidar aerial survey: Tom Weinberg, Steve Elkins, Juan Carlos, and Mark Adams, the crew's sound mixer. Most were new: They included Anna Cohen and Oscar Neil Cruz, archaeologists; Alicia González, anthropologist; Dave Yoder; Julie Trampush, production manager; Maritza Carbajal, local fixer; Sparky Greene, producer; Lucian Read, director of photography; and Josh Feezer, camera operator. Bill Benenson and several other members would arrive later, once camp was established.

Woody proceeded to give us the deadpan, hair-curling lecture about snakes and disease that opened this book. Then it was Sully's turn to speak. Sully, who had spent thirty-three years in the SAS, focused his narrow eyes on all of us with skepticism and disapproval. He finally lasered in on an important expedition member whom he accused of dozing off during the meeting and whose attitude he had judged lackadaisical. "You've got to tune in mentally right away now," he said in a grim Scottish brogue. The poor man looked like a deer in the headlights. "Maybe you just think we're talking for our health up here. Maybe you think you already know all about it. And so when you're out there, you're going to get into trouble—and then what? You're going to be *hurt* or *dead*, that's what. And who's bluidy responsible? *We're* bluidy responsible. So it isn't going to happen on our watch." His squinty gaze swept us all. "*Not on our watch.*"

The whole room fell into a heavy silence as we all strived to appear to be paying the utmost attention. After a long, uncomfortable moment, Sully went over the plans for the next day. Two helicopters, the expedition's AStar and the Honduran military's Bell 412, would fly into the valley to scout out possible landing zones. When landing areas had been chosen, the AStar chopper would drop Woody, Sully, and Spud in with machetes and chainsaws to clear the LZ. If the brush was thick and high, Sully said, the first few crews in might have to abseil (rappel down) from the hovering chopper. Steve had chosen a group of five people, including me, who would be in the first group to land in the forest, and Sully now had to train us how to do it safely.

We followed Sully to the outside patio of the hotel, where he had arranged a duffel bag of gear. He showed us how to put on a climbing harness, how to edge out on the pontoon of a hovering chopper, abseil down a rope using a mechanical slowing device called a descender, unclip, signal, and move away. I had had some experience rappelling down cliffs and frozen waterfalls, but that was always with the security of a vertical face to put my feet on as I descended. Roping down from a hovering chopper in free space seemed less secure, and if you didn't properly release yourself once on the ground, the chopper might take off with you still attached. We each practiced the maneuver multiple times until we had nailed it to Sully's exacting standards.

The small AStar that would go in first could only carry three passengers, or two with gear. The final question was who exactly, out of our lucky five, would get a coveted spot on the very first flight. Elkins had already adjudicated some angry disputes among members of the team as to who would be included. Chris argued successfully that he had to be on the first flight in, because he needed to make sure the LZ was not itself an archaeological site that would be damaged by helicopter landings. Dave Yoder demanded to be on that first flight, so that he could capture the moment when boots first hit the ground; one of his fundamental principles as a photographer was never to shoot a reenactment. Steve assigned the third seat to Lucian Read, the DP (director of photography) of the film crew, so he could record the moment on film.

I would fly in on the second trip with Juan Carlos and a load of essential gear. The five of us and Woody's team would make a primitive camp that night. The rest of the expedition, including Steve, would fly into the valley in the succeeding days. Excited as he was to be fulfilling a lifelong dream, Steve had sacrificed his own early place in the helicopter for us, because he felt it was important to get the filmmakers, the writer, and the scientists into the valley first. He would fly in the following day.

The Honduran military, with their larger helicopter, would have to find a landing zone farther downriver; the soldiers would then have to hike up the river to establish a camp behind ours.

So for that first day and night, we would be on our own.

## CHAPTER 14

### Don't pick the flowers!

On February 16, at dawn, the advance team piled into a van and drove to El Aguacate airport, a shabby jungle airstrip built by the CIA during the Contra war. It was located near the base of the mountains about ten miles east of Catacamas. The two helicopters were waiting: the AStar, brightly painted in candy-apple red and white, which had been flown down from Albuquerque, and a Honduran Bell 412 painted in combat gray. This first flight was to be a visual reconnaissance only, to scout out the two possible landing zones: one below the archaeological site, the other at the junction of the two rivers. There would be no landing in T1 on this aerial mission.

I rode in the Honduran chopper with Dave Yoder, while Elkins rode in the AStar. We took off at 9:45 a.m., heading northeastward, under the agreement that the two birds would stay in visual contact with each other at all times.

The Honduran helicopter I was in had trouble getting off the ground and then immediately began flying erratically, with a tilt. As we flew, various red lights and an alarm went off on the console, and then we turned around and headed back to Aguacate, where the helicopter made a crooked, skidding landing. It turned out a computer controller had gone bad. I'd been in sketchy aircraft before, but a helicopter is another level of concern, because if the engine fails there is no glide; the pilot must try to execute an "unpowered descent," which is a euphemism for dropping out of the sky like a stone. Because helicopters are very expensive to fly and require much maintenance, the Honduran military can't afford to give its helicopter pilots the same number of flying hours that, for example, USAF pilots have. Even less reassuring was the fact that these helicopters were old and had cycled through the air assets of several foreign countries before being acquired by Honduras.

As we waited at the airstrip, the AStar finally returned. Despite the agreement to stick together, the AStar had gone ahead anyway. Elkins bounded out. "Bingo," he said, raising his thumb with a grin. "We can land right at the site! But you can't see the ruins at all—it's so thick."

The Honduran Air Force brought in a replacement Bell, and both choppers made a second reconnaissance later in the day into the valley of T1. This time, the AStar pilot wanted to hover over the potential landing zone and scout it out more thoroughly. The military chopper, on the other hand, would be examining the bigger landing zone downriver, to see if it could accommodate its larger size. As the two LZs were only a few miles apart, the two birds would fly in together and maintain visual contact throughout.

Once again I flew in the military chopper. For half an hour we were flying over steep terrain, but vast areas of the mountainsides had been cleared, even on slopes of forty to fifty degrees. This was all new territory to me: In 2012, we had flown in from the northwest; now we were flying in from the southwest. I could see that the clearing was not for timbering; it appeared that few if any trees had been taken out, and were left lying on the ground to dry out and be burned, as evidenced by the plumes of smoke rising everywhere. The ultimate goal, I could see, was to turn the land into grazing for cattle—which dotted even the steepest hillsides.*

---

\* I later investigated the illegal clearing and who was responsible. The land southwest of Mosquitia—the Olancho valley and environs—is one of the largest beef-producing areas in Central America, with three quarters of a million grazing head. The surrounding ranches—legal

Finally we left the clear-cuts behind and were flying over a virgin carpet of jungle-cloaked peaks.

Once again I had the strong feeling, when flying into the valley, that I was leaving the twenty-first century entirely. A precipitous ridge loomed ahead, marking the southern boundary of T1. The pilot headed for a V notch in it. When we cleared the gap, the valley opened up in a rolling landscape of emerald and gold, dappled with the shadows of clouds. The two sinuous rivers ran through it, clear and bright, the sunlight flashing off their riffled waters as the chopper banked. I remembered it from the lidar flight three years earlier, but now it looked even more splendid.

---

and illegal—produce thousands of tons of meat for overseas markets, especially the United States. I was able to ascertain (through an unimpeachable source in Honduras) that, after passing through several intermediaries, some of this illegal rainforest beef ends up in patties for McDonald's and other American fast-food chains.

When I later queried McDonald's public affairs department about this, within three days people in Honduras reported that McDonald's USA was making intensive inquiries in the country as to the sources of the Honduran beef coming into the United States; the company was demanding to know what was being done to ensure that beef cattle from the Mosquitia region were not coming from "farms that are responsible for such deforestation, or any irresponsible environmental practices," in my source's words. A week later, McDonald's spokesperson Becca Hary wrote me back, saying: "McDonald's USA does not import any beef from Honduras, or any country in Latin America. McDonald's has a proven track record of protecting rainforests in Latin America, ensuring that no cattle from deforested land enters its supply chain."

Towering rainforest trees, draped in vines and flowers, carpeted the hills, giving way to sunny glades along the riverbanks. Flocks of egrets flew below, white dots drifting against the green, and the treetops thrashed with the movement of unseen monkeys. As had been true in 2012, there was no sign of human life—not a road, trail, or wisp of smoke.

In the larger Bell, we followed the winding path of the river. The AStar was ahead and below us, and as we closed in to the upper LZ, the one near the ruins, the AStar went into a hover over an area along the riverbank covered with thick vegetation. We spent twenty minutes circling this LZ and then circled the second one downriver, which was larger and more open. With both landing zones now firmly identified—one for the Bell and the other for the AStar—we headed back to Aguacate.

The next morning, on February 17, we arrived back at Aguacate at dawn for our flight into the valley, where we hoped to land and establish base camp. The airstrip terminal, a shabby, one-room concrete building, its ceiling tiles falling down, was now full of gear: portable generators, stacks of water bottles, toilet paper, plastic bins packed with Mountain House freeze-dried food, tarps, Coleman lanterns, folding tables, tents, chairs, cots, parachute cord, and other necessities.

The AStar took off with Woody, Sully, and Spud, equipped with machetes and a chainsaw to clear the landing zone near the ruins. The chopper returned two hours later, having successfully dropped them into an area alongside the stream where there were only a few trees, with a plant cover six to nine feet deep, which could be easily cleared with machetes. Only a few small trees would have to be cut.

All was going according to plan. It would probably take them four hours to clear it. We would not have to rope down from a hover after all; the chopper would be able to land firmly on the ground.

Chris Fisher, Dave Yoder, and Lucian Read went in the next flight. Two hours later, the chopper returned and refueled, and then Juan Carlos and I walked out onto the hot tarmac to get in. We each had backpacks with all our essential gear, including food and water for two days, as the camp would not be fully stocked for at least forty-eight hours. We would have to be self-sufficient for those first few days. Because the LZ at the site was so small, and the AStar unable to carry more than a tiny amount of equipment, most of it would be ferried into the valley on the Bell, offloaded at the downstream LZ, and from there shuttled in by the AStar in many back-and-forth trips.

Juan Carlos and I stowed our two backpacks in a basket attached to the port side of the helicopter, since there wasn't room inside. Steve Elkins brought out his iPhone, and he taped me as I gave a ten-second video farewell to my wife, Christine, since I would be out of contact for the next nine or ten days. It was strange to think about what might happen before I was next in touch with her. Steve promised to e-mail the video to her when he got back to Catacamas.

Just before we lifted off, I had a chance to chat with our copilot, Rolando Zuniga Bode, a lieutenant in the Honduran Air Force. "My grandmother used to talk about Ciudad Blanca all the time," he said. "She had a lot of stories."

"What stories?"

Rolando dismissed them with a wave of his hand. "You know, the usual old superstitions. She said the conquistadors found the White City and went in there. But they made a mistake: They picked the flowers—and they all died." He laughed and wagged his finger. "Don't pick the flowers!"

Juan Carlos and I donned our helmets and buckled in. He was excited. "When I first saw the images with the buildings, the dimensions of those things—they are *big*—I had ten thousand questions. Now we're about to find the answers."

After the helicopter took off, we fell silent, taking pictures of the amazingly green and rugged landscape unfurling below.

"There's Las Crucitas," Juan Carlos said. "I asked the pilot to take us this way."

I looked down at the remote archaeological site, the largest that had ever been found in Mosquitia before the identification of T1 and T3. In an open, grassy area, I could see a series of sharp mounds, earthworks, and plazas, situated on both sides of the Río Aner. Many had speculated that this was Morde's Lost City of the Monkey God, but of course now we know Morde had found no such thing—and had never even entered this region of Mosquitia.

"It looks a lot like T1, don't you think?" Juan Carlos said.

I agreed. From the air it looked strikingly similar to the lidar images—the same bus-like mounds, same plazas, same parallel embankments.

Beyond Las Crucitas the serious mountains loomed up, some almost a mile high. As we maneuvered our way through them, the clear-cuts gave way to unbroken cover. At one point, with Rolando at the helm, the chopper swerved violently.

"Sorry. I dodged a vulture," he said.

Finally the telltale notch into T1 loomed up ahead, and in a moment we had cleared it and were inside the valley. Two scarlet macaws glided below us as we followed the line of the river. Pressed to the window, I took pictures with my Nikon. In a few minutes the landing zone came into view, a green patch littered with cut vegetation; the chopper turned, slowed, and descended. Woody knelt at the edge of the LZ, signaling the pilot as he came down. The trees and bushes around us thrashed with prop wash as we descended, the river surface whipped into a froth of white water.

And then we were on the ground. We'd been ordered to grab our gear and get clear of the LZ as fast as possible, keeping our heads down. We jumped out and seized our stuff, while Woody and Sully ran to the chopper and unloaded gear and supplies from the basket, throwing them into a pile at the edge of the LZ; in three minutes the chopper was back in the air.

I watched it rise above the trees, pivot, and disappear. Silence descended, soon filled by a strange, loud roaring from the forest. It sounded like some giant machine or dynamo had been started and was cranking up to full speed.

"Howler monkeys," said Woody. "They begin calling every time the helicopter comes in and out. They seem to respond to the noise." The landing zone had been macheted from a thick stand of "lobster claw" heliconia plants, also known as false bird of paradise, their fleshy stumps oozing white sap. The red-and-yellow flowers and dark green leaves were strewn everywhere, carpeting much of the LZ. We hadn't just picked the flowers; we'd massacred them.

A part of me hoped that Rolando hadn't seen this as we landed.

Woody turned to us. "Grab your kit, get a machete, pick out a campsite, and get yourself fixed up." He nodded toward the impenetrable wall of jungle. A small dark hole, like a cave, had been cut into it, offering a path in. I hoisted my pack; Juan Carlos did the same; and I followed him into the green cave. Three logs had been laid across a pool of mud, and beyond that the freshly cut trail went up a five-foot embankment. We came out in a deep, gloomy forest, with trees rising like giant cathedral columns into the unseen canopy. Their trunks, ten to fifteen feet in diameter, were braced with massive buttresses and knees. Many were wreathed in strangler figs, called *matapalos* ("tree killers"). The howler monkeys continued roaring as my eyes adjusted to the dimness. The air carried a thick, heady scent of earth, flowers, spice, and rotten decay. Here, among the big trees, the understory was relatively open and the ground was flat.

Chris Fisher, the archaeologist, appeared, wearing a white straw cowboy hat that shone like a beacon in the gloom. "Hey, you guys, welcome!"

I looked around. "So...what do we do now?" Woody and the other two SAS men were busy arranging supplies.

"You need to find a place to string your hammock.

Two trees, about this far apart. Let me show you." I followed him through the trees to his campsite, where he had a green hammock set up, with a rainfly and mosquito netting. He was lashing together a small table from cut pieces of bamboo and had strung up a tarp to sit under in case it rained. It was a very good camp, efficient and well organized.

I walked fifty yards into the forest, hoping the distance would preserve my privacy after everyone else arrived. (In the jungle fifty yards is a long way.) I found a pleasant area with two small trees the right distance apart. Fisher loaned me his machete, helped me cut a small clearing, and showed me how to hang the hammock. As we worked, we heard a commotion in the treetops. A troop of spider monkeys had collected in the branches above, and they were unhappy. They screeched and hooted, coming down lower, hanging by their tails while shaking branches at us in a rage. After a good half hour of protest they settled down on a limb, chattering and staring down at me as if I were a freak of nature.

An hour later, Woody came by to check on my camp. He found my hammock job wanting and made some adjustments. He paused to watch the monkeys. "This is their tree," he said, sniffing a couple of times. "Smell that? Monkey piss."

But it was getting late and I didn't want to go to the trouble of moving my camp. I was beyond the fringes of the group, and concerned that after dark I would need a good trail so as not to lose my way. I walked back to the LZ, clearing a better trail with the machete, losing my way several times, having to backtrack by following the cut plants. I found Juan Carlos in his newly set-up camp. Along with Chris we went down to the bank of the stream and stared across the river at the wall of trees. It mounted up, tier after tier, a barricade of green and brown, dotted with flowers and screeching birds. Beyond that, no more than two hundred yards away, began the edge of the lost city and the possible earthen pyramid we had seen on the lidar images. They were cloaked in rainforest, completely invisible. It was about five o'clock in the evening. A soft yellow sun spilled into the rainforest, breaking into rays and flecks of gold, scattering coins on the forest floor. A few fluffy clouds drifted past. The stream, about three feet deep and fifteen feet wide, was crystal clear, the limpid water burbling over a pebbled bed. All around us, the rainforest chattered with the calls of birds, frogs, and other animals, the sounds mingling together into a pleasing susurrus, punctuated by the call and response of two scarlet macaws, one in a nearby tree, the other distant and invisible. The temperature was seventy degrees, the air clear, fresh, and not humid, perfumed with the sweet smell of flowers and greenery.

"Have you noticed?" said Chris, holding up his hands and smiling. "There aren't any insects."

It was true. The fearful clouds of bloodsucking insects we had been warned about were nowhere to be seen.

As I looked around, I thought to myself that I had been right and this was not at all the scary place it had been made out to be; it felt instead like Eden. The sense of danger and unease that I had been carrying as an unconscious weight since Woody's lecture subsided. The SAS team had, naturally, tried to prepare us for the worst, but they had overdone it.

As dusk fell, Woody invited us into his little bivouac area, where he had a tiny stove going with a pot of boiling water for tea and for hydrating our evening's freeze-dried dinners. I opened a packet of chicken tetrazzini, poured in boiling water, and then, when it had absorbed the water, spooned it from the bag into my mouth. I washed it down with a cup of tea, and we stood around listening to Woody, Spud, and Sully tell stories of their adventures in the jungle.

Within minutes, night dropped like the shutting of a door—absolute blackness fell upon us. The sounds of the day morphed into something deeper and mysterious, with trills and scratchings and boomings and calls like the cries of the damned. Now the insects began to make their appearance, starting with the mosquitoes.

There was no fire. Woody lit a Coleman lantern that forced back the darkness a little, and we huddled in its pool of light in the great forest while large animals tramped, heard but unseen, in the jungle around us.

Woody said he had spent a large part of his life in jungles all over the world, from Asia and Africa to South and Central America. He said he had never been in one like this, so apparently untouched. As he was setting up camp, before we arrived, a quail came right up to him, pecking in the dirt. And a wild pig also wandered through, unconcerned by the presence of humans. The spider monkeys, he said, were another sign of an uninhabited area, as they normally flee at the first sight of humans, unless they are in a protected zone. He concluded, "I don't think the animals here have ever seen people before."

All three of the ex-SAS team were absurdly bundled up against the insects, covered from head to toe with insect-proof clothing, which included a hood and a head net.

"Is that really necessary?" I asked.

"I've had dengue fever twice," Woody said, and launched into a shockingly graphic description of the disease, which had almost killed him the second time. It is called "breakbone fever," he said, because it is so painful you feel like your bones are breaking.

After his tale was over, I noticed everyone quietly applying more DEET. I did the same. Then, as night deepened, the sand flies came out—in numbers. Much smaller than mosquitoes, they looked like white motes drifting in the light of the lantern, so small that they made no noise, and you normally don't feel them biting, unlike mosquitoes. The more the night deepened, the more sand flies collected around us.

Eager to record some of the stories being told, I hurried back to my hammock on the other side of camp to fetch my notebook. My new headlamp was defective, so Juan Carlos loaned me a crank flashlight. I made my way back without difficulty. But on my return, everything looked different in the dark; I halted, hemmed in by dense vegetation, realizing I had somehow veered off my rudimentary trail. The nighttime rainforest was black and alive with noise, the air thick and sweet, the leaves like a wall surrounding me. My flashlight's feeble beam was fading. I took a minute to frantically crank it up to a greater brightness, and then I played it carefully over the ground, looking for my tracks in the forest litter, or any sign of the trail I'd hacked with my machete earlier in the day.

Thinking I saw tracks, I moved in that direction, walking quickly, pushing aside the undergrowth with a growing sense of relief—only to be blocked by a mammoth tree trunk. I had never seen this tree before. Disoriented, I had stumbled deeper into the jungle. I took a moment to catch my breath and get my heart rate down. I could neither hear my companions nor see the light from where they were gathered. I thought of calling out to them, asking Woody to come get me, but decided not to expose myself as an idiot this early in the expedition. After intently examining the ground and cranking the light up several more times, I finally found my real tracks and retraced them, bent over and peering at the forest floor, each time waiting to advance until I located the next scuffmark or depression. A few minutes later, I spied a freshly cut leaf lying on the ground, its stem oozing sap, and then another. I was back on the trail.

Following the slashed leaves and vines like bread crumbs, I retraced the trail to the center of camp, where I gratefully recognized Juan Carlos's hammock. Thrilled to be safely back in camp, I circled the hammock, probing the wall of forest with my light for the path that would take me to where the rest of the group was chatting. That would be easy: I could now hear the murmur of voices and see the light of the Coleman lantern peeking through the vegetation.

On my second circle of the hammock, I froze as my beam passed over a huge snake. It was coiled up on the ground, just to one side of Juan Carlos's hammock, three feet away from where I stood. Impossible to miss, the snake was the opposite of camouflaged: Even in the dim flashlight beam it looked practically aglow, the patterns on its scaly back brilliantly etched against the gloomy night, its eyes two bright points. It was staring at me, in striking position, its head swaying back and forth, its tongue flicking in and out. I had walked right past it—twice. It seemed mesmerized by the flashlight beam, which was already starting to fade. I hastily cranked it back up into brightness.

I backed up slowly until I was out of the snake's range, which I figured might be more than six feet—some snakes are able to strike their entire body length. I have had many encounters with venomous snakes—I've been struck at several times and hit once (a rattler that bounced off the toe of my boot)—but I had never in my life faced a snake like this: so fully aroused, so keenly focused, so disturbingly intelligent. If he decided to come at me, I'd not be able to escape.

"Hey, guys?" I called out, trying to keep my voice steady. "There's a giant snake here."

Woody responded, "Get back. But keep the light on it."

The snake remained motionless, its gleaming eyes fixed on me. The forest had fallen silent. Woody arrived seconds later, with the rest of the group in tow, their headlamp beams swinging wildly through the murk.

"Jesus Christ," someone said loudly.

Woody said quietly: "Everyone stay back, but keep your torches on him. It's a fer-de-lance."

He pulled his machete from its scabbard and, with a few strokes, transformed an adjacent sapling into a seven-foot snake stick, a long pole with a narrow, forked end.

"I'm going to move him."

He advanced toward the snake and, in a sudden thrusting motion, pinned its body to the ground with the forked end of the stick. The snake exploded into furious action, uncoiling, twisting, thrashing, and striking in every direction, spraying venom. Now we saw just how large it really was. Woody worked the forked stick up its body to its neck as the snake continued to whip about. Its tail was vibrating furiously, making a low humming sound. Keeping the neck pinned with the stick and his left hand, Woody crouched and seized it behind the head with his right hand. The snake's body, thick as his arm, slammed against his legs, its dazzling snow-white mouth gaping wide, unsheathing inch-and-a-quarter-long fangs that pumped out streams of pale yellow liquid. As its head lashed back and forth, straining to sink its fangs into Woody's fist, it expelled poison all over the back of his hand, causing his skin to bubble. Woody wrestled the snake to the ground and pinned its squirming body with his knees. He pulled a knife from his belt and with his left hand, never releasing the snake with his right, neatly sliced off the head. He impaled the snake's head firmly to the ground by driving the knife through it, and only then released the snake. The head, along with its three inches of remaining neck, wiggled and struggled, while the headless snake also began to crawl off, and Woody had to pull it back into the pool of light to prevent its escape into the brush. Through the whole struggle, he never uttered a word. The rest of us had been stunned into silence as well.

He rose, rinsed his hands, and finally spoke. "I'm sorry I wasn't able to move it. I had to wash the venom off right away." (Later, he said he was "a bit concerned" when he felt the poison running into a cut on the back of his hand.)

He held up the headless snake by the tail, blood still dribbling from its neck. Nobody said a word. The snake's muscles were still flexing slowly. Curious to touch it, I reached out and wrapped my hand around it, feeling the rhythmic writhing of muscles under its cool skin, a queer sensation indeed. The snake was about six feet long, its back displaying striking diamond patterns in colors of chocolate, mahogany, and creamed coffee. Everyone stared at it as the sounds of the night returned.

"Nothing like this to sort of concentrate your mind, is there?" Woody said. "Female. They get bigger than the males. This is one of the biggest fer-de-lances I've ever seen." He casually slung the body over his arm. "We *could* eat it, they're quite delicious. But I've another use for it. When the others arrive tomorrow, they'll need to see this. Everyone needs to be fully aware of what they're getting into here."

He added quietly, "There's rarely just one."


When I retired that night to my hammock, I could not sleep. The jungle, reverberating with sound, was much noisier than in the daytime. Several times I heard large animals moving past me in the darkness, blundering clumsily through undergrowth, crackling twigs. I lay in the dark, listening to the cacophony of life, thinking about the lethal perfection of the snake and its natural dignity, sorry for what we had done but rattled by the close call. A bite from a snake like that, if you survived at all, would be a life-altering experience. In a strange way the encounter sharpened the experience of being here. It amazed me that a valley so primeval and unspoiled could still exist in the twenty-first century. It was truly a lost world, a place that did not want us and where we did not belong. We planned to enter the ruins the following day. What would we find? I couldn't even begin to imagine it.

## CHAPTER 15

**All this terrain, everything you see here, has been entirely modified by human hands.**

I lay awake most of the night in my hammock. It was a high-tech contraption, the underside made of thin nylon, with a top of insect netting and a rainfly above. You entered through a zippered seam in the side, but it left me feeling exposed, and it swayed with every movement I made. I had stopped taking my weekly dose of chloroquinone, an antimalarial drug, in a fruitless attempt to alleviate the insomnia it had been causing, a common side effect. I reasoned that there couldn't be any malaria in an uninhabited place like this, cut off from the world.

The night clamor of the jungle was so loud I had to wear earplugs. Chris, on the other hand, confessed to me later that he recorded the night jungle on his iPhone and played it to himself back in Colorado to help calm him down when he was stressed or upset.

Sometime in the middle of the night, I got up to pee. I unzipped the hammock and peered out, probing the ground all around with my flashlight, looking for snakes. A cold and clammy mist had descended, and the forest was dripping with condensation. There were no snakes, but the entire forest floor was carpeted with glistening cockroaches—thousands of them rustling in frantic activity, looking like a greasy, jittering flow—along with dozens of motionless black spiders whose multiple eyes gleamed like pinpoints of green. I peed no more than two feet from the hammock and hastily climbed back in. But even in that brief moment it proved impossible to keep the sand flies from pouring into the hammock's interior space. I spent a good fifteen minutes lying on my back, shining my light around, squishing sand flies as they drifted about or landed on the mosquito netting above me. After I had to get out and pee a second time, I damned the British habit of drinking tea before bedtime and swore I would not do so again.

What little sleep I did get ended for good at around five o'clock in the morning, at first light, when I was awoken by a roaring of howler monkeys, which reverberated through the forest like Godzilla on the march.

When I emerged from the hammock, the forest was enveloped in fog, the treetops fading into the mist, water dripping everywhere. For a subtropical jungle it was surprisingly chilly. We ate a breakfast of freeze-dried scrambled eggs and weak tea (coffee had not arrived yet). Chris, who seemed to be prepared for everything, had brought caffeine pills for just such a contingency and popped a few. (I declined his offer to share.) The AStar couldn't fly in until the fog lifted, which it finally did around midmorning. The first flight brought in Steve Elkins and two members of the film crew, Mark Adams and Josh Feezer.

I greeted Steve after the chopper took off. He was walking with a hiking pole and limping, due to chronic nerve damage in his foot.

"Nice," he said, looking around. "Welcome to the Mosquitia Four Seasons."

Alicia González, the expedition's anthropologist, arrived in the second flight, along with Anna Cohen, a graduate student in archaeology at the University of Washington, who was Chris Fisher's field associate. I soon became friendly with Alicia, who was an amazing font of knowledge. With a PhD from the University of Texas at Austin, Alicia was a small, cheerful, and imperturbable woman of sixty, formerly a senior curator in the Smithsonian's Museum of the American

Indian. Of Mexican, Jewish, and Native American ancestry, she was an authority on Mesoamerican trade routes and the indigenous people of Honduras.

The chopper also brought in Oscar Neil, chief of archaeology for the Instituto Hondureño de Antropología e Historia (IHAH). Neil was an authority on the ancient cultures of Mosquitia. We unloaded the chopper with the usual haste, throwing everything into a heap to be sorted and carried into camp later. The morning was spent moving supplies and equipment and organizing our campsites. I grabbed a tent and set it up next to my hammock, grateful to be on solid ground. The tent's sewn-in waterproof ground cover would keep out the snakes, spiders, and cockroaches. I enlarged my campsite area with a machete, strung a clothesline, and claimed a folding chair from one of the loads, which I set up under my hammock. There, protected under the rainfly of the hammock, I could sit and write in my notebook. And I could store my clothes, books, camera, and journals in the hammock itself, which made a handy waterproof storage compartment.

As the day wore on, Chris Fisher became increasingly impatient, eager to begin our extraordinary task of entering the lost city. I found him down on the riverbank, in his straw cowboy hat, pacing back and forth with a Trimble GPS in his hand. Woody had forbidden anyone to leave camp without an escort, due to the danger of snakes and getting lost. "This is ridiculous," Fisher said. "The site is just *right there*—two hundred yards away!" He showed me the LED screen on the Trimble, which displayed the lidar map and our position on it. I could see that the city was, indeed, right on the other side of the river, completely hidden in the screen of trees. "If Woody doesn't free up someone to take us over there, I'm going by myself—screw the snakes." Juan Carlos joined us at the streambank, hands on his hips, staring at the wall of trees on the far side. He, too, was eager to venture into the ruins. "We don't have a lot of time," he said. It was true: We had only ten potential days to explore the valley, our time being strictly limited by the rental period of the AStar helicopter from Corporate Helicopters in San Diego. Its pilot, Myles Elsing, had to fly it back to the States—a four-day journey—for another assignment.

"Someone's got to talk to Woody," said Fisher. "*This* is why we're here"—he gestured across the river at the hidden city—"not boiling water for frigging tea."

Finally, about three thirty in the afternoon, Woody agreed to lead a reconnaissance into the ancient city. He told us to be at the LZ in a half hour, with our packs fully loaded with the emergency overnight kit. We would have one hour in the ruins—no more.

At the appointed time, we gathered at the stream,

stinking of DEET. There were eight of us in the group: myself, Woody, Chris Fisher with a machete in one hand and GPS in the other; Oscar Neil; Juan Carlos, also carrying a fearsome machete; Lucian Read, with a video camera; and Mark Adams, with a forty-pound field audio kit consisting of a wireless audio mic system, portable audio mixer/recorder, and a six-foot boom mic with windshield. I couldn't believe Mark was going to hump all that through the jungle. Dave Yoder, burdened with heavy camera equipment, followed in watchful silence, ceaselessly shooting. Steve Elkins could not come; the nerve damage, caused by a deteriorating disk in his spine, gave him a condition known as drop foot, in which he was unable to control the position of his foot while walking. He felt the jungle was too thick and the hills too steep to take the risk of injury so early in the expedition. He did not want to be laid up, or worse, have to be evacuated. It was a bitter pill to swallow. "If you guys find anything," he said, waving a two-way radio, "call me."

Woody checked our packs to make sure we had all our emergency supplies, and we set off, wading across the stream. On the far side we encountered a thicket of heliconia that formed a virtually solid wall, but the fleshy stems were easily felled with the swipe of a machete. Woody carved and slashed his way through, one step at a time, the leaves and flowers showering down left and right. The cut vegetation lay so thickly on the ground that there was no possibility of seeing where we were putting our feet. Still shaken by my encounter with the fer-de-lance, I couldn't help but think of all the snakes that must be hiding in that undergrowth. We crossed two muddy channels, sinking up to our thighs, struggling through the morass with sucking sounds.

The embankment beyond the floodplain was precipitous: close to forty degrees. We climbed hand and foot, grasping roots and vines and branches, pulling ourselves up, expecting at any moment to come face-to-face with a fer-de-lance. We could see little beyond a dozen feet in any direction. The embankment abruptly flattened out, and we arrived at a long ditch and mound that Chris and Oscar examined and felt were man-made. They appeared to mark the edge of the city.

And then we came to the base of the presumed earthen pyramid. The only indication that this was artificial was that the ground rose sharply in an unnatural change of slope. Until Chris and Oscar pointed it out to me, however, I would never have recognized it. We could see nothing but leaves. Here we were, at the edge of a lost city, and we had no sense of the layout or distribution of the mounds and plazas so crisply visible on the lidar maps. The jungle cloaked all.

We labored up the side of the suspected pyramid and reached the top. There, in front of us, were some odd depressions and linear features that Chris believed might be the remains of a structure, perhaps a small temple. Oscar knelt and, with a hand tool, dug a *sondaje* or test pit into the soil. He said he saw evidence of deliberate construction. I peered at the layers of earth he had exposed just below the surface, but my untrained eye could make out nothing.

Even at the top of the pyramid, the highest point of the lost city, we were immersed in a disorder of leaves, vines, flowers, and tree trunks. Chris held his GPS over his head, but he had trouble locating satellites because of the trees. I took many pictures with my Nikon, but they all ended up showing the same thing: leaves, leaves, and more leaves. Even Dave struggled to get photographs of something other than an endless green ocean of vegetation.

We descended the side of the pyramid into the first plaza of the city. The lidar images indicated that the plaza was surrounded on three sides by geometric mounds and terraces. As Fisher tried once again to get a GPS reading with his Trimble, in order to start ground-mapping, Oscar gave a shout. He knelt, brushing dirt and vines off the corner of a large stone, almost completely invisible in the riot of plants. The stone had a shaped surface. After pulling back and cutting away some of the vegetation, we began to uncover more such stones—a long row of them, all flat, resting on tripods of round, white-quartz boulders. They looked like altars. "We have to clean these stones," Chris said, "to see if any have carvings, and we need to locate them on the GPS." He pulled out his walkie-talkie and called Elkins, back in camp, to report the news.

They had an excited conversation that we all could hear through the walkie-talkie speaker. Elkins was ecstatic. "This proves," he told Chris, "that they *did* use cut stone for building. It means this was an important site."

The GPS finally located enough satellites for Fisher to begin establishing way points and mapping the city. He charged through the jungle, slashing his way, marking way points, keen and impatient to make the most of our limited time before we had to return to camp. We could hardly keep up. Beyond the altar stones, we reached the central plaza of the city, which had clearly been at one time a large public space. It was as flat as a soccer pitch and more open than elsewhere.

"These were probably once public buildings," said Fisher, indicating the long mounds surrounding the plaza. "Perhaps reserved for an elite class or royalty. All this would have been open and very impressive. I imagine this area was where major ceremonies took place."

Standing in the plaza, I finally began to have a sense of the size and scale of the city, if only barely. Chris cut his way across it, saying that there were three more plazas and a possible ball court farther on, along with a peculiar mound we had called "the bus" because it looked like one in the lidar image. These bus-shaped mounds were prominent in both T1 and T3, well defined, each a hundred feet long, thirty feet wide, and fifteen feet tall. I had also seen several at the site of Las Crucitas. They were a characteristic structure unique to this culture.

While the rest of the team stayed behind, clearing the vegetation from the stones, Woody and I followed Fisher northward, trying to keep him in sight. We came to more mounds and a steep ravine cutting through them. Glancing into the cut, I could see where the erosion had exposed what looked like stone paving forming an ancient surface. Fisher hurried on past the ravine, where the jungle became incredibly dense. I did not want to follow him into that frightful tangle, and neither did Woody. He called to Chris not to go any farther, that it was time to go back, but he didn't seem to hear us. Moments later, we saw his white cowboy hat vanish into the forest. The rhythmic swiping of his machete died away into silence. "Bloody hell," Woody muttered, and again called for him to come back. Silence. He called again. Minutes passed. While Woody was not one to express emotion, I could see a look of irritation and concern gathering on his face. Just when we were thinking Chris was gone, we heard his faint voice drifting through the trees and he emerged back out of the hole he'd cut in the vegetation.

"We were concerned you were lost," said Woody in a clipped voice.

"Not with this," he said, waving his GPS.

Woody called for a return. While we had been waiting for Chris, the others had come up to the ravine. Using his own GPS, Woody identified a more direct route back to camp, hiking down the ravine to the floodplain, where we encountered another barrier of heliconia, which Woody worked his way through, expertly wielding his machete, scattering flowers left and right. We had to cross three parallel channels of sucking mud, once again sinking to our thighs. When we reached the stream, coated with mud, we waded in, rinsing the mud off. While the others went back to camp, I stripped, wrung out my clothes and piled them on the pebble beach, and then I lay back in the cool water and floated on my back, letting the river carry me a ways downstream, watching the treetops lazily move past.

Back in camp, I found Steve on a cot outside his tent, which he had set up next to my camp on the other side of the spider-monkey tree. He was lying on his back, eating peanuts, and gazing straight up with binoculars at the troop of spider monkeys. They in turn were lined up on a limb fifty feet above, staring down at him and eating leaves. It was a funny sight, two curious primate species observing each other with fascination.

Steve was absolutely beaming over the discovery of the altar stones and full of self-reproach for not having gone with us. He asked questions about how tough the hike was, and I assured him that although it was steep and slippery, and the mudholes were appalling, it was only a few hundred yards and I was pretty sure he could do it if he took it slow.

"Screw the leg," he said. "I'm going up there tomorrow, one way or another."

That night, we sat around eating freeze-dried beans and rice to the light of a Coleman lantern. I avoided tea, although I did accept a "tot" of whisky from Woody, rationed out in a bottle cap.

Chris was elated. "It's just as I thought," he said. "All this terrain, everything you see here, has been entirely modified by human hands." In one short reconnaissance, he had confirmed the accuracy of the lidar survey, verifying on the ground every feature seen in the images—along with a great deal more. The "ground truthing" had begun.

A rising wind breathed through the treetops. "That means rain," said Woody. "In ten minutes." Right on schedule the downpour thundered into the treetops. It took a good two or three minutes for the water to work its way down through the canopy and reach us on the ground—and then streams of water came cascading everywhere.

## CHAPTER 16

**I can't move my legs at all. I'm going down.**

After night fell, I crawled in my tent, glad to be on solid ground and out of the dreaded hammock. I read my Dover edition of John Lloyd Stephens by flashlight as the rain drummed down. Despite the rain, snakes, mud, and insects, I felt exhilarated, not just by the lost city, but by the feral perfection of the valley. I had been in many wilderness areas, but never in a place as purely untrammeled as this. The hostility of the environment only added to the feeling of being the first to explore and discover an unknown place.

I awoke at five to the roar of howler monkeys rising above the pounding of rain. It was a morning so dark it didn't seem as if daytime had arrived at all. The forest was wrapped in a twilight gloom, cloaked in mist. Chris was up and as usual impatient to the point of zeal to continue his work. The camp kitchen and gathering area had now been partly erected. We assembled under blue tarps strung up over several plastic folding tables. One camp stove was boiling water and the other heating a pot of coffee, now that the supply of coffee had finally arrived. Outside, the rain was turning the jungle floor into greasy mud that seemed to deepen with every passing hour. The water collected in the hollows of the tarp, which periodically had to be pushed up with poles to dump the puddles of water off the edges.

At breakfast, several people reported having heard a jaguar prowling about the edges of the camp in the dead of night, making a rumbling, purring noise. Woody assured us that jaguars almost never attack humans, although I wondered about that, given Bruce Heinicke's story. Others were concerned that the large animals heard stumbling about might blunder into a tent, but Woody dismissed that as unlikely, explaining that the animals that came out at night could see quite well in the dark.

"There are four more plazas I want to look at," Chris said, gulping his coffee. "Upriver is a weird L-shaped mound. I want to see that. And about a kilometer downriver is another set of plazas I want to see. There's a lot to do—let's get going."

I had donned my raincoat, but the rain was so heavy that water began to trickle in anyway, and wearing it made me sticky and hot. I noticed none of Woody's team were wearing rain gear; they were going about their business completely and cheerfully soaked. "Take it off," Woody said to me. "Best to get it over with all at once. Trust me: Once you're thoroughly wet, you'll be more comfortable."

As soon as I did, I was quickly drenched—and discovered Woody was right.

After breakfast, with the rain still falling, the full expedition team assembled on the riverbank, and we set out for our second exploration of the site. Despite his injured leg, Steve Elkins joined the group, carrying a blue hiking pole. Also included were Alicia González and Anna Cohen. We waded the river and went along the trail cut the previous day. When we reached the second mudhole, Alicia struggled to walk through the muck, got stuck, and—as we watched, aghast—began to sink.

"I can't move," she said with remarkable calmness, even as she was sinking. "I can't move my legs at all. I'm going down. Really, folks, *I'm going down.*" The mud was already at her waist, and the more she struggled, the more it gurgled up around her. It was like something straight out of a B horror film. Woody and Sully jumped in and seized her arms and slowly worked her out. Once she was safe on hard ground, the mud draining off of her, it became clear what had happened: The mud had filled up her snake gaiters as she tried to wade through, creating an instant pair of cement overshoes, which were inexorably dragging her under with every movement she made. "For a moment there," she said afterward, "I thought I was going to be having tea with the snakes."

Elkins, for his part, made it through the mudhole with his hiking pole as a balance and managed to climb up the slippery embankment, using roots and small tree trunks as handholds.

"We'll get fixed ropes in here tomorrow," said Sully.

As we skirted the base of the pyramid, happy shouts and singing echoed from across the river. Sully called Spud in camp on his walkie-talkie and learned that the Honduran Special Forces soldiers, sent to guard the expedition team, had just arrived in good spirits after a hike upstream from the river junction. They had brought nothing but their weapons and the clothes on their backs; they intended to establish camp behind ours and live off the forest, building their shelters from poles and leaves, hunting their food and drinking from the river.

"Give them a tarp," said Sully. "And also some water purification tablets. I don't want a bunch of soldiers with the runs camped near us."

When we reached the altar stones, Elkins knelt and began clearing leaves and debris away from them, running his hand over their carved surfaces. One of the stones had a peculiar quartz vein running through it, which looked like it had been chiseled around to enhance it. It ran due north. Elkins felt this was highly significant, and someone else suggested it might have been used to channel blood from human sacrifices. Chris rolled his eyes. "Let's not get out of hand with the speculation here, folks. We don't have any idea what these are. They could be foundation stones, altar stones, or something else entirely." Chris asked Anna to clear the area and survey the stones while he went northward to explore the four plazas. Alicia González and Tom Weinberg remained behind to work with Anna. Dave Yoder, his gear wrapped up in plastic, stayed back to photograph, along with the film crew, who were also struggling to keep their equipment from getting soaked in the rain. The crew posed Elkins next to the stones, clipped a lavalier mic on him, and rolled an interview.

Chris forged ahead, once again charging through the forest like a maniac, his machete flashing. All the machetes we carried had strips of Day-Glo pink tape on their blades, so they could be seen and avoided. The vegetation was so thick that it was easy to see how someone could get sliced open by a machete-wielding neighbor, and even with the Day-Glo tape there were a couple of close calls. Woody, Juan Carlos, and I tried to keep up with Chris. Beyond the ravine, we explored a second plaza, twice as large as the first, also delineated by mounds, berms, and raised earthwork platforms. On the far side, too, were two low, parallel mounds with a flat area in between, which Fisher mapped out with his GPS. He believed it might have been a Mesoamerican ball court, having a similar geometry and size. This was especially interesting, as it indicated a possible link between this culture and its powerful Maya neighbors to the west and north. Far more than the casual recreation we think of when it comes to games of skill, in Mesoamerican cultures the ball game was a sacred ritual that reenacted the struggle between the forces of good and evil. It might also have been a way for groups to avoid warfare by solving conflicts through a match instead, one that occasionally ended with human sacrifice, including the decapitation of the losing team or its captain.

I followed Chris and Juan Carlos around as they hacked this way and that through the jungle, surveying and mapping the plaza. I was especially intrigued to see the famous "bus" mound, which was so striking on the lidar images. In reality it was a perplexing earthen construction, with a sharply defined base and steep walls.

"What the heck is it?" I asked Chris, as he poked around it, marking way points on his GPS.

"I think it's the foundation of a raised public building or temple," he said, explaining it was situated at the far end of what had once been a big plaza, where it would have been prominently visible. "There was something on top that's gone now, built out of perishable materials."

The rain ceased, but the trees continued shedding millions of drops. The light filtered down, cloudy green, as though passing through pond water. I stood breathing in the rich odor of life, marveling at the silent mounds, the immense trees choked by strangler figs, the mats of hanging vines, the cries of birds and animals, the flowers nodding under the burden of water. The connection to the present world dissolved, and I felt we had somehow passed into a realm beyond time and space.

Soon enough, the peace was broken by another downpour. We continued exploring. It was exhausting, soaking work, pushing through the jungle, unable to see where we were putting our feet, the ground as slippery as ice. We climbed up and down steep ravines and hillsides, made treacherous by mud. I learned the hard way not to grab hold of a stick of bamboo, because it would sometimes shatter into sharp, cutting pieces and dump on me a load of rank water that had accumulated in its hollow stem. Other potential handholds sported vicious thorns or swarms of venomous red ants. Downpour after downpour came and went, like someone turning a tap on and off. Around one o'clock, Woody became concerned that the river might be rising, preventing our ability to cross back to camp, so we returned to where Anna, Alicia, and Tom were working on the row of stones. As they cleared the area, they had discovered, in the corner of the plaza, a stone staircase that went down into the earth, partially buried by slumping mounds. We paused in the rain while Woody passed around a thermos of hot, sweet, milky tea. Everyone was talking excitedly. Even with the minimal amount of clearing, I had a better feeling for what this tiny corner of the city was like, with its row of stones propped upon boulders. They certainly *looked* like altars, but were they places of sacrifice, or seats for important people, or some other thing? And the stone staircase that went nowhere was another puzzle. Where did it go down to—some underground tomb or chamber? Or did it lead up to something that had washed away?

Too soon we had to leave. We set off in single file, back to camp, again skirting the base of the pyramid. It was a route we had taken several times before without noticing anything special. But suddenly Lucian Read, in the back of the line, called out, "Hey! Some weird stones over here!"

We returned to look, and all mayhem broke out.

In a broad hollow area, just poking out of the ground, were the tops of dozens of extraordinary carved stone sculptures. The objects, glimpsed among leaves and vines, and carpeted with moss, took shape in the forest twilight. The first thing I saw was the snarling head of a jaguar sticking out of the forest floor, then the rim of a vessel decorated with a vulture's head and more large stone jars carved with snakes; next to them was a cluster of objects that looked like thrones or tables, some with carvings along the rims and legs that, at first glance, appeared to be inscriptions or glyphs. They were all almost entirely buried, with only the tops visible, like stone icebergs. I was astounded. These sculptures were in beautiful condition and had probably been lying here undisturbed since they had been left centuries ago—until we stumbled across them. This was proof, if we needed it, that this valley had not been explored in modern times.

The crew crowded into the area, jostling each other and exclaiming in astonishment. The camera team was shooting and Dave Yoder was in there, too, photographing like a madman, while I also had my Nikon out, taking pictures in the rain. Chris, the archaeologist, began yelling for everyone to get back, dammit, don't touch anything, quit stomping around, watch your feet for chrissakes! Cursing and driving people out, he finally roped off the area with Spanish crime-scene tape that spelled out CUIDADO, "warning," which he had been carrying (with remarkable foresight) in his backpack.

"Nobody goes past the tape," he said, "but me, Oscar, and Anna."

Steve, leaning on his walking stick, exhausted and in pain from the punishing hike up to the ruins, was astounded. "It's amazing," he said, "that there's this place here, this jewel of a place, as pure as you could find, untouched for centuries!" The rain streamed down all around us, but nobody paid any attention. "When you're here and see how overgrown it is," he continued, "how much has been buried, you see how improbable it would be to stumble upon this. In a metaphysical sense it was like we were led here."

Chris Fisher was also a bit stunned. "I expected to find a city," he told me later, "but I didn't expect *this*. The undisturbed context is rare. It may be an *ofrenda*, an offering or a cache. This is a powerful ritual display, to take wealth objects out of circulation." He was especially impressed by the carved head of what, to him, might be a portrait of a "were-jaguar," showing a shaman "in a spirit or transformed state." Because the figure seemed to be wearing a helmet, he also wondered if it was connected to the ball game. "But this is all speculation: We just don't know." He suspected that much, much more lay below the surface.

And much more did, as later excavation would reveal. The cache was vast, containing over five hundred pieces, but more intriguing even than its size was its existence at all. This particular type of ritual collection of artifacts seems to be a special feature of these lost cities of ancient Mosquitia—they have not been seen in Maya culture or elsewhere— meaning that they could hold a key to what distinguishes the people of Mosquitia from their neighbors and defines their place in history. What was the purpose of these caches? Why were they left here? While similar caches had been reported in Mosquitia before, none had been found so fully intact, offering a rare opportunity for the spot to be systematically studied and excavated. The significance of this offering would prove to be the expedition's greatest discovery so far, one that had important implications far beyond Mosquitia. But it would be a year before we understood the scope of those discoveries.

Even with the intense excitement and high spirits, the hike back to camp was grueling, as the steep hillsides were impossible to descend except in a semi-controlled sort of falling slide. In spite of Woody's worries, the stream had not risen much and remained fordable. The rain abated; the sky began to clear; and we hoped the helicopter would soon be able to come in with more needed supplies for the camp, which was still only partly set up. We lacked food and water, generators to charge up laptops and batteries for the camera gear, and we needed to set up a medical tent and guest tents for scientists who were expected to arrive over the following days.

Back in camp, Chris declared he was now going to explore what appeared in the lidar images to be an earthwork behind our camp. His energy was impressive. We hiked back behind camp, passing through the soldiers' encampment. They were building a communal house using one of our tarps, and paving the muddy floor with thick leaves. They had a fire burning—I had no idea how they managed it in the rain—and one soldier was returning from the hunt with a deer haunch thrown over his shoulder. The deer, it turned out later, was a threatened Central American red brocket deer; a week later, the military ordered the soldiers to stop hunting and began flying in MREs. The soldiers told us it had taken them almost five hours to make the journey to our camp on foot from the lower landing zone at the river junction, a distance of three miles. They had traveled in the river, wading upstream, easier and safer than slashing through the jungle.

Behind the soldiers' camp, a steep slope thrust upward. This was the anomaly Chris wanted to explore. We climbed to the top and came down on the far side, finding ourselves in an oval area with a flat bottom, surrounded by what appeared to be dikes or man-made earthen banks. The area was open, with little understory. It looked like a large swimming pool, with a flat bottom and steep walls. A small outlet at one end led back down to the flat area where we were camped. On the other end, a swale that looked like an ancient road passed down the side of the hill. Chris concluded that these earthworks had probably been a reservoir for collecting water during the wet season, to be released during the dry season to irrigate crops in the area where we were camped. "That whole terrace we're on was probably an agricultural area," he said, that had been artificially leveled. Part of it may have been a cacao grove; Alicia González had identified what she believed were some small cacao trees growing near her campsite.

The dark clouds drifted off, and finally blue sky appeared in patches for the first time that day. A milky sun emerged, sending spears of sunlight through the misty canopy. An hour later we heard the thudding of the incoming chopper, rousing once again a furious chorus from the howler monkeys. We had two visitors: Lt. Col. Oseguera, who had come to check on the situation of his troops, and Virgilio Paredes, the IHAH chief. The colonel went to review his troops while Virgilio retired to the kitchen area and listened with interest as Steve and Chris described to him the discovery of the cache. It was too late in the evening to go back up, so Virgilio and the colonel decided to spend the night and visit the site the next day.

I had first met Virgilio in 2012 during the lidar survey. He was a tall, thoughtful man who, while not an archaeologist himself, asked probing questions and had taken pains to become thoroughly versed in the project. He spoke fluent English. He was descended from an ancient Sephardic Jewish family named Pardes, who left Jerusalem in the nineteenth century and emigrated to Segovia, Spain, where the name was Hispanicized to Paredes. During the Fascist regime of Franco, his grandfather left Spain and went to Honduras. His father went to medical school in Honduras and became a biochemist and a businessman, but now, close to retirement, he was considering making aliyah and moving to Israel. Virgilio was raised Catholic, went to the American School in Tegucigalpa, got a master's degree from the London School of Economics, and lived and studied in diverse places in the world, from Germany to Trinidad and Tobago. He was working for the Ministry of Culture at the time of the 2009 coup, when the interim president asked him to head the IHAH. It was a big change: For the past sixty years the IHAH had been headed by an academic, but the new administration wanted a manager instead. Some archaeologists were unhappy. "The academics were fighting with the tourist sector," Virgilio told me. "If you have the golden chicken, the archaeologists don't want the chicken to produce *any* golden eggs, but the tourist guys, they want to cut it open to get *all* the eggs at once. There should be a balance."

He had known the story of the White City since he was a boy. When he first heard that Steve's group was looking for it, he thought the whole project was "mumbo jumbo." Since taking the job, a steady stream of crazy people had been coming through his office or sending him e-mails about Atlantis or legendary shipwrecks with millions in gold. He thought Steve was in that same category. "I said, 'Tell me another story!'" But when Steve described lidar and how it had the potential to bare the secrets of Mosquitia, Paredes got interested: This was a serious technology and Steve and his team impressed him as capable people.

The rain started again. After dinner and another tot, I retired to my campsite, stripped off my muddy clothes, hung them on the clothesline for the rain to rinse clean, and crawled into my tent. My camp—and everywhere else—was now a sea of mud. Taking a cue from the soldiers, I tried to pave the mud in front of my tent with waxy leaves, a failing strategy. Inside, the mud had worked its way under the tent, and my waterproof floor was squishy like a water bed.

As I settled into my sleeping bag, I could feel insects crawling on me. They must have been on me all along without me realizing it until I stopped moving. With a yelp I unzipped my bag and turned on the flashlight. I was covered with ugly red welts and patches, hundreds of them—but where were the actual bugs? I felt something biting me and pinched it off; it was a chigger the size of a grain of sand, almost too small to see. I tried to crush it but the shell was too hard, so I carefully placed it on the cover of my John Lloyd Stephens book and stabbed it with the tip of my knife, making a satisfying crunch. To my horror I soon discovered more chiggers, not just on my skin but also some that had dropped off inside my bag. I spent a half hour collecting them, placing them on the execution block, and stabbing them. But the tiny creatures were nearly invisible in my bed, so I covered myself with DEET and resigned myself to sleeping with chiggers. By the end of the trip, the book's cover was so full of stab marks that I threw it away.

At breakfast Alicia reported another jaguar as well as hearing a faint, whispery noise creeping alongside her tent that she was sure was a very large snake.

## CHAPTER 17

**This is a very ancient place, a bewitchment place, they say.**

The morning of our third day in the jungle, we hiked to the site of the cache with Virgilio, the colonel, and four soldiers. Even with the fixed ropes that Sully and Woody had strung up, it was tough getting up the hill. Chris asked Anna Cohen to take charge of clearing the cache site of vegetation, marking each object, inventorying, recording, and sketching them all in situ. The soldiers would help her. Chris, Woody, Steve, and I set off to explore the city to the north. With Chris leading, we crossed plaza 1, climbed in and out of the ravine to plaza 2. We chopped our way through tangles of bamboo, vines, and plants. Fisher had a long checklist of features seen in lidar that he wanted to visit on the ground, and his GPS took us into some fiercely dense jungle. In places it was like digging a tunnel through green. We visited more

View of the River Pao. The lost city lies on an unnamed tributary upstream from this river.

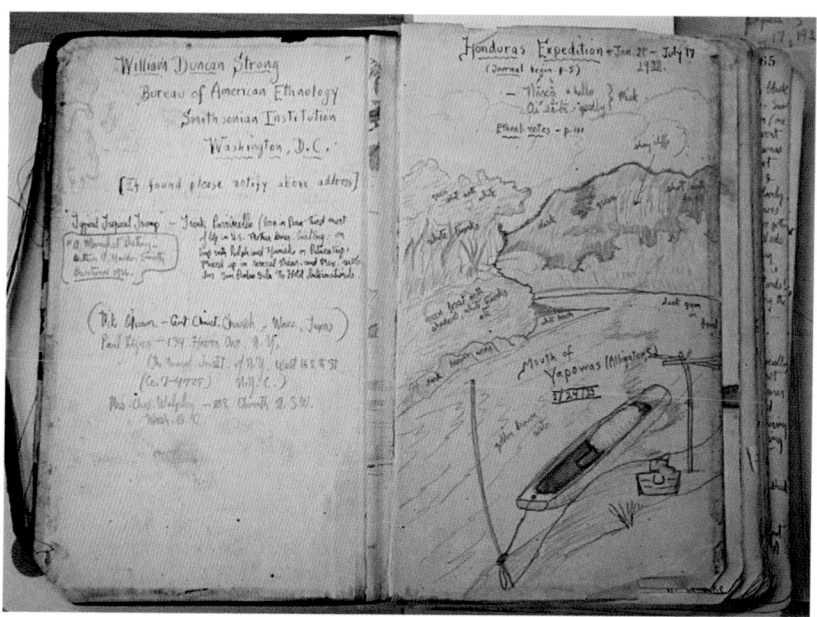

The opening pages of William Duncan Strong's 1933 Honduran journal. Strong was one of the first legitimate archaeologists to penetrate the region.

Sam Glassmire in 1959, hunting for the White City, with one of his guides.

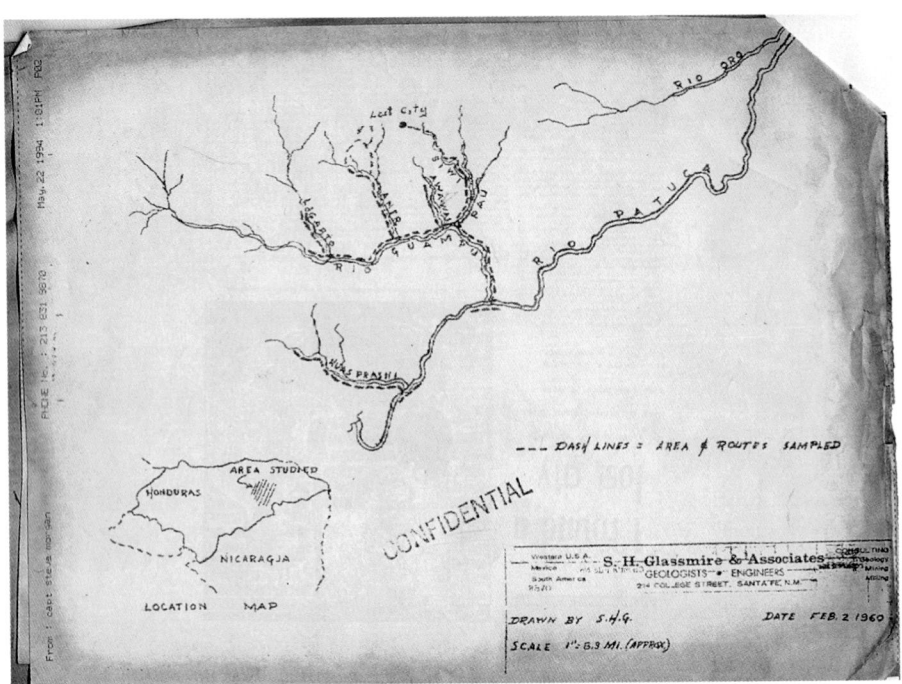

Sam Glassmire's hand-drawn map showing the location of the "Lost City" he discovered on an expedition in 1960.

The valley of T1, deep in Mosquitia and ringed by almost impenetrable mountains, remained one of the last scientifically unexplored places on earth until the expedition arrived there in February 2015.

Theodore Morde traveling up the Patuca River by motorized pitpan, or dugout canoe, Mosquitia, Honduras, 1940.

The Cessna Skymaster containing a million-dollar lidar machine and its highly classified payload being guarded by Honduran soldiers. The plane flew missions over three unexplored valleys in the remote mountains of Mosquitia in 2012.

Dr. Juan Carlos Fernández, engineer from the National Center for Airborne Laser Mapping at the University of Houston and the lidar mission planner, operates the lidar machine during the May 4, 2012 overflight of the T1 valley that discovered the ancient city.

The author jammed in the back of the Cessna, ready to depart on the historic overflight of the T1 valley.

On his first expedition looking for the White City in 1994, Steve Elkins found this carved rock deep in the jungle showing a man planting seeds, and he had a revelation that in Pre-Columbian times a major farming civilization had lived in what is today almost impassible jungle.

Steve Elkins photographed jumping a hedge as he was running to see the first images of the lost city found by lidar in the valley of T1—the culmination of his 20-year search.

In Roatán, Honduras, examining the first lidar image of the lost city, 2012. From left: Steve Elkins; Bill Benenson (behind); Michael Sartori (seated); Virgilio Paredes; Tom Weinberg; and the author, Douglas Preston.

Two lidar images of a hilltop portion of T1, the first in grayscale and the second in a rotated, color-scale format. This large, mountaintop ruin has not yet been explored.

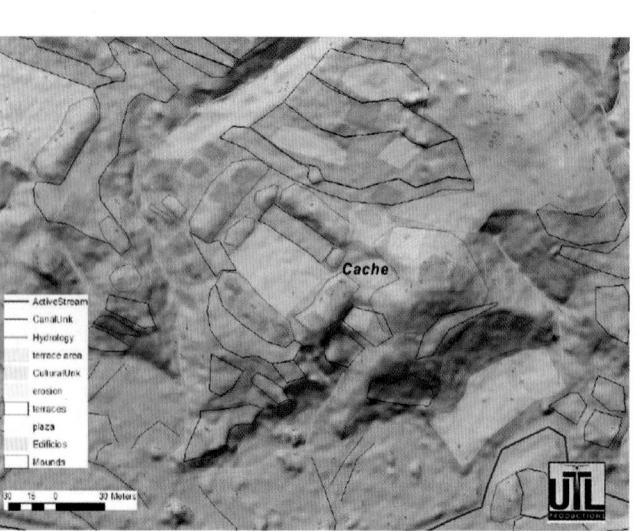

A lidar image of the heart of the city of T1, showing the cache location and other features of importance. In Pre-Columbian times, it had been a landscape entirely modified and engineered by the ancient people of Mosquitia.

Bruce Heinicke, fixer, gold prospector, former drug smuggler for the Colombian cartel, and archaeological looter, who was instrumental in helping find the lost city.

The expedition's Astar helicopter being unloaded in the jungle landing zone below the ruins of T1.

Chris Fisher (behind), the expedition's chief archaeologist, and the author explore the unnamed river flowing through the valley of T1 below the ruins.

Tom Weinberg, the expedition's official chronicler, taking notes on his laptop deep in the jungles of Mosquitia, 2015.

The jungle at dawn, seen from the banks of the unknown river flowing through the valley, 2015.

The author's campsite below the ruins, shortly before it turned into a sea of mud in the relentless rain. A troupe of spider monkeys lived in the trees above and shook branches and screeched at the author, trying to get him to move. At night, the ground was covered with cockroaches and spiders while jaguars roamed about.

A fer-de-lance, one of the world's deadliest snakes, entered the camp the first night and had to be killed. Its fangs were over an inch long. The head was tied to a tree in camp by an expedition leader to impress on everyone the high risk of snakes.

Andrew Wood, ex-SAS leader of the expedition, holding up the headless fer-de-lance that he killed the night before.

Bill Benenson, the filmmaker who financed the search for the lost city, exploring the unnamed river in the valley of T1 below the ruins.

Dr. Alicia González, the expedition's anthropologist, in the Mosquitia jungle, 2015. In the background, from left to right are: Chris Fisher, Anna Cohen, and Andrew Wood.

Chris Fisher exploring the ruins using a Trimble GPS. This photograph was taken in the main central plaza of the lost city, surrounded by mounds and an earthen pyramid. The incredible thickness of the jungle obscured everything.

The "kitchen" area of the expedition's camp deep in the Mosquitia jungle, 2015. The area was so remote, the animals apparently had never seen people before and wandered about, unafraid.

Honduran TESON Special Forces soldiers accompanied the expedition; they are roasting a deer over the fire in their camp, 2015.

Oscar Neil, chief of archaeology for Honduras, discovered the first altar stone in the ruins a few seconds before this photo was taken in February 2015. The altar is barely visible behind his right hand; it proved to be a large, flat stone placed on three quartz boulders, in a long line of altars alongside the main plaza of the city.

The cache or offering of stone objects, vessels, thrones, and figures, with just the tops visible above the surface of the ground. The excavation of this cache would solve one of the greatest mysteries of this enigmatic civilization: What caused its sudden, catastrophic disappearance five centuries earlier?

The were-jaguar as it first appeared emerging from the ground. Photographer David Yoder risked his life to climb up to the cache at night to photograph the artifacts using a special "light-painting" photographic technique.

Archaeologist Anna Cohen excavates stone vessels at the site of the mysterious cache. Visible here is the so-called "alien baby" stone vessel, which may depict a corpse bound for burial, a captive awaiting sacrifice, or a half-monkey, half-human deity.

The mysterious sculpture placed in the center of the cache found at the base of the central pyramid, which archaeologists believe depicts a shaman in a spiritually transformed state as a vulture.

Deforestation on the way to the valley of T1, primarily clearing land for cattle grazing. One Honduran official estimated that illegal clearcutting would have reached the valley of T1 in fewer than 8 years. The expedition and its discoveries, however, motivated the Honduran government to crack down on deforestation in the Mosquitia region.

President Hernández of Honduras and Steve Elkins after his arrival by helicopter at the site of the lost city, 2016.

mounds, the remains of principal houses and ceremonial structures, two more bus-like features, and several terraces. We came to a break in the canopy, where the collapse of a tall tree had brought down a dozen others with it and created an opening to the sky. The understory had run riot in this sudden wealth of sunlight, massing into an impenetrable thicket of bamboo and catclaw vines that we skirted. Visibility in the undergrowth was so limited that Woody, Chris, and I often kept track of each other by sound, not sight, even though we were no more than a dozen feet apart.

When we returned to the cache after a long circuit of the city, we found the company again in a minor uproar. As the soldiers were clearing the area and Anna began to sketch, an annoyed fer-de-lance had shot out from under a log in the midst of everyone, causing panic. It hung around long enough to get itself thoroughly photographed, the video crew delighted to have an unexpected extra on set; but when Sully tried to capture and move it, it escaped back under the log, where it remained, thoroughly irritated. As a result, nobody would go into the area behind the log, which we could see was packed with artifacts.

Virgilio, Steve, Woody, and I continued back to camp. Virgilio flew out on the chopper, anxious to brief the president on the cache discovery. In the meantime, the AStar, which had continued flying in supplies, was nearly brought down by a vulture that afternoon. The pilot had swerved to avoid the bird but it hit one of the rotor blades and its guts were sucked into the transmission space at the base of the shaft. The rotting contents of its final meal created a hideous mess in the transmission and filled the cabin with a frightful odor. The near accident reminded us of how acutely dependent we were on the two helicopters, our only connection to the outside world. If we were stranded, evacuation would have involved an overland journey of weeks, with limited supplies.

While we had been up in the ruins, Alicia had spent the day talking with the Special Forces soldiers in their camp behind ours, and I was curious to hear what anthropological insights she'd learned. Many of the Special Forces soldiers taking part in *Operación Bosque* were from indigenous Indian groups in Honduras. Some came from Wampusirpi, the closest indigenous town, on the Patuca River about twenty-five air miles away, an isolated village normally accessible only by water. What did the soldiers think of all this?

"It was pretty wonderful," Alicia told me. "They said they'd never seen anything like this place, and they said it with such joy. They felt like they were in the middle of a paradise. Of course, some of them just want to get back to their girlfriends. But most are thrilled to be here." Some felt that the fortress-like nature of the valley made it a kind of sacred place. She had persuaded one of the soldiers, who was Pech, to flag the cacao trees so she could map them and see if they were in fact the remains of an ancient, cultivated grove. Chocolate was sacred to the Maya, who treasured cacao and considered it the food of the gods. It was reserved for warriors and the ruling elite, and the pods were sometimes used as money. Chocolate was also involved in the ritual of human sacrifice. Cacao trees and the chocolate trade very likely played an important role in ancient Mosquitia; it would have been a valuable commodity that was traded with the Maya. "He says it's a very ancient variety with small pods," Alicia said. "Mosquitia is full of cacao." (Some doubt was raised in retrospect, never resolved, as to whether these were actually cacao trees or a related species.)

A few days later, some of the soldiers took Alicia to Wampusirpi in the military helicopter, to meet their families. Alicia showed them pictures on her cell phone that she had taken of the deforestation northeast of Catacamas. "They were astounded," she said, and deeply troubled. "They said, 'No wonder the rivers are drying up, the animals are going, the fish are dying!'"

Wampusirpi has an organic cacao cooperative, which produced blocks of pure chocolate, shipped downriver to market. It is said by chocolate aficionados to be some of the finest single-source chocolate in the world. Some of the cacao pods are harvested from wild cacao trees growing in the Biosphere Reserve forests surrounding the town. The men harvest the pods and the women ferment and toast them. Alicia toured the cooperative and they gave her a four-pound brick of pure, bitter chocolate.

In response to her questions about Ciudad Blanca, or Casa Blanca (White House) as the Pech call it, she was introduced to a man in his eighties. He told about it as the children gathered around. "He said the gringos came a long time ago and took all the gold and desecrated Casa Blanca. He said Casa Blanca is way up in the mountains; it's where the *sukia* went, the shamans, and it's controlled by the shamans. This is a very ancient place, a bewitchment place, they say, inhabited by people before the Pech."

The morning of the twenty-first arrived as usual—foggy, dripping, and dank. I had now been in the jungle four days, and it seemed like the time was passing much too fast. At 8:00 a.m. we hiked a quarter mile upriver to look at the L-shaped feature that was so prominent on the lidar images. We walked in the river itself, easier and safer than trying to push through the jungle on either embankment.

The L feature was clearly man-made, a large geometric earthen platform raised about ten feet above the floodplain. Enormous trees grew around and on top of it. One of the trees was truly monstrous, with a trunk at least twenty feet in diameter. I took a slew of photographs of it, some with Steve, and Steve took some of me. According to Chris, the platform probably supported a neighborhood of tightly packed houses, raised above the seasonal flood zone, with cultivated fields on the floodplain below. On the way out, struggling down a steep embankment, I tumbled into the river. I was fine but my Nikon camera didn't survive. Luckily, I was able to recover all the photographs from the card after I returned to civilization. I had my cell phone with its camera flown in the next day.

We hiked downriver about half a mile to a large series of plazas that were prominent in the lidar images. As we journeyed along, the unnamed river revealed itself as one of the loveliest I had ever seen, crystal-clear water running over a cobbled bed, with gravel bars, sunny patches thick with flowers, riffles and pools, and every once in a while a little waterfall. In places, huge trees and other vegetation leaned over the river, turning it into a furtive green tunnel haunted by the sound of water. Every bend disclosed something new—a shimmering rapid, a fern-draped tree trunk, a deep pool flashing with silvery fish, scarlet macaws and snowy egrets rising from the treetops. I regretted not having a camera to record these images.

According to our lidar maps, the river made an extreme hairpin bend about halfway to our goal. Woody decided we could save time with a shortcut straight across. The route plunged us into thick jungle, every inch forward won only with the blade of a machete. We crossed a ridge and came down into a ravine, which we followed back to the river. After an hour, we stopped to rest on a gravel bar opposite the presumed ruins, and we ate lunch.

We talked about how difficult, if not impossible, it would have been to explore the valley and its ruins before the advent of GPS and lidar. Without the lidar maps, we could have walked through the middle of the T1 ruins and not even realized they existed. Only with lidar maps and GPS did we know where to look for features otherwise cloaked in vegetation. The wall of trees on the far side of the river, across a meadow, gave no hint whatsoever of the mounds and plazas we knew were there.

After lunch we waded across the river and pushed into a field of dense, chest-high grass, the idea of snakes never far from our thoughts, as there was no way to see where we were putting our feet. We entered the forest with relief and came upon the first sharp mound, another bus. Parallel mounds extended from it on either side. Chris suggested this site was an extension of the upper city, but Oscar believed it to be a separate settlement entirely. This was not a trivial disagreement. The lidar images showed that there were nineteen major sites strung along the valley, all close together. Were they part of the same polity—the same economic and political unit—a single city? Or were they separate villages, each with its own governance? So far, the evidence suggests that most but not all of them were part of an extended city, but the question remains unresolved.

We explored the site for several hours. It was very much like the first set of plazas, only smaller. We climbed a nearby hill hoping it might be another earthen pyramid, but at the summit Chris and Oscar concluded it was just a naturally conical hill. We found more rows of flat altar-like stones, several leveled plaza areas, and bus-like mounds. On the way out, at the very edge of one of the mounds, we all traipsed, unawares, past a huge fer-de-lance. Lucian (again at the rear) spied it. We had each walked within two feet of it, so close that one of us could easily have stepped on it or brushed it. The snake remained peacefully asleep, its head tucked into its chocolate-colored coils.

It was virtually invisible in the forest litter, although it looked to be five or six feet long, almost as big as the one we killed the first night.

When we returned to camp, more visitors had arrived. Tom Lutz, a writer, literary critic, and founder of the *Los Angeles Review of Books*, was covering the expedition as a freelancer for the *New York Times*. Bill Benenson, the expedition coleader and financial backer, arrived with him.

The rain started again—a massive downpour—and I huddled under my hammock, writing in my journal, before rejoining the group under the kitchen tarp. The atmosphere was one of focused work: Dave Yoder was downloading massive numbers of photographs onto hard drives, while Lucian Read and the film crew fussed with their equipment, cleaning it and working to keep it dry—a never-ending job—and charging batteries with the newly arrived generators. The ex-SAS crew was busy cutting bamboo to lay down paths over the deepening mud. The entire camp area was flooding, and as the mud rose it came oozing in under the tarps.

The rain continued all afternoon. That evening, after the usual freeze-dried dinner, we remained under the tarps, the day's work finally done. Woody tried to light a fire by digging a hole in the ground, soaking a roll of paper towels in gasoline, piling wet wood on top, and lighting it. But the accumulating water soon reached the hole and flooded it, putting out the wretched fire.

A disagreement had flared up that morning about what to do about the cache of artifacts. Steve called a general meeting that evening. We gathered in a semicircle of chairs by the light of the lanterns, stinking of DEET and mildew, drinking tea or coffee and slapping insects, while the steady thrum of rain sounded on the sheltering tarps.

Steve opened the discussion by explaining that the site was in grave danger of being looted. Even if we hadn't found it, he pointed out, deforestation was less than ten miles from the valley's entrance and rapidly approaching. In that sense we had saved it from destruction, but only temporarily. Virgilio had estimated the illegal logging would reach the valley in eight years or less, which would result in the immediate looting of the cache, worth possibly millions of dollars. Even more ominous, the Honduran soldiers had reported a narcotrafficking airstrip being carved out of the jungle beyond the entrance to the valley. Enough people now knew the location of T1, Steve said, that the cat was out of the bag; the narcos had the money and planes; they would loot the site as soon as we left. He felt the team should remove one artifact—to prove what we had found and to use it to raise money for a swift excavation of the site. "We've opened Pandora's box," he said, and now we had a responsibility to protect the artifacts.

Bill Benenson agreed, arguing that the removal of a few objects would not harm the context, that it was a kind of salvage archaeology, and that bringing out a gorgeous item would be an effective fund-raising tool to interest donors in preserving the valley and ruins. And if the site were looted, which seemed possible, at least one artifact would be saved.

After this, Chris Fisher spoke. He was uncompromising. "The whole world will be watching what we do here," he said, his voice raised. He was adamantly opposed to a hasty excavation of even one object. First, he pointed out, we had no excavation permit. Second, and most important, the value of the objects was *in their context*, not in the individual pieces. There were pieces like this already in museum collections, but no cache had ever been excavated in situ. A careful, legal excavation by qualified archaeologists might reveal a tremendous amount about this culture. Chemical analyses could show, for example, if the vessels held offerings of food, like chocolate or maize. There might be royal burials underneath, and those had to be treated with care and dignity. He said that if anyone dug up anything right now, he would immediately resign from the project, as it went against all his professional ethics.

And what if, three weeks from now, the cache was looted? asked Benenson.

"So be it," said Chris. He said we could not engage in unethical behavior in anticipation of the illegal behavior of others. We must not do anything that would be viewed as unprofessional by the archaeological community. And besides, he said, it wasn't our decision; this wasn't our country; this was the national patrimony of Honduras. It was *their* site and *their* decision whether or not to excavate. But he hoped to God the Hondurans wouldn't make the wrong decision, because to excavate hastily, right now, would not only turn the archaeological community against the project but would destroy the primary value of this discovery.

Chris turned to Oscar Neil and asked him in Spanish: "What do you think?"

So far, Oscar had been listening silently. As Honduras's chief of archaeology, the decision to excavate would be his, in consultation with Virgilio Paredes. Replying in Spanish, he strongly agreed with Chris. He pointed out that the same narcotraffickers Steve had mentioned as a threat would actually keep looters at bay—because they didn't want looters on their turf.

"The narcos are the owners of the outlying territory here," he said. The impenetrable forest itself was protection; the artifacts had been there for perhaps eight hundred years, and as long as the forest remained intact they would be naturally safeguarded. The *saqueadores* (looters) were interested in more accessible sites—and there were sites far easier to get to than this one. The narcos wouldn't bother looting it; they had their own much more profitable business. Finally, he said, the Honduran military was already discussing plans to come in, patrol the valley, and establish Honduran government power in what was essentially an area beyond sovereign control.*

Oscar's and Chris's arguments prevailed, and it was decided to leave everything in situ, untouched for now, to await careful and proper excavation.

After the meeting, Sully touched my arm and spoke to me, lowering his voice: "I *know* soldiers. I was a soldier. I can tell you that the danger isn't from some narcotraffickers or outside looters—it's from *right there.*" He nodded to the soldiers' camp in the dark behind us. "They're already planning how to do it. Up there, they were marking every site with GPS. Downriver

---

* Tom Lutz later wrote an interesting account of this discussion in the *New York Times*, in an op-ed piece entitled, "Finding This Lost City in Honduras Was the Easy Part," published March 20, 2015.

they're enlarging their LZ. The military isn't going to let looters in here because they *are* the looters. After you leave, it will be gone in a week. I've seen this kind of corruption all over the world—believe me, *that's* what's going to happen."

He said this to me as an aside, and while I worried he might be right, the decision had been made: The cache would be left untouched. Sully kept his opinion private, and did not share it with Chris and Oscar.

By now, the trails in the campsite had been churned into soupy mud so deep it slopped up to our ankles. I stripped outside my tent, hung up my clothes, and crawled inside. There I picked off the chiggers and stabbed them on my book and squashed the sand flies that had gotten inside. I lay in the dark, miserably wet, listening to the usual nighttime beasts tromping around my tent and thinking that maybe the SAS guys hadn't exaggerated the challenges of this place after all.

## CHAPTER 18

**This was a forgotten place—but it ain't forgotten anymore!**

As usual, it poured all night, sometimes with deafening ferocity, and it was still raining when we awoke to the howler-monkey alarm clock.

As I crawled out of my tent and drew on my sodden clothes, Steve next door was looking up at the spider monkeys, who seemed as miserable as we were. He wondered how they could stand the rain, day in and day out. This was supposed to be the dry season in Honduras, but in this remote area a crazy sort of microclimate seemed to prevail.

At breakfast, the discussion turned to T3. The bad weather would prevent the air reconnaissance of T3 planned for that day. The other city lay about twenty miles to the north, and Chris was passionately eager to see a glimpse of it, at least from the air, if only the weather would break.

We waited for a pause in the rain. When it came, the AStar showed up with two more expedition members: Mark Plotkin, the noted ethnobotanist, president of the Amazon Conservation Team, and author of the bestselling book *Tales of a Shaman's Apprentice*; and his colleague Prof. Luis Poveda, an ethnobotanist from the National University of Costa Rica. Their hope was to record and study the botany of the T1 valley, especially in relation to its ancient inhabitants; they planned to inventory any legacy plants that might remain from pre-Columbian times, as well as identify biologically useful trees and medicinal plants. Almost immediately after the helicopter left, the rains came again. We packed up for another hike into the ruins. This time Juan Carlos carried a huge plastic suitcase strapped to his back. Inside was a $120,000 terrestrial lidar unit, a machine on a tripod, with which he intended to scan the sculpture cache.

While ascending the fixed ropes up the slippery trail, Prof. Poveda, who was in his early seventies, fell and rolled down the hill, pulling a muscle in his leg. He had to be carried back to camp and later evacuated by helicopter. At the cache it was pouring so hard that Juan Carlos had to wait an hour before he dared remove the lidar machine from its box. He set it up on the bottom slope of the pyramid just above the cluster of sculptures. Kneeling in the mud, with a tarp draped over his head, he fiddled with his MacBook Pro, jacked into the lidar unit as a controller. It seemed doubtful his equipment would survive the ordeal. Finally, hours later, the rain let up enough for him to uncover the machine and do an eleven-minute scan of the site. His intention was to do six scans, at different angles, to complete a three-dimensional picture, but a fresh downpour caused a delay and finally shut him down for the day. He left the equipment up there, well tarped, to complete the scans the next day. It poured again all night, and I awoke to the now familiar hammering of rain on the tent fly. My entire tent was now sunken in mud, and water was coming in and starting to pool.

At breakfast, Oscar passed around his cell phone with a picture he had taken that morning from his hammock. Just as he was putting his foot out to step onto the ground, he said, "I had a funny feeling." He withdrew his bare foot and poked his head out of the hammock, peering at the ground below. Directly underneath him, crawling along at a leisurely pace, was a fer-de-lance as long as his hammock. When it passed by, he climbed down and got dressed.

Sully glanced at the picture. "Lovely way to start the day, mate," he said, passing it along.

\*       \*       \*

I spent the morning under the kitchen tarp, writing in my notebook, thinking how fast the days had gone by. We only had a few more before we would have to break down the camp, pack up, and fly everything out. I felt a sense almost of panic that we had hardly scratched the surface. Exploring the city was clearly an undertaking that would take years.

Meanwhile, the camp had turned into a quagmire, the mud six inches deep or more, except where there were ponds of water. The bamboo poles laid down as corrugation over the worst spots sank out of sight as soon as they were trod upon, and disappeared into the muck. Spud would cut more to lay on top, and they, too, would be swallowed.

That afternoon, the weather broke long enough for a quick reconnaissance of T3. Steve joined the flight, along with Dave and Chris. I wanted to go but there wasn't room. The AStar took off in the early afternoon and returned a few hours later.

"Did you see anything?" I asked Steve, as he came back into camp.

"It's beautiful. Unbelievably beautiful. It's like a paradise." The pilot had descended almost to the ground, hovering about a foot off a sandbar, while Dave took pictures. Steve described the valley of T3 as much gentler and more open than T1, a vast, parklike expanse bisected by clear rivers with sandy beaches along the banks. The rivers were surrounded by fields of deep grass, over six feet high, broken here and there by stands of giant trees. Most of the actual ruins stood on benchlands above the river and were hidden in the forest. The valley was bounded on the east by a lofty ridge, where an unnamed river flowed through a gap, heading toward the distant Patuca; T3 was surrounded by peaks on the other three sides as well. He said there were no obvious signs of human habitation, "just forest and grasslands as far as the eye can see." The chopper was able to hover in place for only a few minutes at T3 before heading back to T1.

The following year, Chris and Juan Carlos would attempt a more serious reconnaissance of T3. In mid-January 2016, the Honduran military flew them in a helicopter to T3 and were able to put down the chopper on a sandbar.

"We landed," Chris recalled, "and the pilot said we had a couple of hours." But the grass was so high and thick that it took them an hour and a half to go a mere thousand feet, slashing unceasingly with machetes at the tough, thick-stemmed grass. It was impossible to see anything, and they were in great fear of snakes. But when they finally got out of the floodplain and climbed up to the benchland, they came upon an amazing sight: "It was nonstop plazas," Chris said, "with little mounds around them, and more plazas and little mounds, as far as we could go. It's much bigger than T1. It was huge. There were a *lot* of people living there." The valley of T3, like T1, gave every indication of being another untouched wilderness with no evidence of recent human entry or indigenous use. As of this writing, beyond these two reconnaissance missions T3 remains unexplored.

Around noon, Mark Plotkin arrived back in camp carrying a turtle. I was curious to hear what he, as a rainforest ethnobotanist, was seeing in the valley. "We went upriver," he said. "We were looking for evidence of recent habitation, but we didn't see any. But we saw lots of useful plants." He began rattling them off. A ginger used to treat cancer; a fig-related plant used by shamans; balsa trees; the biggest ramón trees he had ever seen, which produce a fruit and a highly nutritious nut; massive Virola trees used to treat fungal infections and to make a hallucinogenic snuff for sacred ceremonies. "I don't see any trees or plants that would indicate any recent human presence," he said. "I've been looking for chiles—seen none of that. And no *Castilla*." *Castilla elastica*, he explained, was an important tree for the ancient Maya, who used it as the source of latex to make rubber for the balls used in the sacred game. He had also seen no mahogany trees. "What's driving the deforestation near here," he said, confirming what others had told me, "isn't mahogany but clearing the land for cattle."

He had run into a huge troop of spider monkeys upriver, much bigger than the family above my camp. "These are the first animals hunted out," he said. "When you see spider monkeys who don't run away but come and look at you, that is exceptional." Later, Chris Fisher went downriver and ran into another large troop of monkeys, who were sitting in a tree above the river eating flowers. They screeched and shook branches at him. When the inner primate in Chris emerged and he began hooting and shaking bushes back at them, they bombarded him with flowers.

Plotkin was profoundly impressed by the valley. He said that, in all his years wandering the jungle, he had never seen a place like it. "This is clearly one of the most undisturbed rainforests in Central America," he said. "The importance of this place cannot be overestimated. Spectacular ruins, pristine wilderness—this place has it all. I've been walking tropical American rainforests for thirty years and I've never walked up to a collection of artifacts like that. And I probably won't ever again."

I asked him, as an authority on rainforest conservation, what could be done to preserve the valley and site. He said it was a very difficult problem. "Conservation is a spiritual practice," he said. "This place is right up there with the most important unspoiled places on earth. This was a forgotten place—but it ain't forgotten anymore! We live in a world gone crazy for resources. Everybody on Google Earth can look at this place now. If you don't move to protect it, it will disappear. *Everything* in the world is vulnerable. It's amazing to me it hasn't been looted already."

"So what should be done?" I asked. "Create a national park?"

"This is already supposed to be a biosphere reserve. Where are the guards? The problem is people establish a national park and think they've won the war. No way. That's only the first step—a battle in a longer war. The good thing about this expedition is that at least you're bringing attention to this place and it might now be saved. Otherwise, it won't last long. You saw the clear-cutting outside the valley. Absolutely gone in a few years."

That night, the rain continued to fall. I was astounded to see Dave Yoder packing up his camera gear with a set of portable lights, and loading it all on his back. He said he was dissatisfied with his pictures of the cache so far. The daylight filtering down was too flat. He was going to hike up there in the dark with Sully so that he could "light-paint" the artifacts. This is a difficult photographic technique in which the camera, on a tripod, is left with the shutter open while the photographer sweeps light beams over the objects from different angles, to highlight particular details and add a sense of drama and mystery.

"You're crazy," I said. "You're going up there in the pitch dark, with all those snakes, in the rain, wading in mud up to your balls, climbing that hill with a ton of gear on your back in a suitcase? You're going to get yourself killed."

He grunted and hiked off into the dark, his headlamp bobbing around before winking out entirely. As I hunkered down in my tent, listening to the rain, I was damned glad I was just a writer.

The rain stopped in the night and—finally—the morning of February 24 dawned beautifully, with fresh sunlight skimming the treetops. Some of the Honduran soldiers said they had seen petroglyphs downstream, where the river entered the notch on its way out of the valley. An expedition was organized to investigate. Chris Fisher and his crew decided to use the good weather to continue mapping the site, while Juan Carlos hoped to finish up his lidar scan of the cache. Steve and Bill Benenson joined our group heading downriver, along with Alicia and Oscar.

The weather was glorious. I washed my muddy, mildewed clothes in the river and put them back on, then stood on the riverbank in the warm sunlight, holding my arms out and turning about in a hopeless effort to dry my clothes. After so many nights and days of rain, even after laundering they smelled like they were rotting.

The AStar flew our group from our LZ to the Honduran LZ downstream at the river junction. A second group of Honduran soldiers had set up a camp at the junction, with tarps and palm fronds erected for tents, floored with cut bamboo. This was the only landing zone for the Honduran Bell helicopter, and these soldiers helped ferry supplies in and out and served as a backup to the group upstream. A side of deer ribs and two haunches were smoking over a fire, the rule against hunting having not yet been instituted.

We set off hiking downriver, Steve hobbling along, wading in the water with his walking pole, wearing a Tilley hat. The trip down this magical river was one of the most beautiful and memorable journeys of my life. We traveled mostly by wading in the stream, avoiding as much as possible the dense embankments, which we knew were a favorite snake habitat. (Venomous snakes are easier to see and less common in the water.)

Snowy cumulus drifted across a clean blue sky. The area where the two rivers came together opened into a broad grassy field, and for the first time we could look around and actually see the shape of the land. The encircling ridge formed an arc in front of us, covered with trees; the conjoined river made a sharp right turn, running along the foot of the ridge, and then an abrupt left, cutting into the mountains and rushing through a ravine. For the first time, too, we could see the rainforest trees from top to bottom. Inside the rainforest, you can't see the treetops or get a sense of what the trees look like and how tall they are.

After crossing the field, we waded into the river and hiked downstream. A tree had fallen across the river, with a tangle of limbs in and out of the water. The trunk was streaming with excitable, noxious red ants, which were using the tree as a bridge. We carefully wormed our way through its network of branches with the utmost care so as not to disturb them. We were lucky no one had been showered by these ants so far, which would require an evacuation and perhaps even a trip to the hospital. The river made a broad turn against the encircling ridge, running along a steep rocky slope thick with jungle trees that leaned over the river, dropping curtains of vines and aerial roots that trailed in the water, swaying in the current. The water was crystal clear until we stirred up the bottom, when it blossomed opaque with clouds of auburn silt. In some areas the river narrowed and became too strong and deep for wading; we were forced up on the embankment, where we followed the Honduran soldiers as they macheted a path for us, expertly flicking their machetes left and right, the blades going *ping, snick, tang, snap*—each species of plant making a different sound as it was cut.

As usual, we couldn't see where we were putting our feet, and the fear of snakes was never far from our minds. And we did see one: a beautiful coral snake, banded in bright colors of red, yellow, and black, slithering through the grass. This snake has a bite that injects a potent neurotoxin, but unlike the fer-de-lance it is timid and reluctant to strike.

A few times we had to cross the river through rapids; there the soldiers formed a human bridge by linking arms in the water, while we waded through the current hanging on to them for dear life. As we reached the gap, we saw the first evidence of historic human occupation in the valley—a tattered cluster of wild banana trees. Banana trees were not native; originally from Asia, they had been brought to Central America by the Spanish. This was the only sign we ever saw of post-Conquest habitation in the valley.

We neared the gap: two forested slopes meeting in a V notch. The river took a ninety-degree turn at a place of heartbreaking loveliness, with thick stands of flowers giving way to a lush meadow and a beach. The river flowed in a singing curve over round stones and spilled in a waterfall over a ridge of basalt. In the shallows along the stream edge grew fat, blood-red aquatic flowers.

From the turn the river ran in a line as straight as a highway through the gap, faster and deeper, tumbling over rocks and fallen trees, sweeping around sandbars, dappled in sunlight. Rainforest giants leaned over the river from either side, forming a great cave echoing with the calls of macaws, frogs, and insects. The cloying smell of the jungle yielded to a clean scent of water.

Most of the people in our group halted at the opening to the ravine. Steve stretched out on a flat rock at the edge of the river, drying himself in the rare sunlight, not wanting to risk his bad leg by going on. Oscar cut some big leaves and laid them on the ground, making a bed, on which he took a nap. I decided to continue downstream looking for the petroglyphs, along with Bill Benenson, three soldiers, and the video crew.

Beyond the gap, the footing downstream got more treacherous, with waist-deep currents, hidden rocks, sunken limbs, and potholes. In places gigantic moss-covered tree trunks had fallen across the river, spanning the gap. Where the river got too swift, we scrambled up on the steep embankment. A faint animal path ran along the river, and the soldiers identified tapir dung and jaguar scat. The character of the river, now swiftly flowing between cliffs and overhung with trees, had become darker, mysterious, and unsettling. There were many boulders and ledges sticking out of the water, but we found no petroglyphs; the soldiers suspected the water had risen and submerged the rock carvings. We turned back when the river finally became too deep and the ravine walls too steep to continue. At several points I feared one of us might be swept away.

Indeed, once we'd returned to the gap, Bill was nearly carried off by the current while crossing a stretch of deep water. Steve rescued him by sticking out his foot, which Bill seized as a handhold. When I arrived, Steve ruefully handed me his iPhone, which was very hot. He had dropped it in the water and hadn't completely clicked shut the waterproof flap over the charger port. As a result it had fried, and he'd lost all the photographs he had taken of the expedition he had spent twenty years bringing to fruition. (He would spend over a year working with Apple to recover the photos, to no avail; they were gone forever.)

We hiked back to the Honduran LZ, where the AStar picked us up and flew us back to camp. When we arrived, Woody told us that more bad weather was expected. Not wanting to risk anyone getting stranded, he had decided to begin extracting the team from the jungle a day early. He said he had scheduled me for a flight in one hour sharp; I should break down my camp, pack up, and be waiting with my gear at the LZ at that time. I was surprised and disappointed, but he said he'd worked out the evacuation on paper and this was the way it had to be. Even Steve had to come out that day. He clapped me on the shoulder: "Sorry, mate."

The treetops were filling with golden light as the helicopter came in. It upset me that I had to leave when the weather had finally cleared, but I took a certain schadenfreude in the fact that torrential rains might soon be returning to torment those lucky enough to stay. I threw my pack in the basket, boarded, buckled in, and put on my headset; we were airborne in sixty seconds. As the chopper banked out of the LZ, sunlight caught the riffling stream, turning it for an instant into a shining scimitar as we accelerated upward, clearing the treetops, heading for the notch.

As we thundered through the gap, a feeling of melancholy settled over me at leaving the valley. It was no longer a terra incognita. T1 had finally joined the rest of the world in having been discovered, explored, mapped, measured, trod upon, and photographed—a forgotten place no more. Thrilled as I was to have been a member of this first lucky few, I had the sense that our exploration had diminished it, stripping it of its secrets. Soon, the clear-cut mountainsides came into view, along with ubiquitous plumes of smoke, farmsteads with glittering tin roofs, trails, roads, and pastures dotted with cattle. We had returned to "civilization."

## CHAPTER 19

**These are our ancestral fathers.**

We stepped out of the helicopter into dry heat shimmering off the tarmac. It was a blessed relief from the sticky jungle. The soldiers guarding the airstrip were surprised to see us wet and coated with mud because, they said, it hadn't rained at all in Catacamas, seventy air miles away. Before allowing us in the van, they politely asked us to hose ourselves off. I picked and scraped the mud from my boots with a stick; even with the hose it took a good five minutes to get the sticky clay off. Back at the hotel I called my wife, took a shower, and donned a fresh outfit. I bundled my stinking clothes in a sack and dropped it off for the hotel laundry, feeling sorry for whoever was tasked with washing them. I lay back on the bed, hands behind my head, my glumness at having to leave T1 tempered by the glorious sensation of being dry for the first time in eight days, even if covered with bug bites.

Eventually I joined Steve by the pool, where we both sank into plastic chairs and ordered frosty bottles of Port Royal. He looked wrung out. "It's a miracle we all got out of there safely," he said, dabbing his brow with a napkin. "And nobody was bitten by a snake. But, my God, *what* an effort! I started with one simple objective: to prove or disprove the legend of Ciudad Blanca. That was the start, but it led to so much more. Maybe that's what the monkey god wanted, to draw us in."

"What do you think? Did you prove it?"

"Well, what we proved is that there was a large population in Mosquitia with a sophisticated culture that compares to anything in Central America. If we can work with Honduras to preserve this place, I'll feel I've really accomplished something. It's a work in progress. This'll probably go on for the rest of my life."

That evening, Virgilio joined us at dinner. I asked him about the clear-cutting that checkerboarded the jungle we had flown over. He was shocked and concerned by what he'd seen. He said we had found the site in the nick of time, before deforestation and looting reached it. He had discussed the issue with the president, who was determined to halt and even roll back the illegal deforestation. He spread his hands. "The Honduran government is committed to protecting this area, but it doesn't have the money. We urgently need international support."

That support would soon be coming. A year later, Conservation International would investigate the valley as a potential preservation project. The organization sent Trond Larsen, a biologist and director of CI's Rapid Assessment Program, into T1 to investigate how biologically important the valley was and whether it was worthy of special protection. CI spearheads vital conservation efforts across the globe, working with governments and others to save areas of high ecological importance. It is one of the most effective conservation organizations in the world today, having helped protect 2.8 million square miles of inland, coastal, and marine areas across seventy-eight countries.

The Honduran military flew Larsen into the valley, where he did a five-mile transect, explored the ridges, and journeyed north and south along the unnamed river. His interest was solely in the biology, not the archaeology.

Larsen was deeply impressed by his visit. "For Central America, it is unique," he told me, a "pristine, undisturbed forest" with "very old trees" that "has not seen a human presence in a very long time"—perhaps for as long as five hundred years. He said it was a perfect habitat for jaguars, as evidenced by all the tracks and scat everywhere. It was also, he noted, an ideal habitat for many sensitive rainforest animals, especially spider monkeys. "The fact that they're very abundant is a fantastic indicator of forest health," he told me. "They are one of the most sensitive species of all. That is a really good sign that there has not been human presence for a while." He shared photos he had taken of the spider monkeys with the celebrated primatologist Russell Mittermeier. Mittermeier was intrigued, because he felt the markings on these monkeys were unusually white and might indicate they are an unknown subspecies, although he cautioned he would have to observe live specimens to be sure.

This brief exploration impressed Conservation International so much that its vice chair—Harrison Ford, the actor—sent a letter to President Hernández of Honduras praising him on his preservation efforts. Ford wrote that CI had determined it was one of the "healthiest tropical forests in the Americas," and that the valley of T1 and surroundings were an "extraordinary, globally significant ecological and cultural treasure."

The night after our emergence from the jungle, Virgilio told me that the president wanted to get the news of our finds at T1 out to the world as soon as possible, before rumors and inaccurate stories leaked out. He asked if *National Geographic* could post something on their website. The next day, I submitted a short, eight-hundred-word story to the *Geographic*, which was published on March 2, 2015. The story read, in part:

## EXCLUSIVE: LOST CITY DISCOVERED IN THE HONDURAN RAIN FOREST

**In search for legendary "City of the Monkey God," explorers find the untouched ruins of a vanished culture.**

An expedition to Honduras has emerged from the jungle with dramatic news of the discovery of a mysterious culture's lost city, never before explored. The team was led to the remote, uninhabited region by long-standing rumors that it was the site of a storied "White City," also referred to in legend as the "City of the Monkey God."

Archaeologists surveyed and mapped extensive plazas, earthworks, mounds, and an earthen pyramid belonging to a culture that thrived a thousand years ago, and then vanished. The team, which returned from the site last Wednesday, also discovered a remarkable cache of stone sculptures that had lain untouched since the city was abandoned.

The piece touched a nerve. It went viral and garnered eight million views and hundreds of thousands of social media "shares," becoming the second most popular article *National Geographic* had ever published online. The story was picked up and became front-page news in Honduras and across Central America. Inevitably, many news outlets reported that the White City had been found.

President Hernández ordered a full-time military unit to the site to guard it against looters who might have figured out its location. Several weeks later, he helicoptered in to see it first-hand. After he came out, he pledged that his government would do "whatever it takes" to protect the valley and the surrounding region. He promised to halt the illegal deforestation that was creeping toward the valley. "We Hondurans," the president said in his speech, "have the obligation to preserve our culture and ancestral values. We must get to know and learn from the cultures that came before us; these are our ancestral fathers who enriched our nationality. For this reason my government will do whatever it takes to begin the investigation and exploration of this new archaeological discovery."

Patrick Leahy, a senator from Vermont who takes

a special interest in Honduras, gave a speech on the Senate floor calling for the United States to support Honduran efforts to "secure and preserve" the site of T1.

While this was going on, controversy erupted. Christopher Begley of Transylvania University (the archaeologist in *Jungleland*) and Rosemary Joyce of Berkeley began circulating a letter criticizing the expedition and inviting their colleagues and students to sign it. The letter alleged that the expedition had made "false claims of discovery" by exaggerating the importance of the site; that it had not acknowledged previous archaeological research in Mosquitia; and that it had disrespected indigenous people by failing to recognize that they already knew of the site. It criticized the stories published in *National Geographic* and the *New Yorker*, saying they displayed "rhetorical elements that represent antiquated and offensive, ethnocentric attitudes" that were "at odds with anthropology's substantial efforts at inclusion and multivocality." They were concerned about language that felt like a throwback to the bad old colonialist, Indiana Jones days of archaeology.

The letter made some valid points. There are certain phrases associated with the archaeology of the past that the profession has now banished. The sad truth is that, until recently, many archaeologists were shockingly insensitive and arrogant in the way they conducted fieldwork, riding roughshod over the feelings, religious beliefs, and traditions of indigenous people. They dug up burials without permission, sometimes looting the graves of the freshly interred. They put human remains and sensitive grave goods on public display in museums. They hauled off sacred objects to which they had no legal right of ownership. They talked about "prehistoric" Indians as if they had no history until the Europeans arrived. They lectured native people on what their past was and where they came from, dismissing as myths their own origin beliefs. They claimed to have "discovered" sites that were already well known to native people. The ultimate offense was the idea that Europeans "discovered" the New World to begin with, as if the people living here didn't exist before Europeans saw them. Phrases like "lost cities" and "lost civilization" were uncomfortably associated with the archaeology of the past.

While I agree with most of this argument and am delighted that modern archaeological vocabulary is increasingly nuanced and sensitive, it poses a challenge for those of us writing about archaeology for a lay audience, since it is nearly impossible to find work-arounds for common words like "lost" and "civilization" and "discovery" without tying the English language up into knots.

But the letter went far beyond a critique over word usage. The accusation that the team was ignorant of—or worse, deliberately ignoring—previous archaeological research in Mosquitia seriously angered some academics. It was also false. Steve Elkins and his researchers had researched archives in both Honduras and the United States, collecting copies of every published and unpublished paper, report, photograph, map, diary, accession record, and scribbled note they could find regarding Mosquitia going back almost a century. And my 2013 *New Yorker* piece on the lidar discovery featured Begley and his work, extensively quoted Joyce and other archaeologists, and contained an overview of Mosquitia archaeology. The *National Geographic* reports on the discovery linked to that article. No one had been ignored.

Begley also claimed that nobody from the team had contacted him, but this, too, was not true. Tom Weinberg had in fact enlisted Begley's help in the late 1990s—as a string of e-mails and reports prove—but Steve later dropped him from the project. After the successful lidar mission in 2012, Begley sent several e-mails to Steve offering his expertise, writing: "I'd be glad to help on the ground truthing and any other way I can." Steve declined on the advice of others involved with the project—who asked Steve not to include Begley for reasons touched on below.

*American Archaeology* magazine sent a reporter, Charles Poling, to cover the controversy. He interviewed Begley and several other signers. Begley expanded at length on the accusations in the letter. He said the publicity attending the discovery was not justified. He told Poling: "This site is not actually any different from what archaeologists have found there for years, either in size, or the stone artifacts on the surface. What merits the publicity?" He objected to the involvement of filmmakers in the discovery and called it a "B movie fantasy" that was resurrecting the "trope" of "the big hero explorer." He said that, while he was not privy to the location of the site, he was nevertheless "certain that local folks know about the site and the area"—and he also suggested that he, himself, had probably explored the ruins. Other signatories were equally dismissive. Joyce told *American Archaeology* that in her view the expedition was an "adventure fantasy trip." Mark Bonta, an ethnobotanist and cultural geographer at Penn State University who specializes in Honduras, said about the expedition: "One day it's this, the next day it's Atlantis. It's almost like it's a reality show." Another letter signer, John Hoopes, chair of the Department of Anthropology at the University of Kansas and an authority on ancient Honduran culture, posted on his Facebook page a lidar image of a section of T1 that had been released by UTL, and ridiculed its small size. "Are the 'lost cities' in Honduras actually Lilliputian in scale?" he asked sarcastically. Begley and others joined in posting mocking comments on the small size of the site—until Juan Carlos pointed out to Hoopes that he had misread the scale bars on the lidar image by a factor of ten: What he thought was a hundred meters was actually a kilometer.

The *American Archaeology* reporter pointed out that Begley himself had for years been leading filmmakers and celebrities to sites in Mosquitia, that he had earlier publicized his own search for Ciudad Blanca and the "Lost City," and that an article on his website referred to him as the "Indiana Jones of archaeology." How was that any different? Begley responded: "I am not against popular media. I do it, but I do it differently." He said about the expedition: "That kind of treasure-hunting, lost-city-finding mentality puts archaeological resources at risk." Begley went on to complain about the expedition in his blog, comparing it to "children playing out a movie fantasy" and saying that "most scholars are disgusted" by the "colonialist discourse."

The ten PhD scientists who had taken part in the expedition were stunned. The vociferousness of the criticism went far beyond the usual academic tiff or a dispute over language, and they were amazed that these scholars, who had never been to the site and had no idea where it was, would make claims like these with such certainty. But they understood that a letter signed by two dozen professors and students, including respected scholars like Joyce and Hoopes, had to be taken seriously. Seeing that the letter contained errors of fact, Juan Carlos, Chris Fisher, and Alicia González drafted a FAQ about the expedition, trying to respond to their critics. "The ultimate goal of our work is to highlight the rich cultural and ecological patrimony of this endangered region so that international cooperation and resources can be brought to bear to help initiate effective conservation... The team urges those archaeologists and others concerned about Honduras and its unique cultural patrimony to please join us in this crucial effort, which will take the synergy of collaboration and goodwill among all involved." The letter noted that none of the sites found in T1 or T3 had been "previously registered with the Honduran Government in its database of cultural patrimony."

A number of news outlets, including the *Washington Post* and the *Guardian* (UK) ran articles on the controversy that repeated the charges and quoted Begley and others questioning the significance—and even the very existence—of the find. "Interestingly," Chris wrote me, "many reporters, after I made them aware of the FAQ, were uninterested in reading it. They only wanted salacious quotes from everyone involved to help 'fuel' a controversy."

"I feel as though we're on trial," Alicia González wrote me. "How dare they? Rubbish!"

Chris Fisher told *American Archaeology* that the charges were "ridiculous." "Our work has resulted in protection for the area. We're preparing academic publications on the material. The map digitizes the archaeological features we saw. The overarching goal was to confirm what we saw on the lidar. I don't think that's adventuring." He was particularly dismayed that Begley had called him a "treasure hunter," the dirtiest insult in archaeology. Chris said to me, "Where are Begley's peer-reviewed publications? Where's his scholarship? I can't find a single peer-reviewed article he's published. And if he claims he's visited these ruins, where's the map? Where's the site report?" Chris continued: "When you do archaeology, you survey, you make maps, you take photos, notes, et cetera. If he [Begley] had those locations they should have been turned over to the IHAH, as it is their cultural patrimony. To not do so is colonial and unethical." But in the past twenty years, according to IHAH, Begley had not deposited any reports of his work, in violation of Honduran regulations.

The National Geographic Society posted the expedition's response: "We hope our colleagues will realize the enormous contribution and attention that this project has brought, not only to the academic community working in the area but to the people and government of Honduras, and we hope that together we will be able to foster and encourage greater academic research in the area."

Virgilio Paredes, in his capacity as director of IHAH, wrote a letter of support that the expedition posted with the FAQ. In private he was upset at the academic attacks. He told me that he had checked IHAH records and they showed that, indeed, Begley hadn't pulled an archaeological permit in Honduras since 1996, even though he continued to "illegally" conduct research and exploration, as well as guide celebrities, filmmakers, journalists, and adventure-tourists to remote archaeological sites for pay. When I gave Begley an opportunity to refute that serious charge, in an exchange of e-mails he was unwilling or unable to do so, saying only that I was "being misled." He wrote in his defense: "All of my trips to Honduras have either had necessary permission or they did not involve any activities that legally or by the regulations of the IHAH would require a permit." He declined to provide any specifics, and he would not clarify the nature of his work in Honduras since 1996—whether it was archaeological, commercial, or touristic. He shut down our e-mail correspondence by writing: "I hope that this can put an end to this line of inquiry... That is really all I have to say on this matter."

"They criticized," Virgilio said to me, "because they were not involved. Come on! They should be saying, 'How can we get involved and help?' This is a project for my country, Honduras—for my children's children."

Juan Carlos Fernández mused, drily: "They're upset because we invaded their sandbox."

Originally it seemed that the contretemps came from a concern about academic purity and incorrect assumptions, whether willful or not, about where the site was located. But I eventually learned that there were deeper reasons for the academic rhubarb, unwittingly revealed to me by one of the letter signers, who asked to remain anonymous. Many of the signatories had been supporters of the Zelaya administration. After Zelaya was deposed in the 2009 military coup, the new government removed the previous director of IHAH, Dario Euraque, and replaced him with Virgilio Paredes. The source complained to me that, because of the coup, the present government of Honduras is illegitimate and Virgilio Paredes "is in charge illegally" and "I will not work with him." Euraque, who teaches at Trinity College in Connecticut, was one of the leading critics and complained to the *Guardian* that the expedition was "irrelevant," a publicity stunt, and he claimed it had "no archaeologists of any name."

All this made it clear that the protest letter was, in part, a proxy attack on the present Honduran government, an example of how the coup and its aftermath left the Honduran archaeological community angry and divided. We would see more evidence of this when excavations began the following year, reigniting the controversy. Many of the letter signers have found it difficult to let go of the dispute and continue to disparage the project.

## CHAPTER 20

**The key in tying together the Americas**

Our too-short exploration of the ruins was only the beginning of understanding the significance of the site and its treasures. The excavation of the cache—and the revelation of its secrets—would come only once the team was able to return to the jungle during the following year's dry season. But before we could understand the importance of the city itself, we needed to answer the more immediate question: Who were the people who built it? A hint of the answer lies in the stupendous Talgua Caves in the Agalta Mountains north of Catacamas.

In April 1994, two Peace Corps volunteers living in Catacamas, Timothy Berg and Greg Cabe, heard about some caves along the Talgua River, in the mountains about four miles outside of town. The caves were a popular picnicking spot with the locals, and the men were curious to explore them. Joined by two Honduran friends, Desiderio Reyes and Jorge Yáñez, Berg and Cabe hitched a ride to the end of the closest road and hiked up the river. The four stopped to explore the largest cave, a giant cleft in the limestone cliffs a hundred feet up. An underground stream tumbled out of the opening, dropping in waterfalls to the river below.

The friends climbed up to the cave and ventured inside with flashlights, walking in the shallow stream. The cave was broad and spacious, with a flat floor, offering an easy hike deep into the mountain. About half a mile in, one of them spied a ledge about twelve feet above the cave floor, which looked like it might lead somewhere. They boosted a person up to take a look, and he hauled up another.

To their surprise, the two young men found the ledge littered with pre-Columbian artifacts, including broken pottery. It seemed no one had climbed up there before, at least in recent history. As they searched around for more pottery pieces, they spied another ledge, twenty feet higher up. Beyond that, there appeared to be an enigmatic opening.

Returning three weeks later with a ladder and ropes, they reached the higher ledge. It was indeed the gateway to a new cavern system. And as they stood on its threshold they beheld a mind-boggling sight. As Berg wrote later, "We saw many glimmering bones scattered along the floor of the passageway, most of them were cemented in place, and a number of ceramic and marble vessels. This was all complemented by many spectacular formations, hidden crevices filled with more bones and of ceramics shards in piles of fine dust." The skulls were strangely elongated and frosted like sugar candy, covered with glittering crystals of calcite.

They had discovered a spectacular ancient ossuary, which would turn out to be one of the most important archaeological finds in Honduras since the discovery of Copán.

By sheer coincidence, the discovery had happened back when Steve Elkins was in Honduras with Steve Morgan, filming and searching for the White City. At that moment, they were shooting the excavation of an archaeological site on a Honduran island called Santa Elena, adjacent to Roatán. Elkins received a radio call from Bruce Heinicke, who had gotten word of the discovery through his grapevine. On the way back from the island in a boat, Elkins and his team excitedly discussed what the crystal-covered skulls might mean. Steve Morgan coined a name for the site: the "Cave of the Glowing Skulls." Even though it wasn't entirely accurate (the skulls do not actually glow), once the name was suggested it stuck, and that is how the site is known today.

The young discoverers reported the find to George Hasemann, the director of IHAH at the time. Hasemann had been working with Elkins on the White City project, and the two discussed what to do. Elkins, who by this time was on his way back to LA, wired money to IHAH so that the institute could hire security for the cave to prevent looting and conduct a preliminary exploration. When Hasemann got inside, he too was stunned by what he saw. He and Elkins contacted a renowned Maya cave archaeologist named James Brady. Together, Hasemann and Brady organized a joint Honduran-American exploration of the necropolis, which commenced the following September in 1995, with Brady as the lead archaeologist.

Brady and his team explored the ossuary, which occupied a labyrinth of holes, alcoves, and side caves packed with bones. Deep in the complex, they spied yet another hole in the ceiling of one chamber, climbed up to it, and entered what appeared to be the central burial chamber. It was a cavern one hundred feet long, twelve feet wide, and twenty-five feet high. As they played their lights around the chamber, they saw a breathtaking space of intricate stalactites, dripstone, and translucent sheets of calcite hanging like drapery from the ceiling. Every ledge, crack, and shelf was stacked with human bones and gaping skulls, covered with a hoarfrost of dazzling white crystals. Bones rarely survive long in the tropics, but in this case the coating of calcite had preserved them. "We have never before seen or heard of skeletal material preserved on such a tremendous scale," Brady wrote. "The archaeological record is laid out like an open book for us to read."

Placed among the bones were gorgeous artifacts, including delicate marble and painted ceramic bowls and jars, jade necklaces, obsidian knives, and spearpoints. Some pottery bowls had holes punched in the bottom, which was a curious but widespread practice in pre-Columbian America, the ritual "killing" of an object placed in a grave to release its spirit so that it could follow its owner to the underworld.

Brady and his team determined that these stacks of bones were secondary burials. The corpses of the dead had been interred elsewhere and then, when the flesh had decayed, the bones were removed, scraped clean, painted with red ochre, brought to the cave, and piled up with grave goods. Many of the artifacts were later additions, left years later as offerings to the dead.

In the months between the discovery and Brady's survey, despite security efforts, vandals and looters had decimated many of the deposits. "Even as we were trying to work there," Brady told me recently, "they were going in and looting it. Each time we would go back, there were pretty dramatic changes in the amount of destruction. They'd been rooting through the skeletal material, breaking it up into little bits, looking for some kind of treasure."

As spectacular as this find was, the real shock came when the bones were carbon-dated. The oldest ones were three thousand years old, far older than anyone had assumed, and the burials had taken place over a period of a thousand years. That made the ossuary the earliest evidence of human occupation in Honduras and one of the oldest archaeological sites in Central America.

As Brady recalled, a few days into their work "it dawned on me that this was not a Maya burial pattern." Although the cave was situated on the Maya frontier, it appeared to belong to an entirely different and virtually unknown culture. While the Maya also buried their dead in caves, the way in which these bones were arranged and the kinds of artifacts that had been left with them were different from what one would expect from Maya cave burials. The ossuary was the work of a sophisticated, socially stratified, and artistically advanced culture, one that developed astonishingly early, even before the Maya. Said Brady: "If we only knew who these people were!"

But the Maya and these unknown people, Brady said, did seem to share a similar cosmological view. In both cultures, "there is a focus on the sacred, animate earth, which is the most important force in the universe." In contrast to the Old World idea that the dead live on in the heavens, in Mesoamerican belief the dead live within the earth and mountains. Caves are sacred, as they are a direct connection to that underground spiritual world. The ancestors living underground continue to take care of the living, watching over them. The living can contact the dead by going deep into the caves, leaving offerings, conducting rituals, and praying. The cave is a church, in essence, a place where the living come to petition their ancestors for favor and protection.

The Cave of the Glowing Skulls and similar cave ossuaries discovered around the same time remain the earliest evidence of human occupation in Honduras. But were these people the *actual* ancestors of those who, a thousand years later, would build the cities in Mosquitia we had found at T1 and T3?

"Shit, I don't know," Brady said. "We have very little knowledge in this sea of ignorance. And of course the Mosquitia is farther into the frontier, and it's even less known." Three to two thousand years ago, he said, we have the burials but not the settlements; and then a thousand years later we have the settlements but not the burials.

After Talgua Caves, the archaeological record falls silent for a thousand years. People lived in eastern Honduras during that time, but no trace of them has yet been found.

Following that thousand-year gap in our knowledge of Honduran prehistory, small settlements begin to appear in Mosquitia starting around AD 400 to 500. Archaeologists believe the people of Mosquitia spoke a dialect of Chibchan, a group of languages that encompasses Lower Central America down into Colombia. This suggests that Mosquitia was more connected to its southern neighbors than to the Maya, who spoke an unrelated set of languages.

The major Chibchan-speaking civilization, the Muisca, lived in Colombia. It was a powerful chiefdom known for intricate goldwork. The Muisca confederation was the source of the El Dorado legends, based on a real tradition in which a new king, smeared in sticky mud and then covered with gold dust, would dive into Lake Guatavita in Colombia, washing off the gold in the lake as an offering to the gods.*

---

* In past centuries many efforts to drain the lake and recover the gold were made, some of which salvaged extraordinary gold sculptures and ornamental art. The lake is now protected by the Colombian government from further treasure-hunting efforts.

The original people of Mosquitia may have come from the south or been influenced from that direction. But that southward orientation would change as the Maya city of Copán, two hundred miles west of Mosquitia, rose in power and prestige. The appearance of modest settlements in Mosquitia around AD 400 to 500 roughly coincides with the founding of the ruling dynasty of Copán. We don't know whether the two events were linked. We do know a great deal about the establishment of Copán, one of the most studied cities in the Maya realm. The people of Copán achieved remarkable heights in art, architecture, mathematics, astronomy, and hieroglyphic writing, and the city's magnificent public monuments contain many inscriptions telling the story of its founding and history. The influence of Copán would eventually reach into Mosquitia.

In AD 426, a ruler named K'inich Yax K'uk' Mo' (Sun-Eyed Resplendent Quetzal Macaw) came down from the Maya city of Tikal, in Guatemala, and seized control of the settlement of Copán in a coup or invasion. He became Copán's first "Holy Lord" and launched a dynasty of sixteen lords that would elevate Copán into a glorious city dominating the area for centuries.

Quetzal Macaw and his elite force of Maya warriors imposed themselves on a local population already living in the Copán valley. These original people may have been Chibchan-language speakers related to those in Mosquitia. Archaeological work at Copán suggests that after Macaw's conquest it was a multiethnic city. Some neighborhoods at Copán had metates decorated with animal heads like those found in Mosquitia. Macaw married a Copán woman, probably the daughter of a local lord, no doubt to secure his legitimacy and form an alliance with the local nobility, just as European kings once did.

Copán is as far south as the Maya appear to have reached. Perhaps they were stymied by forbidding mountains and jungle. Perhaps they met resistance. As a result, even after the Maya invasion of Copán in the fifth century, Mosquitia was left to develop on its own. The two civilizations were not, however, isolated from each other. On the contrary, there was probably a vigorous trade between them, and possibly even warfare. From many bragging inscriptions of glorious combat and deeds, we know the Maya city-states were belligerent and engaged in frequent battles with each other and with their neighbors. These conflicts only intensified as the wealth and populations of the Maya city-states increased, swelling their hunger for resources.

In 2000, archaeologists found Quetzal Macaw's tomb. For centuries, a bend in the Copán River had cut into the central acropolis of the city, and although its course was altered years ago, the old cutbank remained. The erosion had exposed layer upon layer of buildings erected as the city grew. Each main temple at Copán had been built over and around the previous one, creating a series of buildings nested together like Russian matryoshka dolls.

In a feat of clever detective work, archaeologists located the tomb by examining the cutaway embankment and identifying the original floor of the oldest building platform. They then tunneled in from the cutbank, following the floor, until they came to a filled-in staircase that led up into the original temple, which had been covered over by eight subsequent temples. They cleared the staircase and found at the top a sumptuous burial chamber containing the skeleton of a man. He was about five feet six inches tall and between fifty-five and seventy years old. Inscriptions, grave offerings, and other evidence confirmed this was the tomb of Quetzel Macaw.

The Holy Lord's remains were covered with gorgeous jade and shell jewelry, and he wore a peculiar goggle-eyed headdress made of cut shell. His bones showed that he had taken quite a beating over the course of his life: His skeleton was peppered with healed fractures, including two broken arms, a shattered shoulder, blunt trauma to the chest, broken ribs, a cracked skull, and a broken neck. The physical anthropologist who analyzed his remains wrote that, "In today's world, it would appear that the deceased had survived an auto accident in which he had been thrown from the vehicle." But in the ancient world, the injuries were probably caused by playing the famed Mesoamerican ball game called *pitz* in classical Mayan. (Maya warfare, which used piercing weapons such as the spear and atlatl and close-quarter engagement involving thrusting, stabbing, and crushing, would likely have produced a different mix of injuries.) We know from early accounts and pre-Columbian illustrations that the game was extremely fierce. One sixteenth-century friar, a rare eyewitness, spoke of players being killed instantly when the five-pound ball, made of solid latex sap, hit them on a hard rebound; he also described many others who "suffered terrible injuries" and were carried from the field to die later. The ball game was a vital Mesoamerican ritual, and playing it was essential to maintaining the cosmic order and keeping up the community's health and prosperity. Because most of Quetzal Macaw's injuries occurred when he was young, before he arrived in Copán, he might have achieved his leadership role by playing the ball game; alternatively, it is possible that he was required to play the game because of his high status. Either way, the burial confirmed he had not ascended dynastically to the throne from a local elite; he was definitely a foreigner to Copán. Symbols on his shield and the Groucho Marx–style goggle-eyed headdress connected him to the ancient city of Teotihuacan, located north of Mexico City, which in his day was the largest city in the New World. (Today it is a magnificent ruin containing some of the greatest pyramids in the Americas.) An analysis of isotopes in his bones, however, showed he had grown up not in Teotihuacan, but probably in the Maya city of Tikal, in northern Guatemala, two hundred miles north of Copán. (Drinking water, which varies from place to place, leaves a unique chemical signature in the bones.)

Four centuries after Macaw's rule, at its apex around AD 800, Copán had become a large and powerful city of perhaps 25,000 inhabitants, spread out over many square miles. But all was not well; a creeping rot—environmental, economic, and social—had been undermining its society for some time and would eventually lead to destruction. Scholars have long debated the mystery surrounding the collapse and abandonment of Copán and the other magnificent cities of the Maya realm.

Skeletons speak with eloquence, and the many graves unearthed at Copán show that after AD 650, the health and nutrition of the common people appeared to decline. This happened even as the ruling classes apparently swelled in size over succeeding generations, with each generation larger than the last—in what archaeologists call the "increasingly parasitic role of the elite." (We see the same process today in the gross expansion of the Saudi royal family into no fewer than fifteen thousand princes and princesses.) This proliferation of noble lineages may have triggered vicious internecine warfare and killing among the elite.

Jared Diamond, in his book *Collapse*, argues that the destruction of Copán was caused by environmental degradation combined with royal neglect and incompetence. Beginning around AD 650, the rulers of Copán engaged in a building spree, erecting gorgeous temples and monuments that glorified themselves and their deeds. As is typical of Maya inscriptions, not a single one at Copán mentions a commoner. Working folk had to build all those buildings. Farmers had to feed all those laborers along with the holy lords and nobles. This type of class division usually works when everyone believes they are part of a system, with each person occupying a valued place in society and contributing to the vital ceremonies that maintain the cosmic order.

In Maya culture, the holy lords had a responsibility to keep the cosmos in order and appease the gods through ceremonies and rituals. The commoners were willing to support this privileged class as long as they kept up their end of the bargain with effective rituals. But after 650, deforestation, erosion, and soil exhaustion began reducing crop yields. The working classes, the farmers and monument builders, may have suffered increasing hunger and disease, even as the rulers hogged an ever-larger share of resources. The society was heading for a crisis.

Diamond writes: "We have to wonder why the kings and nobles failed to recognize and solve these seemingly obvious problems undermining their society. Their attention was evidently focused on their short-term concerns of enriching themselves, waging wars, erecting monuments, competing with each other, and extracting enough food from the peasants to support all those activities." (If this sounds familiar, I would note that archaeology is thick with cautionary tales that speak directly to the twenty-first century.)

Other archaeologists say this conclusion is too simple, and that the holy lords did indeed see things were going awry. They tried to solve these problems with solutions that had worked in centuries past: increased building projects (a jobs program) and more raiding (resource acquisition), both of which involved moving workers from outlying farms into the city. But this time the old solutions failed. The ill-advised building projects speeded up the deforestation that was already reducing rainfall, and it accelerated soil loss, erosion, and the silting of precious farmland and rivers.

A series of droughts between AD 760 and 800 seem to have been the trigger for famine that hit the common people disproportionately hard. It was the last straw for a society teetering on the edge of alienation and conflict. Here was proof the holy lords were not delivering on their social promises. All building projects halted; the last inscription found in the city dates to 822; and around 850, the royal palace burned. The city never recovered. Some people died of disease and starvation, but the majority of the peasant and artisan classes appear to have simply walked away. Over the centuries the region experienced a relentless population decline, and by 1250, the Copán valley had largely returned to jungle wilderness. The same process occurred in the other Maya city-states, not all at once, but in a staggered fashion.

From AD 400 to 800, during the rise of Copán, small settlements in Mosquitia sprang up and grew at a modest rate. But when Copán fell apart, the civilization in Mosquitia experienced the opposite: a tremendous flowering. By AD 1000, even as most of the Maya cities had been left to the monkeys and birds, the ancient inhabitants of Mosquitia were building their own cities, which were starting to look vaguely Maya in layout, with plazas, elevated platforms, earthworks, geometric mounds, and earthen pyramids. This is also when they seem to have adopted the Mesoamerican ball game.

How were these ancient people of the Mosquitia rainforest able to settle and thrive in a snake- and disease-ridden jungle, an area far more challenging than most lands settled by the Maya? What was their relationship to their powerful neighbors, and what allowed them to flourish even as Copán was crumbling? In other words, how did they survive what the Maya couldn't—and what eventually brought them down?

While the Maya are the most studied of ancient cultures in the Americas, the people of Mosquitia have been among the least—a question mark embodied by the legend of the White City. This culture is so little known that it hasn't even been given a formal name. In this context, the discovery and continued exploration of T1 and T3 become enormously significant, bringing the region to the world's attention and representing a turning point in our understanding of these vanished people. It was a formidable civilization, occupying over ten thousand square miles of eastern Honduras, at the crossroads of trade and travel between Mesoamerica and the powerful Chibchan-speaking civilizations to the south.

The excavation of T1 is shedding light on this culture, but also deepening its mystery. "There is much we don't know about this great culture," Oscar Neil told me. "What we don't know is, in fact, almost everything." Only a small number of archaeological sites have been identified in Mosquitia, and none have been fully excavated. The archaeology that has been done is not enough to answer even the most basic questions about the culture. As one archaeologist said, "There aren't a lot of people who want to undergo the kind of pain it takes to work out there." Until the lidar images of T1 and T3 were made, not a single large site in Mosquitia had even been comprehensively mapped.

We do know from recent archaeology in other rainforest environments—such as the Maya lowlands and the Amazon basin—that complex farming societies were able to thrive in even the toughest rainforest areas. Human ingenuity is boundless. Rainforest farmers developed clever strategies for enriching soil. In the Amazon, for example, they overcame the poor rainforest soils by mixing them with charcoal and other nutrients to create an artificial soil called *terra preta*, or "black earth," built into raised beds for intensive farming. There may be as much as fifty thousand square miles in the Amazon covered in this artificially enriched black soil—a staggering accomplishment that tells us Amazonia was densely settled in pre-Columbian times. (If a lidar survey were done of the Amazon basin, it would be, without doubt, an absolute revelation.) So far, almost no research has been done on how the people of Mosquitia farmed their rainforest environment. At T1, we found probable irrigation canals and a reservoir that would have helped make farming possible during the quasi-dry season from January to April. But beyond that there is much, much more to be learned.

The ancient people of Mosquitia were neglected by researchers partly because of their very proximity to the Maya, as John Hoopes acknowledges. "In this area, these people are in the shadow of the Maya," he told me. "There are only a few really high-profile archaeological cultures in the world: Egypt and the Maya. That draws people and resources away from the surrounding areas." This disregard, Hoopes feels, has hurt our understanding of the region, which he believes "holds the key in tying together the Americas," because it occupies the frontier between Mesoamerica and Lower Central and South America.

Another reason for this neglect is that the jungle-choked mounds in Mosquitia are, at first glance, not nearly as sexy as the cut-stone temples of the Maya or the intricate gold artwork of the Muisca. The people of Mosquitia, even though they left behind impressive stone sculptures, did not erect great buildings or monuments in stone, the kind of structures that become dramatic ruins wowing people five centuries in the future. Instead, they constructed their pyramids, temples, and public buildings out of river cobbles, adobe, wattle and daub, and probably tropical hardwoods. They had gorgeous woods at their disposal such as mahogany, purple rosewood, aromatic cedar, and sweet gum. We have reasons to believe their weaving and fiber technology was truly spectacular. Imagine a temple made out of highly polished tropical hardwoods, with adobe walls that had been skillfully plastered, painted, incised, and decorated, the interiors draped in richly woven and colored textiles. Such temples might well have been just as magnificent as those of the Maya. But once abandoned, they dissolved in the rain and rotted away, leaving behind unimpressive mounds of dirt and rubble that were quickly swallowed by vegetation. In the acidic rainforest soils, no organic remains survive—not even the bones of the dead.

Most intriguingly, around the time of the fall of Copán, the people of Mosquitia began to adopt aspects of Maya culture.

The simplest and most convincing theory about how Maya influence flowed into Mosquitia has it that when Copán was struck with famine and unrest, some of the original Chibcha people of Copán simply packed up and left, seeking refuge in Mosquitia where they had linguistic ties and possibly even relatives. We know that most of the population of Copán walked away; Mosquitia was probably one destination. Some archaeologists take this further: They think that during the chaos of the Maya collapse, a group of warriors marched over from Copán and seized control of Mosquitia. As proof they cite the fact that, when the early Spanish arrived in Honduras, they found tribes of Nahua/Aztec-speaking Indians in Honduras southwest of Mosquitia who may have been a remnant of one such invasive group. (Others think those tribes were descended from Aztec traders, not invaders.)

One of the most intriguing theories about why Mosquitia began to look Maya involves what archaeologists call the "esoteric knowledge" model. In many societies, the elites rule over the common people and get them to do what they want by displaying their sanctity and holiness. This ruling class of priests and lords awe the populace with arcane rituals and ceremonies using secret knowledge. The priests claim, and of course themselves believe, that they are performing rites that are essential to appease the gods and gain divine favor for everyone's benefit—to avert disaster, sickness, and defeat in battle, while encouraging fertility, rainfall, and bountiful crops. In Mesoamerica and probably also in Mosquitia, these rituals were dramatic and involved human sacrifice. Those noble lords with access to the "ultimate truths" leveraged that knowledge to control the masses, avoid physical labor, and amass wealth for themselves.* Part of the allure and prestige of esoteric knowledge, the theory goes, is its association with distant and exotic lands—in this case, the lands of the Maya. The "Mayanization" of Mosquitia, therefore, may not have required an invasion; it might instead have been a method for local elites to gain and hold supremacy over the common folk.

The city of T1 at the height of its power would have been impressive indeed. "Even in this remote jungle," Chris Fisher said to me, "where people wouldn't expect it, there were dense populations living in cities—thousands of people. That is *profound*." T1 consisted of nineteen settlements distributed throughout the valley. It was an immense human-engineered environment, in which the ancient Mosquitia people transformed the rainforest into a lush, curated

---

* We see this phenomenon in Western society not only in established religions and cults like Scientology, but also in the quasi-religious practice of capitalism: specifically, in extremely high CEO compensation (necessary because of esoteric knowledge), and on Wall Street, where bankers dismiss criticism by claiming that the common people do not understand the complex, important, and multilayered financial transactions they are engaged in as they do "God's work"—to quote the CEO of Goldman Sachs.

landscape. They leveled terraces, reshaped hills, and built roads, reservoirs, and irrigation canals. In its heyday T1 probably looked like an unkempt English garden, with plots of food crops and medicinal plants mingled with stands of valuable trees such as cacao and fruit, alongside large open areas for public ceremonies, games, and group activities, and shady patches for work and socializing. There were extensive flower beds, because flowers were an important crop used in religious ceremonies. All these growing areas were mixed in with residential houses, many on raised earthen platforms to avoid seasonal flooding, connected by paths. "Having these garden spaces embedded within urban areas," said Fisher, "is one characteristic of New World cities that made them sustainable and livable."

Even the vistas were tended, with view lines opened up to sacred architecture. The pyramids and temples needed to be seen from afar, so the people could appreciate their power and watch important ceremonies. The entire effect of all this might have been something like Frederick Law Olmsted's vision for Central Park, only wilder.

While the valley is spectacularly isolated now, in its heyday it was a center of trade and commerce. "When you're here today," Chris said, "you feel so disconnected. It's a wilderness, and it's hard to imagine you're even in the twenty-first century. But in the past, it wasn't isolated at all. It was in the midst of an intense network of human interaction." Situated in a fortress-like valley, the city of T1 would have been a highly defensible place of retreat, something akin to a medieval castle that was normally a bustling center of trade but, if threatened, could raise its drawbridge, arm the battlements, and defend itself from attack. Because of this, T1 might have been part of a strategic zone of control in pre-Columbian times, possibly an anchor that defended the interior from invaders coming inland from the coast. It may also have been a bulwark against attacks from the Maya realm.

And then, around 1500, this culture collapsed. But unlike the Maya, who experienced a multitiered collapse, with various city-states declining at different times, the Mosquitia civilization vanished everywhere all at once—in a sudden, civilization-wide catastrophe. "We have only a glimpse of this great culture," said Oscar Neil, "before it vanished in the forest."

## CHAPTER 21

**The vulture—the symbol of death and transition—was placed in the middle.**

The undisturbed cache of sculptures was an outstanding find—but just how important would only be revealed by excavation. While similar caches of objects had been found in large ruins in Mosquitia going back to the 1920s, not a single one had ever been professionally excavated; archaeology in Mosquitia is, as I've noted before, a dangerous, expensive, and arduous activity. By the time archaeologists found most of these caches, they had already been dug into or partially looted. Even the few somewhat in-situ caches still existing today—perhaps four or five—have been irredeemably disturbed. What this means is that the experts have never been able to study them properly and coax them into yielding their secrets, the clues to what makes Mosquitia so special. To date, archaeologists had no idea what the caches were for, why they were created, or what the sculptures meant. Chris hoped that a meticulous, scientific excavation of the cache in T1 might change that.

When Chris and his team returned to the jungle, they began excavating the cache as soon as the next dry season hit, in January of 2016, and within a month they had uncovered a trove of over two hundred stone and ceramic artifacts, many in fragments, with hundreds more still buried. This was an incredible concentration of wealth piled in an area of only a few hundred square feet—out of an archaeological site several square miles in extent. To the ancient people of Mosquitia, this small place was clearly of supreme ritual importance.

The cache, Chris concluded, was an offering, a kind of shrine. These were precious objects, carved by artisans out of hard rhyolite or basalt. There were at least five kinds of stone from different areas, suggesting a network of trade in fine stone with other communities. Having no metal tools to chisel with, these ancient sculptors shaped them using a laborious grinding process, using handheld rocks and sand to abrade a block of stone into the desired form. Archaeologists call these "ground stone" objects, as opposed to objects carved using traditional hammers and chisels. A tremendous amount of labor, skill, and artistry went into creating each sculpture. Only a specialized class of artisans could have created them.

The offerings had been placed in the cache area, at the base of the pyramid, all at the same time, on a floor of red, claylike soil. The clay floor had been specially smoothed and prepared to display these objects. Analysis revealed that it was a type of red earth called laterite, which forms much of the basement soil of the valley—an intriguing echo of Cortés's Old Land of Red Earth.

The offering or shrine was far from a disorganized heap: Everything had been carefully arranged on the clay foundation. The pieces had been organized around a key central sculpture: an enigmatic standing vulture with drooping wings. Surrounding that were ritual stone vessels, whose rims were decorated with vultures and snakes. Some vessels had carvings depicting a bizarre, humanoid figure with a triangular head, hollow eyes, and an open mouth, perched on a small, naked male body. Dozens of metates had been arranged around this central cluster of artifacts, including the were-jaguar. Many of them were beautifully made and decorated with dramatic animal heads and tails, the legs and rims incised with glyph-like markings and designs.

No carbon dating of the cache could be done, as the high acidity and wetness of the jungle environment had destroyed any organic artifacts and bones. But based on style and iconography, the objects date to the Mesoamerican Post-Classic phase, between AD 1000 and circa 1500, also called the Cocal Period by archaeologists who prefer not to use the Mesoamerican dating system for a non-Mesoamerican culture.

Most of the objects in the cache were metates. Normally the word "metate" describes a stone for grinding corn. But these metates, found not only in Mosquitia but across Lower Central America, are different, and nobody knows exactly what they were for or how they were used. They are indeed shaped like tables or platforms for grinding, and they are found with stone grinding rollers. The puzzle is that most of these metates are too large and awkward to be used for efficient grinding. Archaeologists believe instead that they might have been thrones or seats of power. Pottery figurines have been found that depict people sitting on big metates. That they were designed to resemble real corn-grinding stones might be because corn was sacred in the Americas; a Maya creation myth says that human beings were formed from corn-meal dough. Because metates are sometimes found on top of graves, almost like tombstones, some believe they may have also been used as seats for carrying the dead to their final resting place.

The triangular-headed humanoid figures found on

the rims of some jars in the cache, which Chris and his team fondly called alien babies, presented another conundrum. Chris believes they might depict a "death figure," perhaps the bundled-up corpse of an ancestor. They might also represent bound captives, ready for sacrifice; captives were often depicted in humiliation with their genitals exposed.

But these metates and jars might have served an even darker purpose. I sent some of the images to John Hoopes, who is a leading authority on Central American ceramics. Despite being a critic of the project, he was impressed and was willing to share with me his ideas, which he emphasized were speculative. "I think they may also have been grinding bones," he said, referring to the metates. The Chibchan-speaking people farther south in Costa Rica and Panama, he said, collected trophy heads and bodies. "Perhaps they were using those metates," he said, "to pulverize heads and bodies" of their enemies as a "way of terminating that individual permanently." He pointed out that in the Maya realm, when a king was defeated, before being executed he was sometimes forced to witness the killing of his entire family and the desecration of his family's tombs, in which the corpses were removed and ritually destroyed in a public place. "He sees not only his family being destroyed," Hoopes said, "but his entire dynasty being erased." Some metates in Costa

Rica, he noted, are decorated with tiny trophy heads, which might connect them to ceremonies of bone grinding and erasure. The depiction of what look like bound captives on some jars supports this idea.* Eventually the jars and metate surfaces will undergo "residue analysis," which could determine what offerings might have been inside them, or what substances, if any, were ground up on them.

I also showed pictures of some of the artifacts to Rosemary Joyce, another critic willing to share her thoughts. Joyce is a leading authority on iconography in pre-Columbian Honduran art, and she disagreed with all the above. The humanoid figure, she said, is not a body bundled for burial or a captive. The key, she points out, is that the figure appears to have an erection. This, she said, is typically how monkeys are portrayed in ancient Honduran pottery: shown as part human and part animal, with round circles for eyes and mouth—and an erection. In the mythology of some indigenous tribes in Honduras, monkeys were the first people, banished into the forest when humans arrived. Monkeys played a central role in the creation of the world and in Honduran stories and myth. This is probably where the idea of a "City of the Monkey

---

* When I ran this idea of bone grinding by Chris Fisher, he said: "That's just beyond crazy. Don't print that."

God" came from; some early reports from explorers say the Indians told them stories of monkey gods and half-monkey, half-human beings living in the forest, who terrorized their ancestors, raiding villages and stealing human women to maintain their hybrid race.

The cache is rich in animal imagery: vultures, snakes, jaguars, and monkeys. Joyce explained that, throughout the Americas, traditional shamans and priests claim special relationships with certain animals. The "were-jaguar" head is a classic example of half-human, half-animal beings portrayed in ancient pottery and sculpture. According to creation stories and myths, jaguars, monkeys, vultures, and snakes were all seen as animals with great power, and were adopted by shamans as their avatars or spiritual doppelgängers.

Each species of animal has a spiritual being, a "master," who watches over and protects them. The human hunter must appease this master of animals in order to successfully hunt that particular kind of animal. After killing it, the hunter must ask forgiveness of the master and make an offering. The master ensures that human hunters do not wantonly kill the animals under his protection, and he rewards only those hunters who are respectful, observe the rituals, and take just what they need.

A shaman who has adopted an animal as his power

spirit can communicate (sometimes using hallucinogens) with that master. This is where the shaman's power comes from: his ability to transform himself into a were-jaguar, for example, and communicate with the master of jaguars. Through the master he can influence all jaguars in the realm. Each master of animals acts as a spiritual channel to his particular species. Given this, many anthropologists believe the metates with animal heads were seats of power used by shamans or holy lords as a way to move between the earthly and spiritual planes, a doorway to the power of their particular animal.

According to Joyce, the vulture that was found in the place of honor at the center of the T1 cache, its wings hanging down like arms, is a human who has become part vulture, a shaman who has been transformed into his spirit animal. In Central American pottery and sculpture, vultures were often shown feasting on human corpses or guarding the severed heads of enemies killed in battle. And since vultures were believed to have the ability to cross from the terrestrial to the heavenly realm, the central vulture may be associated with death, transfiguration, and the transition to the spirit world. All this suggests that the meaning of the cache somehow involved death and transition. But the death and transition of whom, or what?

The motifs carved on some of the metates provide another clue. Joyce interprets the double spiral motif on one T1 metate as representing the mist that emerges from caves in the mountains, which symbolize ancestral origin places. The crossed bands, she says, appear to show entry points into the sacred earth: doorways to a place of origin or birth. The "Celtic knot" motif so common on the T1 artifacts is a quincunx, a geometric arrangement representing the four sacred directions and the center point of the world—a symbol of the universe itself. (The metates also display many additional, puzzling motifs that could be some form of idiographic writing, yet to be deciphered.)

Following this line of reasoning, it would appear that the focus of the cache was on birth, death, and transition to the spirit world. But why would the people of this city leave in this place such a concentrated mass of sacred and powerful objects, probably owned by the ruling elite, the shamans and holy lords?

Chris made two key findings that helped unlock this mystery. The first is that this was not an accumulation of offerings deposited over many years or centuries: They had all been left at the same time. The second clue is even more telling: Most of the objects were broken. Were these artifacts broken naturally over the centuries by giant forest trees falling on them? Or were they deliberately broken? In the cache, Fisher and his team found a massive mano or grinding roller carved out of basalt and polished. It is over three feet long, an awkward size and too finely finished to have been useful for actual grinding, indicating it was a ritual object. Even though it is anything but fragile, it was found shattered into six pieces. Mere falling trees are not likely to have broken up this stone so thoroughly. Nor does it seem possible, by sheer numbers, that so many of the other artifacts made out of hard basalt could have broken naturally over time. These artifacts, Chris concluded, must have been deliberately smashed. They were destroyed for the same reason the pots found in the Cave of the Glowing Skulls had been ritually "killed"; ancient people engaged in this ceremonial destruction at gravesites so that objects could journey with the deceased to the afterworld. This was true not just of pots and artifacts, but also involved the ritual destruction of sacred buildings, and even roads. In the American Southwest, for example, parts of the great Anasazi road system and its way stations were closed in the thirteenth century by burning brush and smashing sacred pots along its length, when the ancestral Pueblo people abandoned the region.

Taken together, these clues imply the cache was assembled during a ritual closing of the city at the time of its final abandonment. In this scenario, the last remaining inhabitants of the city gathered up all their sacred objects and left them as a final offering to the gods as they departed, breaking them to release their spirits.

It's reasonable to think that the other caches of artifacts noted in Mosquitia may have been left for the same purpose, during the abandonment of those settlements. It seems that a civilization-wide catastrophe involving the "death" of all these cities occurred at approximately the same time, around 1500—the time of the Spanish conquest. Yet the Spanish never conquered the region; they never explored or even penetrated these remote jungles.

Which leads us to the overwhelming question: If not because of Spanish invasion or conquest, why was the city and the rest of Mosquitia abandoned? The organized cache suggested the last inhabitants simply walked away from their jungle home, going to parts unknown, for reasons unknown. For the answer to these mysteries, we have to revisit the legend, and the curse, of Ciudad Blanca.

## CHAPTER 22

## They came to wither the flowers.

The myths of the White City, the City of the Monkey God, a Casa Blanca or Kaha Kamasa, have a similar arc: There was once a great city in the mountains struck down by a series of catastrophes, after which the people decided the gods were angry and left, leaving behind their possessions. Thereafter it was shunned as a cursed place, forbidden, visiting death on those who dared enter.

A legend, certainly, but legends are frequently based on the truth, and this one, so persistent and long-lasting, is no exception.

To dig the truth out of the myth, we have to go back in time, to the discovery of the New World by Europeans. In October of 1493, Columbus set sail on his second voyage to the New World. This expedition was very different from the first. That one, with three ships, had been a voyage of exploration: This one was primarily aimed at subjugation, colonization, and conversion. Columbus's enormous flotilla on that second voyage consisted of seventeen ships carrying fifteen hundred men and thousands of head of livestock, including horses, cattle, dogs, cats, chickens, and pigs. But on board those ships was something far more threatening than soldiers with steel arms and armor, priests with crosses, and animals that would disrupt the New World ecology. Columbus and his men unwittingly carried microscopic pathogens, to which the people of the New World had never been exposed and against which they had no genetic resistance. The New World was like a vast, tinder-dry forest waiting to burn—and Columbus brought the fire. That European diseases ran rampant in the New World is an old story, but recent discoveries in genetics, epidemiology, and archaeology have painted a picture of the die-off that is truly apocalyptic; the lived experience of the indigenous communities during this genocide exceeds the worst that any horror movie has imagined. It was disease, more than anything else, that allowed the Spanish to establish the world's first *imperio en el que nunca se pone el sol*, the "empire on which the sun never sets," so called because it occupied a swath of territory so extensive that some of it was always in daylight.

Columbus had boasted on his first voyage that "no

one had been sick or even had a headache," except for an old man with kidney stones. The second voyage, carrying soldiers from different parts of Spain and teeming cargo of livestock, was a Noah's ark of pestilence. Even during the Atlantic crossing, hundreds of men and animals on board Columbus's flotilla began to sicken. When they reached the outer islands of the Caribbean, the ships, carrying their ripe payload of disease, made a grand tour of the islands, landing on Dominica, Monserrat, Antigua, and other islands of the Lesser Antilles before sailing on to Puerto Rico and Hispaniola, where most of the men disembarked. Even while he and his men were getting sicker, Columbus took a smaller fleet that then explored Cuba and Jamaica before returning to Hispaniola.

Columbus's first descriptions of Hispaniola reveal a wondrous and fertile place, an island "larger than Portugal with twice the population," which he extolled as "the most beautiful land I have ever seen."* Hispaniola (today divided between the countries of Haiti and the Dominican Republic) was richly inhabited by Taíno Indians, but how many is disputed by historians. Bartolomé de las Casas, the early Spanish chronicler who wrote a largely eyewitness account of the colonization

---

* It is actually slightly smaller. Portugal had a population of about a million in 1500.

of the Indies, said that the Indian population of Hispaniola when Columbus arrived was about a million, which he later revised upward to three million. Many modern historians believe las Casas exaggerated the numbers and that the actual population was perhaps around half a million. Regardless, Hispaniola and all the big islands of the Caribbean were astoundingly prosperous. In nearby Jamaica, Columbus encountered "all the coast and land filled with towns and excellent ports" where "infinite numbers of Indians followed us in their canoes."

All that was about to change.

On that fateful second voyage, Columbus himself became so ill that he almost died, and for weeks he stopped writing in his log. The flotilla reached Hispaniola on November 22, 1493, and reestablished a Spanish settlement to replace the one that had been destroyed by Indians in their absence. Many of the Spanish by this time had fallen sick, and quite a few had died, due to the unsanitary conditions on board ship and the impossibility of escaping contagion. In a few years, fully half of Columbus's fifteen hundred soldiers would be dead of disease. But that was nothing compared to what happened to the native populations.

In their wandering passage through the Caribbean, the ships with their sick crews unknowingly spread epidemics of illness at many of the ports they visited. By 1494, these epidemics merged into a plague raging across Hispaniola and the rest of the Caribbean. "There came among [the Indians] such illness, death and misery," Bartolomé de las Casas wrote, "that of fathers, mothers and children, an infinite number sadly died." He estimated that a third of the population died in the two years from 1494 to 1496.

A table of statistics for the island of Hispaniola tells the story:

| Date | Native Population |
| --- | --- |
| 1492 | ~500,000 (disputed) |
| 1508 | 60,000 |
| 1510 | 33,523 |
| 1514 | 26,334 |
| 1518 [before smallpox] | 18,000 |
| 1519 [after smallpox] | 1,000 |
| 1542 | 0 |

Not all of these deaths were caused by disease, of course; forced labor, starvation, cruelty, murder, rape, enslavement, and relocation also contributed mightily to the extinction of the Taíno Indians of Hispaniola and the other peoples of the Caribbean. But the overriding factor was European disease, against which the New World had almost no resistance. Modern epidemiologists have studied the old accounts to figure out what diseases struck down the Indians during these first epidemics. Their best guesses are influenza, typhus, and dysentery. Many later diseases joined the first in triggering wave after wave of mortality, including measles, mumps, yellow fever, malaria, chicken pox, typhoid, plague, diphtheria, whooping cough, tuberculosis, and—deadliest of all—smallpox.

These epidemics did not stay in the islands. Las Casas described a "drag-net" of death that spread to the Central American mainland "and devastated all this sphere." Native traders may have first spread contagion to the mainland before 1500; people may have begun dying there even before Europeans arrived. But we know for certain that Columbus, on his fourth voyage in 1502, inadvertently unleashed disease on mainland America.

While probing for a passage westward to the Indies, Columbus reached Honduras's Bay Islands on July 30, 1502. After spending a few weeks in the islands, he sailed on to the Central American main, becoming the first European to touch land there. He anchored in a harbor near the present-day town of Trujillo, and he christened the new land "Honduras" (the Depths) because of the very deep water he had encountered near shore. After disembarking on the Honduran mainland, he and his men held a Christian mass on August 14, 1502, and claimed the land for Isabella and Ferdinand of Spain.

After meeting with friendly Indians, Columbus, who was ill yet again (with what we are not sure), continued exploring southward with his many sick men, sailing along the coastline of Honduras, Nicaragua, and Panama, stopping frequently along the way. Like spot fires set in a forest, disease spread outward from these points of contact, burning deep into the interior lands, far outracing actual European exploration. We do not know how many died in these first epidemics; the natives who witnessed them did not leave any accounts, and there were no European chroniclers.

But the real apocalypse was yet to come. That arrived in the form of smallpox. Las Casas wrote that "it was carried by someone from Castile," and it arrived in Hispaniola in December of 1518. "Of the immensity of peoples that this island held, and that we have seen with our own eyes," Las Casas wrote, only "a thousand" were left by the end of 1519. In January it spread to Puerto Rico, and from there it raged across the Caribbean and jumped to the mainland. By September of 1519, smallpox had reached the Valley of Mexico.

Traditional Indian remedies against illness—sweats, cold baths, and medicinal herbs—were ineffective against smallpox. Indeed, many efforts at healing only seemed to hasten death. In Europe, at its worst, smallpox killed about one out of three people it infected; in the Americas the death rate was higher than 50 percent and in many cases approached 90 to 95 percent.

Epidemiologists generally agree that smallpox is the cruelest disease ever to afflict the human race. In the century before it was eradicated in the 1970s, it killed more than half a billion people and left millions of others horribly scarred and blind. It inflicts unbearable suffering, both physical and psychological. It usually starts like the flu, with headache, fever, and body aches; and then it breaks out as a sore throat that soon spreads into a body rash. As the disease develops over the subsequent week, the victim often experiences frightful hallucinatory dreams and is racked by a mysterious sensation of existential horror. The rash turns into spots that swell into papules, and then fluid-filled pustules that cover the entire body, including the soles of the feet. These pustules sometimes merge, and the outer layer of skin becomes detached from the body. In the most deadly variety of smallpox, the hemorrhagic form, called the bloody pox or black pox, the skin turns a deep purple or takes on a charred look, and comes off in sheets. The victim often "bleeds out," blood pouring from every orifice in the body. It is extremely contagious. Unlike most other viruses, smallpox can survive and remain virulent for months or years outside the body in clothing, blankets, and sickrooms.

The Indians were in abject terror of it. It was like nothing they had ever experienced before. The history of the Conquest contains many Spanish eyewitness accounts attesting to the horrors of the pandemic. "It was a dreadful illness," wrote one friar, "and many people died of it. No one could walk; they could only lie stretched out on their beds. No one could move, not even able to turn their heads. One could not lie face down, or lie on the back, nor turn from one side to another. When they did move, they screamed in pain... Many died from it, but many died only of hunger. There were deaths from starvation, for they had no one left to care for them."

These epidemics of disease weakened Indian military resistance, and in many instances it aided the Spanish in their conquest. But overall, the Spanish (and Columbus personally) were deeply dismayed by the vast die-offs; the deaths of so many Indians interfered with their slaving businesses, killed their servants, and emptied their plantations and mines of forced labor. When smallpox arrived, the Indians often responded with panic and flight, abandoning towns and cities, leaving behind the sick and dead. And while the Spanish were less susceptible to these epidemics, they were not immune, and many also died in the general conflagration.

Epidemics cleared out huge swaths of the New World even before Europeans got there. There are numerous accounts of European explorers arriving in a village for the first time, only to find everyone dead, the houses full of rotting, pustule-covered corpses.

Historians once marveled at how Cortés, with his army of five hundred soldiers, defeated the Aztec empire of over a million people. Various ideas have been advanced: that the Spanish had crucial technological advantages in horses, swords, crossbows, cannon, and armor; that the Spanish had superior tactics honed by centuries of fighting the Moors; that the Indians held back, fearful the Spanish were gods; and that the Aztecs' subjugation and misrule of surrounding chiefdoms had created conditions ripe for revolt. All this is true. But the real conquistador was smallpox. Cortés and his troops occupied the Aztec capital city of Tenochtitlan (the future Mexico City) in 1519, but this cannot be counted as a conquest: The uneasy Aztec emperor, Moctezuma, invited Cortés into the city, unsure if he were god or man. Eight months later, after Moctezuma was murdered under murky circumstances (perhaps by the Spanish, perhaps by his own people), the Indians rose up and handily drove the Spanish from the city, in the so-called *Noche Triste*, the "Night of Sorrows." In this crushing rout, many Spanish soldiers either were killed or drowned as they fled the island on which the city was built, because they had overloaded their pockets with gold. After their flight, the Spanish encamped in Tlaxcala, thirty miles east of Tenochtitlan, licking their wounds and wondering what to do next. At that moment, smallpox invaded the Valley of Mexico.

"When the Christians were exhausted from war," one friar wrote, "God saw fit to send the Indians smallpox." In sixty days, smallpox carried off at least half of the inhabitants of Tenochtitlan, which had a pre-contact population of 300,000 or more. Smallpox also killed the very capable successor to Moctezuma, the emperor Cuitláhuac, who in his brief, forty-day rule had swiftly been building military alliances that, had he survived, would very likely have repelled Cortés. But with at least half the population dead and the city and surrounding countryside engulfed in chaos by the epidemic, Cortés was able to retake the city in 1521. The worst effect of smallpox was the complete demoralization of the Indians: They saw clearly that disease decimated them while largely sparing the Spanish, and they concluded they had been cursed and rejected by their gods, who had shifted to the side of the Spanish. As the Spanish marched into the city, one observer wrote, "The streets were so filled with dead and sick people, that our men walked over nothing but bodies."

At the same time that smallpox was ravaging Mexico, it burned southward into the Maya realm before the Spanish arrived. While the Maya cities were no longer inhabited, the Maya people were spread out over the region and were still known for their fierceness and military prowess. The contagion paved the way for the conquest of Guatemala four years later by one of Cortés's captains.

In the ten years following the first outbreak of smallpox in the New World, the disease had stretched deep into South America. The pandemics also felled several of the great pre-Columbian kingdoms in North America. From 1539 to 1541, explorer Hernando de Soto passed through a powerful and flourishing chiefdom called Coosa, which occupied territory encompassing parts of Tennessee, Georgia, and Alabama, and had a population of perhaps 50,000 people. But twenty years later, by the time the next European came through, Coosa had been almost entirely abandoned, the landscape littered with empty houses, the once-abundant gardens overgrown with thistles and weeds. In the Mississippi River Valley, de Soto had found forty-nine towns, but the French explorers La Salle and Joliet, a century later, encountered only seven wretched settlements, a decline of 86 percent. Most of southeastern North America had been cleared out by a massive die-off from disease.

Though the figures are hotly disputed, scholars estimate that, before Columbus's arrival, the population of North America was about 4.4 million, Mexico around 21 million, the Caribbean 6 million, and Central America another 6 million. But by 1543, the Indian peoples of the main Caribbean islands (Cuba, Jamaica, Hispaniola, Puerto Rico) had become extinct: almost six million dead. In the smaller islands, a few shattered native populations clung to a precarious existence. The fall of Tenochtitlan, the general collapse of native populations everywhere, and the continuing waves of pandemics allowed the Spanish to quickly crush Indian resistance throughout most of Central America.

Compare this to the Spanish conquest of the Philippines, which occurred at the same time. The Spanish were just as ruthless there, but the conquest was not aided by disease: Filipinos were resistant to Old World diseases, and the islands experienced no mass die-offs or population crashes. As a result, the Spanish were forced to accommodate and adjust to coexistence with the indigenous people of the Philippines, who remained strong and retained their languages and cultures. Once the Spanish left, the Iberian influence largely faded away, along with the Spanish language, which is today spoken by few.

But did this catastrophe reach Mosquitia, and if so, how did it get into the remote interior, so far from Spanish contact? We don't have much source material on how the 1519 smallpox epidemic affected Honduras specifically. Common sense tells us that, with smallpox raging both north and south, Honduras must have been badly afflicted. Ten years after smallpox, another dreadful pandemic swept the New World: measles. This we know ravaged Honduras with exceptional cruelty. For Europeans, measles is a far milder disease than smallpox; although easily spread, it rarely kills. But when it reached the New World it proved to be almost as deadly, killing at least 25 percent of the affected population. The conquistador Pedro de Alvarado sent a report from Guatemala to Charles V in 1532: "Throughout New Spain, there passed a sickness which they say is measles, which struck the Indians and swept the land, leaving it totally empty." The measles pandemic coincided with epidemics of other diseases in Honduras, among them possibly typhoid, flu, and plague.

Antonio de Herrera, another Spanish chronicler of the period, wrote that "at this time [1532] there was such a great epidemic of measles in the Province of Honduras, spreading from house to house and village to village, that many people died...and two years ago there was a general epidemic of pleurisy and stomach pains which also carried away many Indians." Oviedo wrote that half the population of Honduras died from disease in the years from 1530 to 1532. One Spanish missionary lamented that only 3 percent of the population of the coast had survived and "it is likely the rest of the Indians will in short time decay."

The British geographer Linda Newson produced a magisterial study of the demographic catastrophe in Honduras during the Spanish period, entitled *The Cost of Conquest: Indian Decline in Honduras Under Spanish Rule*. It is the most detailed analysis of what happened in that country. Precise figures of the original population are hard to come by, especially for eastern Honduras and Mosquitia, which remained uncolonized, but Newson evaluated a vast amount of evidence and provided the best possible estimates—despite, she noted, being hampered by the lack of good archaeological work.

Drawing on early narratives, population estimates, cultural studies, and ecological data, Newson concluded that the areas of Honduras first colonized by the Spanish started with a pre-Conquest population of 600,000. By 1550, only 32,000 native people remained. This is a population collapse of 95 percent, a staggering statistic. She broke down the figures like this: 30,000 to 50,000 were killed in wars of conquest, while another 100,000 to 150,000 were captured in slave raids and transported out of the country. Almost all the rest—over 400,000—died of disease.

In eastern Honduras, which includes Mosquitia, Newson estimated a pre-Conquest population density of about thirty people per square mile, establishing the population of the interior mountains of Mosquitia at about 150,000. However, the discovery of large cities like T1 and T3—which Newson did not know about when she wrote her book in 1986—significantly revises that calculus. Regardless of the actual numbers, though, we now know this was a thriving and prosperous region, linked to its neighbors by extensive trading routes; it was not at all the remote, sparsely inhabited jungle we find today. We have the testimony of Cortés and Pedraza of extensive and rich provinces, and we have the evidence from T1 and T3, Las Crucitas, Wankibila, and other former cities in Mosquitia.

The mountain valleys like T1 were too deep in the jungle to be of interest to conquistadors or slavers; the people living there should have continued to flourish long after the Europeans arrived. Many of these areas weren't opened up until the twentieth century or later, and, as we now know, parts remain unexplored even today. But given how diseases spread, it is virtually impossible for the T1 valley to have escaped the general contagion. Almost certainly, epidemics of European disease swept T1, T3, and the rest of Mosquitia sometime between 1520 and 1550. (More and better archaeology is needed to refine this; perhaps the continuing excavations at T1 will help.)

Those pathogens invaded Mosquitia via two pathways. The first was through trade. When Columbus landed in Honduras's Bay Islands, he described a memorable sight: a huge trading canoe, eight feet wide and sixty feet long, manned by twenty-five paddlers. The canoe had a hut built amidships and it was heaped with valuable trade goods: copper, flint, weapons, textiles, and beer. There was extensive maritime trade throughout the Caribbean and Central America. Some historians say the canoe Columbus saw must have been operated by Maya traders, but it's more likely they were Chibcha traders, given that the Bay Islands were settled not by the Maya but by Chibchan-speaking people who had ties to Mosquitia. These merchants, whoever they might be, were certainly trading with the mainland, as well as with Cuba, Hispaniola, and Puerto Rico—some archaeologists believe they may have reached as far north as the Mississippi River delta. And the two main highways into Mosquitia—the Río Plátano and the Río

Patuca—flow into the sea not far eastward of the Bay Islands. During the time of plagues in the Caribbean, there can be little doubt these traders, peddling goods from the islands and coasts, carried European pathogens up the rivers into Mosquitia, where the microbes escaped into the local populations and burned deep into the hinterlands.

A second likely track of infection was the slave trade. Before slavery was restricted by the Spanish crown in 1542, slaving parties scoured Honduras, kidnapping Indians to work plantations, mines, and households. The first Indians enslaved came from the islands and coasts. As disease wiped out these early captives, the Spanish raiders went deeper into the countryside to find replacements. (The African slave trade also ramped up at this time.) By the 1530s, the slavers were ravaging the Mosquito Coast and the Olancho Valley, where Catacamas is today, destroying villages and rounding up people like cattle. On three sides—west, north, and south—Mosquitia was surrounded by brutal slave raids. Thousands of Indians fleeing their villages took refuge in the rainforest. A great many disappeared into the mountains of Mosquitia. Some of these refugees, unfortunately, carried European disease into the otherwise well-protected interior valleys.

If we follow this hypothetical scenario to its

conclusion, then sometime in the early 1500s several epidemics of disease swept T1 in close succession. If the mortality rates were similar to the rest of Honduras and Central America, about 90 percent of the inhabitants died of disease. The survivors, shattered and traumatized, abandoned the city, leaving the cache of sacred objects behind as a final offering to the gods, ritually breaking many to release their spirits. This was not a grave offering for an individual; it was a grave offering for an entire city, the cenotaph of a civilization. The same abandonment, with broken offerings, occurred across the region.

"Think about it," Chris Fisher said. "Even though they were suffering from the ravages of those diseases, for them to go and make that offering really underscores the importance" of the place where the cache was found, and the paramount meaning of the cache itself. "These places were ritually charged and remained that way forever." And so it was until half a millennium later, when our little group stumbled over the cache—a tragic memorial to a once-great culture.

As it turned out, one of the answers to the mystery of the White City had been lying before us the whole time: The various myths of Ciudad Blanca, its abandonment and cursed nature, probably originated in this grim history. Viewed in the light of these pandemics, the White City legends are a fairly straightforward description of a city (or several) swept by disease and abandoned by its people—a place that, furthermore, may have remained a hot zone for some time afterward.

We have few accounts giving the native point of view of these pandemics. One of the most moving is a rare contemporary eyewitness description, called the *Book of Chilam Balam of Chumayel*, which recalls the two worlds, before and after contact. It was written by an Indian in the Yucatec Mayan language:

> There was then no sickness; they had no aching bones; they had then no high fever; they had then no smallpox; no stomach pains; no consumption...At that time people stood erect. But then the *teules* [foreigners] arrived and everything fell apart. They brought fear, and they came to wither the flowers.

## CHAPTER 23

**Four members of the expedition have become
ill with the same symptoms.**

In the weeks after our return from the jungle in February 2015, I and the other members of the expedition settled back into our everyday lives. The power of the experience stayed with us; I felt humbled and awed by the glimpse we'd had of a place completely outside the twenty-first century. We all shared a sense of relief, too, that we had emerged from the jungle unscathed.

A few days after our return from Honduras, Woody sent everyone a broadcast e-mail. It was part of his standard follow-up to any expedition he leads into the jungle, and it included this excerpt:

All, if you find anything at all, feel slightly unwell, develop a slight fever that goes away or any of your multitude of bites appear not to be

317

healing I would advise seeking medical advice as soon as possible, explaining where you have been etc. Better safe than sorry.

At the time, I was completely covered, like everyone else, with bug bites that itched awfully, but that gradually began to fade. A month later, in March, I took a vacation with my wife to France, where we went skiing in the French Alps and visited friends in Paris. While walking around Paris, I began to feel a stiffness in my legs, as if they were sore from excessive exercise. At first I attributed it to the skiing, but over several days the stiffness grew worse, until I could hardly walk without becoming exhausted. When I developed a fever of 103, I went online to the website of the Centers for Disease Control, to check the incubation period for various tropical diseases I might have been exposed to. Thankfully, I was beyond the normal incubation period for chikungunya, Chagas' disease, and dengue fever. But I was smack in the middle of it for malaria, and my symptoms matched those described at the CDC website. I was furious at myself for prematurely stopping my malaria medication. What the hell had I been thinking? But then I wondered how I could have gotten malaria, a disease transmitted between humans via mosquitoes, when the valley of T1 was uninhabited. Mosquitoes do not usually travel more than a few hundred yards in their entire lifetime, and the nearest humans potentially with malaria were many miles away.

My Parisian friends made some phone calls and found a hospital a short metro ride away with an infectious-disease lab that could test for malaria. I went that evening, they drew blood, and ninety minutes later I had the results: no malaria. The doctor thought I had a common virus, unrelated to the Honduran trip, and assured me it was nothing to worry about. My fever had vanished even while I awaited my test results. Two days later I had fully recovered.

Another month passed. The bug bites on my legs eventually faded away, along with the itching. But one bite did not go away. It was on my upper left arm, midway between elbow and shoulder, and it seemed to be getting redder and bigger. I didn't worry about it at first because, unlike the other bites, it didn't itch or bother me.

In April I had an outbreak of sores in my mouth and on my tongue, accompanied by another sudden fever. I went to the local emergency room in Santa Fe. The doctor who examined me thought it was herpes and gave me a prescription for an antiviral medication. I showed him the bug bite on my arm, which was getting uglier. He suggested I treat it with antibiotic ointment. That fever went away quickly and the mouth sores disappeared soon after. The antibiotic cream, however, did nothing for my arm.

Over the next few weeks, the bug bite expanded and developed a vile crust. I discussed it with Steve Elkins, and he said that Dave Yoder and Chris Fisher reported having similar bites that wouldn't heal. Steve suggested that we all photograph our bites and e-mail the pictures around, to compare. Dave, who lived in Rome, sent me a picture of his bite, which was on the back of his leg. It looked like mine, only worse. Dave was frustrated: He had gone to the ER in Rome three times, and the doctors kept diagnosing it as an infection and giving him antibiotics, which didn't work. "It doesn't *look* like a normal infection," he told me. "It looks like a miniature volcanic crater. It just won't heal."

Dave began researching what he might have. "I try not to Google images of disease on the web," he said. "I've given myself two health scares caused by Googling. But this time I did, because I *knew* my doctors were wrong."

The pictures that popped up made him think he might have the tropical disease leishmaniasis.

He e-mailed pictures of his bug bite to two fellow photographers at *National Geographic* who had gotten leishmaniasis while on assignment. One was Joel Sartore, who contracted the disease while shooting in the Bolivian rainforest and who almost lost his leg as a result. Both photographers told Dave that what he had "sure looked like leish."

Dave sent me an e-mail:

*Have you considered the possibility of leishmania-sis? It can be a serious thing. I'm pretty sure that's what I have, at this point. I'm investigating the situation right now.*

I immediately Googled the disease and read about it with fascination and disgust. The images of leish in the early stages did indeed look like my bug bite. The pictures also showed me what it could develop into, and that was a perfect horror. Leishmaniasis is the second deadliest parasitic disease in the world, behind only malaria, and it affects twelve million people worldwide, with around one or two million new cases every year. It kills sixty thousand people a year. Of the leading "neglected tropical diseases" (NTDs) in the world leishmaniasis is one of the most prominent, if not number one. But because it almost always affects poor people in rural areas of the tropics, there is little economic incentive for pharmaceutical companies to develop vaccines or treatments.

Meanwhile, Bill Benenson and Steve began circulating e-mails to the entire group, asking if anyone else had bug bites that weren't going away. Mark Adams, the sound engineer, reported he had a lesion on his knee. Tom Weinberg had a suspicious ulcer on his knuckle. Mark Plotkin had an unexplained rash. Sully and Woody both had bug bites that were turning into sores.

A few days later—this was in late April 2015—fed up with his local doctors and the Italian ER, Dave went to the largest hospital in Rome and demanded to see a tropical disease specialist there. At the beginning of the examination, when Dave opined that it was leish, the doctor snapped, "No it isn't." But by the end of the examination, the doctor agreed that he did indeed appear to have the disease. He suggested Dave return to the States for a more precise diagnosis, since leish is notoriously difficult to identify; it is not a single disease but a suite of diseases caused by some thirty different parasitic species carried by several dozen kinds of sand flies.

On May 2, 2015, Dave sent an e-mail to the group in which he reported on his visit to the tropical disease doctor in Rome and offered some advice:

> *Brothers in the leish:*
> *Despite the fact nobody from the group has been diagnosed with anything, I'm going to perhaps jump the gun and address one elephant in*

*the room directly. There may be cause to explore the possibility of leishmaniasis in my case, and as I understand the situation, possibly others from the group.*

He said he had decided to return to the States for a firm diagnosis and treatment.

This set off a minor panic. Dozens of messages circulated among the expedition members discussing symptoms, real and imagined. Even those without evident signs of leish rushed to their doctors, worried about various complaints—rashes, fevers, headaches, and other ailments. Stomach-turning photographs of everyone's expanding ulcers were circulated, and circulated again.

Steve Elkins remained exasperatingly healthy, but Bill Benenson had discovered two jungle ticks on himself when he returned to California. While that had not led to anything serious, he was shaken up, and he was very concerned about what was happening to others. He sent out an e-mail:

*I feel we should all share our relevant medical information together, if possible and comfortable, to help ourselves and for all future Explorers as well. Let's remember, we've not only made history together in February but that we're still discovering a great deal that's new and exciting, about a lost place in a very threatened environment.*

I was now thoroughly alarmed about my own sore. Steve Elkins dug up the name of a tropical disease specialist in New Mexico who might be able to help me: Dr. Ravi Durvasula at the Veterans Affairs Medical Center in Albuquerque. Dr. Durvasula was a specialist in "Old World" leishmaniasis. I called the VA hospital hoping to speak to him. An hour later, after multiple phone calls and a mind-boggling number of transfers from one wrong office to another, after being told that no such doctor existed, that the doctor worked there but didn't take patients, that I wasn't allowed to speak to his office without a referral, and that the doctor did not take referrals, I gave up. (I can't imagine how our wounded soldiers negotiate this same telephone system.)

"Forget calling the VA," Steve said to me. "Send him an e-mail. Be sure to play up the whole expedition thing, the lost city, *National Geographic*, all that sexy stuff."

So I did:

*Dear Dr. Durvasula,*

*I am a journalist for* National Geographic *magazine and* The New Yorker... *I recently returned from an expedition into an extremely remote area in the La Mosquitia rainforest, exploring a large, unknown pre-Columbian ruin. We were in the jungle from February 17-26. Since that time, four members of the expedition have become ill with the same symptoms... I live in New Mexico and I had heard you were a specialist in leishmaniasis and that is why I'm contacting you to see if you might be willing to take my case.*

Dr. Durvasula e-mailed me back immediately. He couldn't have been more helpful and concerned—in contrast to the VA staff. We arranged a phone call, and he asked me some questions.

"Does the area have a whitish, pearlescent appearance, surrounded by red?"

"Yes."

"Does it itch?"

"No."

"Does it hurt or feel sore at all?"

"No."

"No discomfort?"

"None at all."

"Ah, well. I am afraid those *are* the classic signs of leishmaniasis."

He asked me to e-mail him a photo. When he got it, he confirmed it certainly appeared to be leish. He suggested I seek help at the National Institutes of Health (NIH), the best place in the world, he said, for leishmaniasis study and treatment.

In the meantime, Dave Yoder explored treatment options in the States. He, too, zeroed in on the National Institutes of Health and contacted them. At the NIH, Dave reached Dr. Thomas Nutman, deputy chief of the Laboratory of Parasitic Diseases. Nutman was fascinated by the story of the expedition to the lost city and the mass outbreak of disease. He wrote Dave:

> *Dear Dave,*
> *I think there is a very high likelihood that this is Leishmania and because of the strains in Honduras there is a small but real chance that this could turn into mucocutaneous disease depending on the strain… The big issue is defining which strain of Leishmania you have and tailoring treatment to that particular strain… We have taken care of a number of National Geographic folks in the past.*

The National Institutes of Health's overall mission is to "seek fundamental knowledge about the nature and behavior of living systems," and then leverage that knowledge to "enhance health, lengthen life, and reduce illness and disability." It is strictly a research institution, and anyone admitted for treatment must be part of a research study. Each of its projects has a set of rules that outline who can be treated, why, and how their treatment will contribute to medical knowledge. If a potential patient meets the criteria and is enrolled, the care is free. It even includes financial help with transportation and lodging. In return, the patient agrees to follow the rules and donate to medical research any tissue samples, cells, blood, parasites, and so forth. A participant can withdraw at any time, for any reason. .

The NIH doctors were keenly interested in our situation. The mass outbreak of disease was unusual, the valley of T1 seemed extraordinarily "hot," and the region was unknown medically, all of which made the expedition an enticing medical study. The doctors offered to treat us all for free. It was nice to be wanted.

In late May, Dave flew from Rome to Washington for a firm diagnosis. "Hopefully," he joked, "we'll all turn up negative, and it'll turn out to be a minor staph infection from Woody's jungle stew that is easily treated with an application of cayenne sauce."

The doctor in charge of the project, who would be treating Dave, me, and the other potential "brothers in the leish," was Theodore Nash, principal investigator in the Clinical Parasitology Section, Laboratory of Parasitic Diseases, National Institute of Allergy and

Infectious Diseases. Nash was one of the country's leading experts in leishmaniasis treatment, having worked under Dr. Frank Neva, a pioneer in leishmaniasis treatment who came to the NIH from Harvard. After Neva's retirement, Nash became the chief clinical researcher into leish at the NIH, and over the past decades he advanced its treatment with new drugs and formulations.

At NIH, doctors took a biopsy of Dave's lesion, looked at it under a microscope, and saw it was teeming with round, microscopic leishmania parasites. But Dave's treatment would depend on what kind of leish it was. A special lab at NIH began the process of sequencing the parasites' DNA.

Leishmaniasis has a long and terrible history with human beings, stretching back as far as human records exist and causing suffering and death for thousands of years.

A few years ago, a hundred-million-year-old piece of Burmese amber was found to have trapped a sand fly that had sucked the blood of a reptile, most likely a dinosaur. Inside this sand fly, scientists discovered leishmania parasites, and in its proboscis, or sucking tube, they found reptilian blood cells mingled with the same parasites.

Even dinosaurs got leishmaniasis.

Leishmania has probably been around since the final breakup of the primordial continent known as Pangaea. As these ancient landmasses eventually drifted apart to become the Old and New Worlds, the populations of that sand fly ancestor were separated and continued to evolve independently, eventually giving rise to the two basic strains of the disease in the Old World and the New. At some point the disease made the leap from reptiles to mammals. (Modern reptiles still get leish, and there has been a medical debate over whether reptilian leish can be transmitted to humans; the answer is probably not.)

Unlike many diseases that afflict human beings, leish was global from the very outset, and it was dreaded by our ancient ancestors in both hemispheres. Archaeologists have found leish parasites in Egyptian mummies dating back five thousand years, and in Peruvian mummies going back three thousand years. A description of leish appears in one of the earliest written human documents: the cuneiform tablets of King Ashurbanipal, who ruled the Assyrian Empire 2,700 years ago.

Leishmaniasis comes in three main varieties, each with distinct symptoms.

The most common form is cutaneous (i.e., skin) leishmaniasis, which is found in many parts of the

Old World, especially Africa, India, and the Middle East. It is also widespread in Mexico and Central and South America, and it recently popped up in Texas and Oklahoma. Some US troops returning from Iraq and Afghanistan contracted cutaneous leish during their deployments and nicknamed it the Baghdad boil. This kind of leish starts as a sore at the location of the bite, which grows into a weeping lesion. If left alone, it usually goes away, leaving only an ugly scar. It can usually be treated by burning, freezing, or surgically removing the ulcer.

In visceral leishmaniasis, the second type—also from the Old World—the parasite invades the body's internal organs, particularly the liver, spleen, and bone marrow. It is sometimes known as black fever, because it often turns its victim's skin black. This variety is deadly; without treatment it is always fatal. But treatment of visceral leish is quick and reliable, requiring a single infusion of an antibiotic drug that yields a cure rate of about 95 percent. Most of the deaths in the world from leish are caused by the visceral form, among poor children who don't have access to treatment.

The final form of leish is the mucocutaneous or mucosal variety, the major New World form of the disease. It starts as a skin sore like the cutaneous kind. Months or years later, the sores can reappear in the mucous membranes of the nose and mouth. (The sores I had in my mouth, however, were probably unrelated.) When leish moves to your face, the disease gets serious. The ulcers grow, eating away the nose and lips from the inside and eventually causing them to slough off, leaving the face horrifically disfigured. The parasite continues to devour the bones of the face, the upper jaw, and teeth. This form of leish, while not always lethal, is the most difficult to treat, and the treatment itself involves a drug that has toxic—and sometimes fatal—side effects.

The pre-Columbian inhabitants of South America were plagued by mucosal leish, which they called *uta*. The grotesque disfigurement of the face terrified the Moche, Inca, and other ancient cultures. They may have considered it a punishment or a curse from the gods. Archaeologists have uncovered burials in Peru and elsewhere of people whose disease was so advanced that they had a caved-in hole where the face used to be—the disease had eaten away everything, including the facial bones. Ancient Peruvian pots so faithfully record the disfigurations that researchers can identify in them the actual clinical stages of the disease, from the early soft-tissue destruction of the nose, to the general destruction of the nose and lips, and finally to the disintegration of the hard palate, nasal septum, upper jaw, and teeth. The Peruvian custom of punishing people by mutilating the nose and lips may have been intended to imitate the facial deformities caused by the disease, perhaps to mimic what they believed was divine retribution.

Acute fear of the disease may have even driven human settlement patterns in South America. The archaeologist James Kus, a retired professor at California State University, Fresno, believes that the Inca site of Machu Picchu may have been chosen, in part, because of the prevalence of mucosal leish. "The Incas were paranoid about leishmaniasis," he told me. The sand fly that transmits leish can't live at higher altitudes, but it is widespread in the lowland areas where the Inca grew coca, a sacred crop. Machu Picchu lies at just the right altitude: too high for leish, but not too high for coca; at Machu Picchu the king and his court could rule from a place of safety and preside over the rituals associated with coca cultivation, without the risk of getting this most dreaded disease.

When the Spanish conquistadors arrived in South America in the sixteenth century, they were horrified at the facial deformities they saw among native people in the lowlands of the Andes, especially among the coca growers. The Spanish thought they were looking at a form of leprosy and called the disease *lepra blanca*, "white leprosy." Over the years, mucosal leish has acquired many nicknames in Latin America: tapir nose, hoarse voice, spongy wound, big canker.

Mucosal leish didn't exist in the Old World. But the even deadlier visceral form, the kind that invades the internal organs, had long plagued the Indian subcontinent. It first gained the attention of Western medicine as the British extended their empire into India. Eighteenth-century writers described it as "kala-azar" or "black fever." Visceral leish easily spreads from person to person via the bite of sand flies, using human beings as its primary reservoir host. It was so deadly and spread so fast that in certain regions of India in the nineteenth century, leishmaniasis would sweep through an area, killing everyone and leaving a landscape of empty villages, entirely bereft of human life.

The British also noted the cutaneous form of the disease in India and the Near East and gave it various names: Aleppo evil, Jericho button, Delhi boil, Oriental sore. But doctors did not recognize a connection between the two strains until 1901. William Boog Leishman, a doctor from Glasgow who was a general in the British Army, was posted in the town of Dum Dum, near Calcutta, where one of his soldiers fell ill with a fever and a swollen spleen. After the man died, Leishman looked at thin sections of the man's spleen under the microscope and, using a new staining method, discovered tiny round bodies in the cells—the leishmania parasite. Leishman called it Dum Dum fever. A few weeks after Leisham published his discovery, another British doctor, named Charles Donovan, also stationed in India, independently reported the results of his own research. He, too, had spied the offending parasite, and between the two of them the disease "leishmaniasis" was identified. Leishman got the dubious honor of having the disease named after him, while Donovan was gifted with the species' name: *Leishmania donovani*. Doctors figured out in 1911 that it was transmitted by the sand fly, and later they realized that a bewildering number of mammals could be reservoir hosts for the disease, including dogs, cats, rats, mice, gerbils, hamsters, jackals, opossums, foxes, monk seals, and, of course, humans. This astonishingly broad range of host animals makes it one of the most successful diseases on the planet.

I was still trying to decide whether I should go to NIH or not when the DNA analysis of Dave's parasites came back. It showed he was infected with a species of leish parasite known as *Leishmania braziliensis*. This was bad news for Dave and the rest of us, because *L. braziliensis* causes the third, mucosal variety of the disease, and is considered to be one of the most difficult of all to cure.

Dr. Nash decided to begin Dave's treatment immediately. He would use a drug called amphotericin B, administered by slow infusion. Doctors have nicknamed the drug "amphoterrible" because of its nasty side effects. It is considered a last resort, most commonly given to patients with fungal infections of the blood when other drugs have failed; most of these patients are extremely ill with AIDS.

Dr. Nash would give Dave and the rest of us a formulation of the drug called liposomal amphotericin. In this form, the toxic drug is encapsulated in microscopic spherules made of lipids (fats). This makes the drug safer, reducing some of the most dangerous side effects. But the lipid droplets can cause disturbing side effects of their own.

The length of treatment depends on how well the patient tolerates the drug and how quickly the ulcer begins to heal. The ideal course, which Dr. Nash had determined over many years of experience, was seven days—long enough to halt the disease but not so long as to harm the patient.

Shortly after Dave was diagnosed with leish, Tom Weinberg learned from the CDC that he, too, had the disease. Chris Fisher, Mark Adams, and Juan Carlos Fernández went to the NIH and were also diagnosed with it. All were treated except Juan Carlos; Dr. Nash recognized that his immune system appeared to be fighting it off and decided to delay treatment. It was the right decision, and Juan Carlos ended up leish-free without going through the rigors of amphotericin B.

From the UK we heard that Woody had contracted leish, as had Sully, despite bundling themselves up so scrupulously every evening. Sully was going to be treated at the Royal Centre for Defence Medicine at Birmingham Heartlands Hospital, while Woody was starting treatment at the Hospital for Tropical Diseases in London. Both would get a new drug, miltefosine. Word soon came back from Honduras that many Honduran members of the expedition had also fallen ill with leishmaniasis. These included Oscar Neil, the archaeologist; the commanding officer of the military contingent, Lt. Col. Oseguera; and nine soldiers.

When the news of our mini-epidemic began to spread among members of the expedition, accompanied by gruesome photos of weeping ulcers, it was hard not to think about the centuries-old legend and its oft-cited "curse of the monkey god." All those flowers we chopped down! Gallows humor aside, though, many of us were privately aghast at having walked so blithely into that hot zone, and then having congratulated ourselves, prematurely, for emerging from the jungle unscathed. The jokes petered out quickly in the face of this dramatic disease, which had the potential to alter the course of each of our lives. This was deadly serious.

Because amphotericin is expensive and not available in Honduras, the Honduran members of the expedition were being treated with an older drug, a pentavalent antimonial compound. Antimony, a heavy metal, is directly below arsenic in the periodic table of elements and is similarly poisonous. This drug kills the parasite while sparing (one hopes) the patient. As bad as ampho B is, this one is worse: Even in the best scenarios it has dreadful side effects. We heard from Virgilio that Oscar, who had been bitten on the right side of his face, had almost died of the treatment and was recovering in seclusion in Mexico. He would have a nasty scar for life; he later grew a beard to cover it up and declined to speak of his experience or do any further work at T1.

After Dave was diagnosed with mucosal leish, I finally understood that I had to stop procrastinating and get treated. As bad as the treatment sounded, I wasn't willing to take a chance with the disease itself, or with my face.

So finally, at the end of May, I called the NIH and set up an appointment for early June to get a biopsy and diagnosis. By this time my bug bite had turned into an oozing crater the size of a quarter, fiery red and disgusting to look at. It didn't bother me; I'd had no more fevers and I felt fine. Dr. Nash said he doubted my fevers had been caused by the leish anyway; they were, he thought, coincidental viral infections, perhaps opportunistic because my immune system had been shaken up by leish, which hijacks white blood cells.

As my date approached, I heard that Dave's treatment with liposomal amphotericin had gone very badly. He had suffered serious kidney damage and Dr. Nash had halted it after only two infusions. He remained hospitalized at the NIH under observation while the doctors debated what to do next.

## CHAPTER 24

**My head felt like it was in flames.**

The National Institutes of Health occupies a verdant campus of several hundred acres in Bethesda, Maryland. I arrived alone on June 1, a gorgeous summer day, the smell of freshly cut grass drifting in the air, birdsong pouring from the trees. Sandals and jeans seemed to outnumber lab coats, and the place had the relaxed air of a college. As I walked up the drive toward the clinical center complex, I could hear from faraway a lone bugler playing taps.

I entered the center, and after wandering around more lost than I'd ever been in the jungle, I managed to find the patient processing area. There I signed paperwork agreeing to be studied, and a kindly nurse took thirteen vials of my blood. I met Dr. Ted Nash and my second doctor, Elise O'Connell, and was reassured by their warmth and professionalism.

In the dermatology lab, a photographer arrived with a Canon digital camera. He affixed a little ruler just below the ulcer on my arm and took dozens of photographs. I was ushered into an examination room where the lesion was inspected by a gaggle of earnest medical students, who took turns peering, palpating, and asking questions. Next, in the biopsy lab, a nurse cut two wormlike plugs of flesh out of the lesion, and the holes were stitched up.

When the biopsy came back it would offer no surprise: Like Dave and everyone else, I had *Leishmania braziliensis*. Or at least that's what the doctors initially believed.

Our primary doctor, Theodore Nash, was seventy-one years old. He did his rounds in a white lab coat with a roll of papers precariously shoved into a side pocket. He had curly salt-and-pepper hair brushed back from a domed forehead, steel-rimmed spectacles, and the kindly, distracted air of a professor. Even though, like most doctors, he was fantastically busy, his manner was unhurried and relaxed, and he was gregarious and happy to answer questions at length. I said I wanted to hear the straight story without any window dressing. He said that was how he preferred to work with all his patients. He was refreshingly, even alarmingly, direct.

The National Institutes of Health has been conducting clinical studies on leishmaniasis since the early 1970s, treating recent immigrants and people who had picked up the disease while traveling. Many of the patients were Peace Corps volunteers. Dr. Nash participated in the treatment of most of them. He had written the upgraded leishmaniasis treatment protocol for the NIH in 2001, and it is still in use today. He shifted treatment away from the antimonial drug, which he thought was too toxic, to amphotericin and other drugs, depending on the parasite species and the geographic variety. Nash knew as much about leish treatment as any doctor in the United States. This is not a simple disease, and treatment is more an art than a science. The clinical data aren't deep enough to give doctors a precise formula, and there are too many forms of leish and many unknowns.

Dr. Nash had spent almost his entire medical career in the parasitology section of the NIH—forty-five years—going back, he said, to the time when parasitology was "the backwater of science, no one was interested, and no one would work with you." Because most people who get parasites are poor, and because infectious-disease medicine is not usually fee-based, parasitology is one of the lower-paying of all the medical specialties. To go into the field, you have to truly care about helping people. Your extremely expensive, ten-year medical education gives you the privilege of working long hours for modest pay among the poorest and most vulnerable people in the world, encountering a staggering amount of misery and death. Your reward is to relieve a small bit of that suffering. It takes a rare kind of human being to become a parasitologist.*

Nash's early research focused on schistosomiasis and then giardia, a common, worldwide, waterborne parasite. Today the main focus of his work is a parasitic disease called neurocysticercosis, in which the brain is invaded by tapeworm larvae that originate in undercooked pork. The larvae circulate in the bloodstream and some get stuck in the tiny vessels in the brain, where they form cysts, leaving the brain peppered with grape-sized, fluid-filled holes. The brain becomes inflamed and the victim suffers seizures, hallucinations, memory failure, and death. Neurocysticercosis affects millions of people and is the world's leading cause of acquired epileptic seizures. "If only we had the smallest fraction of the money that is devoted to malaria," he declared to me in anguish, "we could do so much to stop this disease!"

In our first meeting, Nash sat me down and explained why he thought our team had become

---

* I ran this paragraph by Dr. Nash before publication and he objected. "Please amend and take the halo off my head," he wrote me. I toned it down but I couldn't remove the halo.

infected, how leishmaniasis works, what its life cycle is, and what I had to expect from treatment. The disease requires two animals: a "reservoir host"—an infected mammal whose blood is teeming with the parasite—and a "vector," which is the female sand fly. When the sand fly bites a host and sucks its blood, it also draws in parasites. Those parasites proliferate in the sand fly's gut until it bites another host. The parasites are then injected into the new host, where they complete their life cycle.

Each host animal lives out its life as a Typhoid Mary, infecting the sand flies that drink its blood. The parasite, while it can devastate a human being, generally does not "cost" the host animal very much, although some host mammals get lesions on their noses. A good guest does not burn down the house he's staying in; leishmania wants its host animal to live long and prosper, spreading as much disease as possible.

In the isolated valley of T1, far removed from human habitation, sand flies and an as-yet-unknown mammalian host—it could be mice, rats, capybaras, tapirs, peccaries, or even monkeys—had been locked in a cycle of infection and reinfection going on for centuries. "And then," said Nash, "*you* intruded. You were a mistake." By invading the valley, we were like clueless civilians wandering onto a battlefield and getting shot to pieces in the crossfire.

When an infected sand fly bites a person, the fly unleashes hundreds to thousands of parasites into the person's tissue. These tiny single-celled animals have flagella so they can swim around. They are small; it would take about thirty to span a human hair. But they are positively gargantuan compared to bacteria and viruses that cause disease. Almost a billion cold viruses, for example, could be packed into a single leishmania parasite.

Because it is a complex, single-celled animal, its methods are more subtle and devious than a virus or bacterium. When a sand fly injects leishmania, the human body, sensing the intrusion, sends an army of white blood cells to hunt down, swallow, and destroy the parasites. White blood cells, which come in many types, usually deal with bacteria and other foreign bodies by engulfing and digesting them. Unfortunately, this is exactly what the leishmania parasite wants—to be swallowed. Once inside the white blood cell, the parasite drops its flagellum, becomes egg-shaped, and starts to multiply. Soon the white blood cell is bulging with parasites like an overstuffed beanbag, and it bursts, releasing the parasites into the victim's tissues. More white blood cells rush to attack and engulf the loose parasites, and they are in turn hijacked into producing more parasites.

The ulcer that forms around the infected area

isn't caused by the parasite per se, but by the body's immune system attacking it. The inflammation, not the parasite, is what eats away the person's skin and (in the mucosal form) destroys the face. The immune system goes nuts trying to get rid of the parasite that is blowing up its white blood cells, and this fight trashes the battlefield, inflaming and killing the tissues in the bite area. As the parasite slowly spreads, the lesion expands, destroying the skin and leaving a crater exposing the raw flesh below. The ulcer is usually painless—nobody knows why—unless it occurs over joints, when the pain can be intense. Most deaths from mucosal leish occur from infections invading the body through this unprotected doorway.

Nash then talked about the drug that I would be taking, amphotericin. He said it was the gold standard, the drug of choice, for this kind of leish. While miltefosine was a newer drug and could be taken in pill form, he didn't want to use it. And besides, there was none available.* There had been too few clinical

---

* Nash had been using miltefosine in a clinical trial with the drug company that was seeking approval for it, but when it was approved for use in the United States, the company closed the trial and the drug was suddenly unavailable in the United States, while the company ramped up production. It would take another two years for the drug to finally be available to Americans, due to a crazy combination of slowness in making the drug, bureaucratic bungling by the FDA, and the fact that treating leish in the United States is neither profitable nor a medical priority.

trials to make him comfortable with it, and in one trial in Colombia it seemed to be ineffective against *L. braziliensis.* He also said you never really knew what kind of side effects might pop up until at least ten thousand people had taken a drug, and miltefosine had not reached that benchmark. He had had long experience with amphotericin B, and it produced an approximately 85 percent remission rate, which was about "as good as it gets" in any drug treatment. The drug works by binding to the parasite's cell membrane and tearing open a tiny hole in it, causing the organism to leak and die.

Nash told me what I might experience in taking the drug. He didn't sugarcoat his comments. The side effects of liposomal amphotericin, he said, can be dramatic and "are almost too numerous to mention." There are acute reactions that occur instantly upon receiving the drug, and there are dangerous long-term side effects that occur days later. Many of these side effects are complex and poorly understood. When he started using it around fifteen years ago, things went well at first, and then, all of a sudden, his patients began to experience acute reactions when the drug went into the body. It turns out that some people tolerate the drug and some don't. These reactions, he said, initially panicked him because they mimicked symptoms of an acute infection—fever, chills, pain, soaring heart rate, chest pressure, and difficulty breathing. On top of that, the drug had a mysterious psychological effect on a few patients. Within seconds of receiving the drug they became overwhelmed by a feeling of impending doom that, in the worst cases, made them believe they were actually dying. In those, he had to halt the infusion and sometimes administer a narcotic to calm down or knock out the patient. That acute reaction, however, usually went away quickly, and Nash emphasized that many patients experienced no reaction at all. I might be one of the lucky ones.

He reeled off other common side effects: nausea, vomiting, anorexia, dizziness, headache, insomnia, skin rash, fever, shaking, chills, and mental confusion; other physical effects include electrolyte imbalances, decreases in white blood cell count, and liver function abnormalities. These outcomes were so frequent, he explained, that I could expect to get at least some of them. But the most common and dangerous side effect is that the drug damages the kidneys, degrading renal function. The harm tends to be worse the older you are; old people, he said, lose renal function naturally as they age. I asked Nash if I was, at fifty-eight, in the "old" category, and he thought that was funny. "Oh, ho!" he cried. "So you're still telling yourself you're middle-aged? Yes, we all go through that period of denial." As a general rule of thumb, he would stop administering the drug when kidney function had dropped to 40 percent of baseline.

The whole process, he said, is "stressful for the patient and stressful for the doctor."

When I asked him if the disease was curable, he hemmed and hawed a bit. It's curable in the sense that the symptoms go away. But it's not curable in the sense that the body is completely rid of the parasite—what doctors call a "sterile cure." Like chicken pox, which can come back years later as shingles, the parasite hides in the body. The point of the treatment is to beat down the parasite enough to allow the body's immune system to take over and keep it in check. Rather than mounting a frontal attack on the body, a Pickett's Charge, the parasite hides and shifts about, sniping from cover. But white blood cells talk to each other using chemicals called cytokines. The cytokines tweak how white blood cells respond to a leishmania attack, eventually "training" them to mount a better defense.

But the mucosal and visceral forms of the disease can come roaring back if your immune system goes downhill. That can happen, for example, if you get HIV or undergo cancer treatment or an organ transplant. In *L. braziliensis*, recurrences of the disease are not uncommon in people with good immune systems. But even in the best-case scenario your body must engage in low-level warfare with the parasite for the rest of your life.

While I was in the hospital for my biopsy, I visited Dave, who was recovering from his aborted treatment. He was installed in a large private room with a fine view of rooftops, trees, and lawns. Eager to see him for the first time since we left the jungle, I found him sitting on the side of the bed, dressed in a hospital gown. Even though I knew he'd been through hell, his appearance was a shock: Dave looked shattered, a far cry from the robust, sardonic professional who, festooned with cameras and cracking jokes, had a few months earlier tramped around the jungle in the pouring rain shoving lenses in our faces. But he managed to greet me with a wan smile and a sweaty handshake, not rising from the bed, and told me what had happened.

Because amphotericin damages the kidneys, before starting him on the drug, Nash and his team had analyzed Dave's kidney (renal) function and decided it was not as strong as they would like. They checked him into the hospital for the duration of the treatment so that his renal function could be closely watched. There is a substance in the blood called creatinine, a waste product of muscle use, which the kidneys filter out at a regular rate. When creatinine levels rise, it means the kidneys are not functioning properly. By checking creatinine levels daily, the doctors at NIH can monitor how much kidney damage is taking place. In the early stages such damage is almost always reversible.

Dave then described what it was like to get the drug, which echoed many of Nash's warnings. The total process, he said, took seven to eight hours. After the nurses settled him comfortably into a lounge chair and attached an IV, they conducted a battery of blood tests to make sure his numbers were good. Then they ran a liter of saline solution into his body, diluting his blood so that the kidneys would be able to flush the drug through quickly.

The saline drip took an hour, followed by a fifteen-minute infusion of Benadryl, to tamp down any allergic reaction he might have to the amphotericin. Meanwhile, the nurses hung an evil-looking opaque brown bag, which contained the liposomal amphotericin.

When all is ready, Dave said, they turn a valve that starts the amphotericin. The liquid is expected to spend three or four hours creeping out of the bag and into the patient's arm.

"So what happened when you got the drug?" I asked.

"I watched that limoncello-colored solution come down through the tubes and go into me," Dave said.

"And within seconds—*seconds!*—of it entering my veins, I felt a big pressure on my chest and a pain in my back. I felt this profound tightness in my chest, with really difficult breathing, and my head felt like it was in flames."

Dr. Nash had immediately stopped the flow of the drug. These were, in fact, common side effects of starting the infusion, caused not by the amphotericin itself but by the tiny lipid droplets that, for mysterious reasons, sometimes fool the body into thinking a gigantic foreign cellular invasion is taking place. The symptoms usually go away fairly quickly.

In Dave's case, the doctors let him recuperate for a few hours, and then they pumped him full of more antihistamines and started him on the amphotericin again, at a slower rate. This time he made it through. They gave him a second infusion the following day. But late that evening, Dr. Nash came in with bad news: "You flunked amphotericin." Dave's creatinine levels had soared; his kidneys had taken a serious hit. The doctors had decided to halt the treatment for good.

They were going to keep him there, he said, for the rest of the week, monitoring his renal function to make sure he was properly recovering.

"So what now?" I asked. "How are you going to get cured?"

He shook his head. "Fuck if I know." He said the doctors were going to wait and see if the two doses had knocked out the leish, which was possible but unlikely. It was a slow-acting disease and there was no need to rush into another potentially toxic treatment. In the meantime, the NIH would try to get the newer drug, miltefosine, for him. A course of miltefosine can cost close to twenty thousand dollars, compared to around six or eight thousand for ampho B. Even though miltefosine was unavailable in the States, Dr. Nash was going to see if it could be brought in under a special permit as an experimental treatment.

I had been listening to all this with rising dismay, realizing that I had no alternative but to take the same journey myself. My own treatment was scheduled for the end of the month.

## CHAPTER 25

**They try to have tea with your immune system.**

O n June 22 I returned to the National Institutes of Health. In the interim, Chris Fisher had also been through the treatment, while most of the others were scheduled after me. His initial reaction to the drug had been as bad as Dave's—sudden pain, a feeling of pressure and suffocation, and a panicked feeling that he might be dying. But luckily those side effects went away in less than ten minutes. Chris's body had tolerated the amphotericin better than Dave's, and he managed to get the full, seven-day course. Even so, he had a rough time. The treatment left him feeling nauseated, exhausted, beaten up, and "totally without ambition." After he returned to Colorado he got a rash on his body so terrible that the NIH doctors wanted to hospitalize him (he refused). He was sick all summer and unable to work into the fall semester, which caused him professional difficulties with his university department. The leish ulcer then started to come back, and only went away after Chris applied heat treatments to it. Over a year later, Chris's rash still hadn't completely healed.

Dave's and Chris's experiences were in the forefront of my thoughts as I filled out the usual paperwork at the NIH. My wife, Christine, had come with me, and we were escorted into one of the hospital rooms used for infusions. It was a very pleasant space, although the furniture was bizarrely oversized. I felt like I'd landed in Swift's imaginary kingdom of Brobdingnag. The nurse explained that the NIH was researching morbid obesity, and we were in one of the rooms specially built for those patients.

I took my seat in the infusion chair, stressed and anxious. Since the infusions took a total of six to eight hours a day for seven days, I had brought a backpack stuffed with twenty pounds of my favorite comfort books, far more than I could ever read—Edgar Allan Poe, Arthur Conan Doyle, Wilkie Collins. I imagined being trapped for hours with a terrifying Nurse Ratched hovering about. But a perverse part of me was also curious about the effects of the drug. What would it be like to believe I was dying? Maybe I'd see the face of God, or the light at the end of the tunnel, or the Flying Spaghetti Monster.

An agreeable, totally un-Ratched nurse arrived, inserted the IV, and drew blood; then she started me on the saline drip. My actual ulcer would not be messed with, although they would examine it every day to see if it began to heal.

The bloodwork came back an hour later and all was good: I had strong kidney function. With both Drs. Nash and O'Connell in watchful attendance, the evil brown bag of amphotericin B was hung on the IV rack next to a bag of Benadryl. Fifteen minutes of a Benadryl infusion left me feeling groggy, and then the stopcock was turned and the ampho started down the tubes.

Dave, our honorary Italian, had compared it to limoncello. To me it looked like the color of urine. Watching it creep down the tube toward my vein only raised my anxiety levels, so I forced myself to avert my eyes. I chatted with the doctors and my wife, pretending nothing was happening, but all the while bracing myself for the sudden pain, the pressure, my head erupting in flames, God, or Baal. I could see my two doctors were also chatting about nothing with excessive cheer, trying to cover up their own nervousness.

The yellow liquid went in and then—nothing happened. I experienced none of the side effects that Dave and Chris did. It was a total anticlimax. Everyone was relieved, but I was also slightly disappointed.

From there, my treatment proceeded uneventfully. I arrived at the clinical center every morning around eight, got stuck with an IV, was subjected to a battery of blood tests, and then infused. After the third day, I asked my doctors to stop the Benadryl (aimed at blocking an allergic reaction to the drug) because it made me sleepy. They did so with no problems. After a few days the inevitable nasty side effects of the ampho did begin to creep in: I got a persistent headache and started to feel nauseated. Beyond that, I had a vague mental uneasiness that something was going badly wrong inside me, but I couldn't put my finger on what. The side effects worsened until the sixth day, when I felt I was dragging around the world's worst hangover—headache, nausea, lethargy, and muddled thinking. Toward the end of my treatment, Mark Adams, the sound engineer, started his. Mark had been on both expeditions, the 2012 lidar search and the 2015 jungle foray. He had been one of my favorite people, soft-spoken and cheerful even while hauling forty pounds of sound equipment and a long boom mic through dense jungle in the pouring rain. We asked to be together in the same room, where we passed the time chatting and reminiscing about our adventures. Mark also tolerated the ampho well, experiencing none of the scary side effects.

Awful as I felt, the nausea and apathy were among

the most common and mildest side effects of ampho-tericin. I was extremely lucky. My doctors gave me anti-nausea drugs, ibuprofen, and a vile-tasting drink to restore my electrolyte balance. But on the sixth day, Nash and O'Connell told me my kidney function had dropped into the danger zone and they were going to discontinue the infusions. They wanted me to wait and have the final infusion after my kidneys had recovered. I received that infusion a few weeks later, closer to home, arranged by the NIH and my brother David, who is a doctor.

The hangover went away after about a week of the initial round, and in the following months the lesion dried up, flattened out, and turned into a shiny scar. At one point I asked Dr. Nash about the risks of going back into the jungle, which, despite everything, part of me remained eager to do if I could. He said that research indicated that 75 to 85 percent of people who got leish were thereafter immune; he felt I should be much more concerned about other diseases rife in the area for which there are no preventatives—dengue fever, chikungunya, and Chagas' disease. (At this point Zika had not yet arrived in Honduras.)

I returned to the NIH three months later, in September 2015, for a follow-up. Nash and O'Connell looked me over, poked at the scar, took some blood, and concluded that the disease had been drubbed into remission. I was cured, at least as far as was possible. While neither doctor could talk about the other members of the expedition due to medical confidentially, I did learn that I was one of the lucky ones, and that some of my fellow travelers (who have asked me not to identify them) have not been cured and require additional courses of treatment using miltefosine or other drugs. Some are still struggling with the disease. (Unfortunately, at the time of this writing, my own leish appears to be returning, although I haven't told my doctors yet.)

Meanwhile, I had become curious about the NIH's leishmania research, said to be the most advanced in the world. I wondered what their scientists had learned, if anything, from studying our particular parasite. So I took the opportunity to pay a visit to the leishmania laboratory on the campus, where researchers maintain a live colony of infected sand flies and mice. It is one of the few laboratories in the world breeding and raising infected sand flies—a tricky and dangerous business.

The leish lab is officially called the Intracellular Parasite Biology Section. It keeps a biological archive of live leishmania parasites of many different strains and species, some going back decades. The parasites are cultivated from biopsied tissue samples taken from people like me. These bits of tissue are placed on a blood agar plate, where the parasites are teased into multiplying. Then they are transferred into bottles filled with a liquid nourishing medium and stored at seventy-seven degrees, the body temperature of the sand fly. In the bottles, the parasites go about their business, fooled into thinking they are swimming around inside the gut of a host fly.

The sand fly has a much lower body temperature than human beings. Cutaneous and mucosal leish parasites do not like the higher heat of the human body; that is why they normally remain on the skin or seek out the mouth and nasal membranes, where the body temperature is a few degrees lower. (This is not true of visceral leish, which tolerates heat and goes deep into the body.)

Every strain in this library of parasites must be regularly recycled through mice to keep up its virulence. Otherwise it becomes "old," weak, and useless for study. The protocols for animal research try as much as possible to avoid inhumane treatment; the suffering of the mice involved in the research, while mitigated as much as possible, is necessary in order to study and combat the disease. There are no alternatives to live research.

The sand flies and mice are kept in a biosafety level 2 lab. BSL-2 is for biological agents of "moderate potential hazard." (There are four biosafety levels, BSL-1 to BSL-4.) I arrived at the lab during mealtime for the sand flies. A lab assistant brought me into the BSL-2 lab, which was a small room with a sealed door, a biohazard warning sign pasted on it. Below the symbol, taped to the door, was a soiled piece of paper with a giant picture of a sand fly and the name PHIL'S PHLY PHARM written underneath. Phil, I learned, was a scientist, long gone, who had helped develop the sand-fly feeding techniques.

No biohazard suit was necessary. I entered with some trepidation, glancing around nervously for loose flies, but they were safely shut away in stainless-steel, climate-controlled lockers. However, outside the lockers, a clear plastic box sat on a lab table, and inside was an off-putting sight: two anesthetized mice lying belly up, paws in the air, twitching. They were completely covered with feeding sand flies, whose tiny guts were expanding into bright red berries of blood. I shuddered, thinking of lying in my own tent, belly up and asleep, while the sand flies sucked my blood. These particular sand flies had not yet been infected with leish; once infected, they are handled more cautiously, not only because they can transmit disease but because they have become more valuable to science.

Later, these sand flies would be infected artificially,

a complicated process. A delicate, hand-blown, tiny glass bottle has a piece of raw chicken skin stretched over it like a drumhead. This skin is moistened with mouse blood to fool the flies into thinking it is mammalian skin. The liquid inside the bottle is also mouse blood, seeded with the parasite. The sand fly jabs its proboscis through the chicken skin into the bottle and sucks up the blood and parasites. Once a sand fly is infected, the lab workers must then coax it into biting a live mouse, to transfer the infection. The target mouse is put in a tight Plexiglas box and its ear is held in a clamp attached to a small vial containing the infected flies. The hungry females fly down a tube, land on the mouse's ear, and suck blood, transmitting the parasites to the mouse.

At the end of my tour, a lab assistant brought out two bottles of live leishmania parasites for me to look at under the microscope. They were living in a cloudy, reddish-orange nutrient broth. I peered into one of the bottles with a binocular microscope. As I focused the eyepieces, the parasites sprang into view, thousands of them in ceaseless motion, bumping into each other and going this way and that. They had elongated, pointy-headed bodies and whiplike flagellae, which are on the front of the cell and draw it forward instead of pushing it along from behind. For a while I watched the wriggling little buggers go about their business, thinking of the havoc they had wreaked on us.

The lab's chief is Dr. David Sacks, a lean, handsome, plain-talking scientist who occupies a cluttered office in the basement. "These flies are just *desperate* for blood," he told me. "They're seeking any source and you folks just happened to be in the right place at the right time."

Why, I asked, didn't we all get sick? Why only half of us?

"I think *all* of you were bitten and infected," he said. "I wouldn't be surprised if a hundred percent of you were exposed, given the frequency of bites you seem to have had. So it's actually more interesting why some of you *didn't* develop lesions."

He explained that one of medicine's greatest mysteries is why some people get sick and others do not, given the same exposure. Environment and nutrition play a role in infection, but genetics are paramount. This is the very question at the heart of why so many New World people died of Old World disease. What was the actual genetic machinery that made some more susceptible than others?

With gene sequencing, Sacks said, we finally have the tools to figure out why some people are more vulnerable than others. Scientists are sequencing people's entire genomes and comparing them, one against the other, to see what genetic differences pop out between those who, exposed to an infection, got sick and those who didn't. We finally have the tools to understand the biology behind the great die-off and how such pandemics might be prevented in the future, but the research is still in its infancy.

During our exchange, when I made an offhand comment about how disgusting the flies were, he chided me: "Of course *we* don't think they are disgusting at all. We love our flies."

The leish lab, Sacks said, has been working for years on charting every stage in the life cycle of leishmania, looking for chinks in its armor that could be exploited by a vaccine. It's harder to design a vaccine against a protozoan than against a simpler virus or bacterium; in fact, not one major parasitic disease has a reliable vaccine yet. Leish is very sophisticated in how it infects the body. It is, as one parasitologist said, "the royalty of the disease world." Instead of wreaking carnage like many viral and bacterial diseases, and thus triggering a massive immune response, the parasites "try to have tea with your immune system." Sacks and his team have identified the essential proteins the parasite uses during its life cycle inside the sand fly—and they've created mutant forms of those proteins that might block development. But figuring out how to exploit those vulnerabilities is hard, and getting from there to a vaccine is even harder.

As is too often true, the biggest hurdle is money. Vaccines cost hundreds of millions of dollars to develop, test, and bring to market. Human trials involve thousands of subjects. "It's difficult to get companies to partner in trials," Sacks told me. "They don't see any market in it, because the people who have leishmaniasis have no money."

Over the past decade the World Health Organization sponsored a series of clinical trials to test a simple leish vaccine, in which parasites were heat-killed and injected into people. Doctors hoped the dead parasites would prime the immune system to attack live parasites when they arrived. The trials failed, but it is unclear why. Other possible vaccines are in the early stages of testing.

One of the biggest discoveries Sacks and his team made was that the leish parasites have sex inside the sand fly. Previously it was thought the parasite could only reproduce by division—clonal reproduction. By having sex they can recombine their genes. This gives them a way to hybridize and adapt. It explains why there are dozens of leish species and why, even within a species, there are so many different strains. The ability to have sex gives leishmania a tremendous evolutionary advantage. It is the main reason it has thrived and spread for a hundred million years, infecting dinosaurs and people, becoming one of the most successful diseases (from its own point of view) in the world.

With leishmaniasis so prevalent in the valley of T1, I wondered how ancient people might have coped with the disease. Could they have controlled it by clearing vegetation or killing the animals that acted as hosts? I posed the questions to Sacks. He pointed out it would have been difficult for the people of T1 to identify the sand fly as the vector and certainly impossible for them to know a host animal was necessary; assailed daily by biting insects, they probably would not have made the link between a sand fly bite and a lesion that developed weeks later. (The link between mosquitoes and malaria, for example, wasn't made until 1897. Previously, malaria was thought to be caused by the "bad air" of nighttime—which is what *mal aria* means in Italian.)

Nor could leishmaniasis have been a reason for the abandonment of T1, since the disease in pre-Columbian times was too widespread; there was nowhere the people of T1 could escape to. They would have lived with the disease, just as hundreds of millions do today.

When our team members were diagnosed, biopsies

were taken from our lesions and sent to another lab at NIH, called the Molecular Parasitology Section, where the lab's director, Michael Grigg, had originally identified the parasite as *L. braziliensis* by sequencing part of its genome. I called up Grigg to find out if he had found out anything unusual.

"The type of leish you have was very hard to grow," he recalled. In fact, like some difficult strains, it wouldn't grow at all. He smeared tissue samples from our biopsies on blood agar plates, but the parasites refused to multiply. Because of that, his lab wasn't able to tease enough parasites clear of human tissue to sequence the entire genome at the time—there was too much human DNA mucking up the works.

Instead, he explained, they initially sequenced one gene or marker: a characteristic one that reveals the species. That marker matched *braziliensis*. But later, Grigg sequenced five markers—which he described as "five little windows into the parasite." He got a big surprise. In two "windows" he found genetic sequences different from any known species of leish. In another window, he found that the DNA resembled another species called *L. panamensis*, an equally bad mucosal strain. But that gene also had a couple of mutations.

Our parasite, he said, might have been a hybrid between *panamensis* and *braziliensis*, in which the two species mingled in a sand fly gut, mated, and produced hybrid offspring. That hybrid was then isolated and began to evolve into a new strain or possibly even a new species. There were enough mutations, called "snips," at the five sites to indicate that this particular species had been isolated for a period of time.

How long? I asked.

"That's a tough one. There are not a lot of snips, so I'd say it's been hundreds of years, not thousands or tens of thousands."

I had a sudden idea. I explained to Grigg that the valley had once been the site of a bustling city with active trade networks. But about five hundred years ago, the city had been abandoned and the valley suddenly cut off from the rest of the world, with people no longer coming and going to spread the disease. Could that abandonment be the moment when the parasite was isolated? And if so, could the parasite's molecular clock be used to date the time of abandonment?

He thought about it and declared it a reasonable hypothesis. "When you get rates of change of one or two snips, we're looking at an isolate of hundreds of years. It's relatively recent. It's consistent with your theory."

All species have what is known as a molecular clock. This clock measures how fast random mutations accumulate over the generations. Some species, like cold viruses, have fast clocks, while some, like humans, have slow. By counting the number of mutations, the molecular clock will tell how long that species has been isolated. It's like the game of telephone; you can tell how far you are from the original message by hearing how garbled it has become.

Later I sketched out to Sacks the same idea about dating the death of T1 by using the parasite's molecular clock.

"That would make sense to me," he said. "These phylogenetic trees are published, so when you find a new species you stick it on that tree to find the genetic distance." And that would give you the time period of isolation.

If true, this might be the first instance in which an archaeological site could be dated by molecular clock; our disease might actually hold clues to the fate of T1. The research, however, has yet to be done.

## CHAPTER 26

## La Ciudad del Jaguar

After our expedition departed the valley of T1 in February 2015, the ruins lay undisturbed for almost a year. A rotating contingent of Honduran soldiers remained in our old campsite, guarding the city. Within weeks, soldiers began coming down with leishmaniasis, something that the Honduran military had not experienced elsewhere in the country. The military considered pulling them out, but in the end it dealt with the problem by rotating the soldiers frequently in hopes that would minimize exposure. The soldiers cleared the brush and vegetation in the camp area, leaving only the trees, in an effort to reduce the habitat for sand flies. To make the rotations simpler and quicker, the military built a barracks at the Aguacate airstrip.

The excavation of the artifact cache at T1 became

a priority. Even Chris understood that leaving every-thing in the ground was not a long-term option. With archaeological looting a widespread problem in Hon-duras, and the cache worth millions of dollars, it would have to be guarded indefinitely by the military. That was not realistic, given the expense, the frequent changes in government, and the raging leishmaniasis that made a permanent human presence in the valley problematic.

At the same time he fought his grueling battle with leish, Chris prepared a plan of work and began assem-bling an expert team of archaeologists and technicians to excavate the cache. The idea wasn't to remove the entire offering, but only to take out artifacts that were sticking out of the ground and in danger of being dis-turbed. He planned to leave the rest of the site covered and hidden so the material remaining underground would be safe. He hoped a partial excavation would help us begin to understand the meaning of the cache and any answers it held to the many mysteries sur-rounding this culture. (Later, Honduran archaeolo-gists continued the excavation and have at the time of writing recovered over five hundred artifacts.)

The academic controversy about the expedition did not die down, as many on the team had hoped it would. Many months after the 2015 expedition, Juan Carlos gave a talk in Tegucigalpa about the expedition's lidar work, and a group of protestors showed up to heckle. Their leader, Gloria Lara Pinto, a professor at Universidad Pedagógica Nacional Francisco Morazán in Tegucigalpa, arrived late. She stood up during the question-and-answer period and challenged Juan Carlos, saying that he was not an archaeologist and had no business passing himself off as one, and that his talk (which was for a general audience) lacked scientific rigor. Juan Carlos pointed out that he had made precisely those disclaimers at the beginning of his lecture and that it was a shame she had arrived late and missed them. "I acknowledged," he told me later, "that I was not an archaeologist or an anthropologist, but as a Honduran I do have the right and the obligation to understand more of my country's geography and history, and as a PhD researcher I do have the basic tools to do historical research." After his response, he said, the audience booed Professor Pinto and her group of hecklers.

The cost of the return trip and the excavation amounted to almost a million dollars, much of it again due to the expense of operating helicopters. With Chris's help, Steve Elkins and Bill Benenson worked to raise the funds, receiving contributions from the Honduran government and the National Geographic Society. *National Geographic* magazine once again hired me to cover the team's work. I was apprehensive about going back but intensely curious to see what was in the cache. Wisely or not, I was no longer worried about leish: I was, in fact, far more concerned about poisonous snakes and dengue fever. The size, power, and lethality of that first fer-de-lance we encountered had been an experience I would never forget. Instead of reusing my old Kevlar snake gaiters, I went online and bought a $200 pair of snake guards said to be the finest made. The manufacturer had posted a video of the snake guards repelling repeated strikes from a big diamondback rattler. I called and asked if they'd ever tested them against a fer-de-lance, and I was told they had not, nor would they guarantee them against that kind of snake. I bought them anyway.

I also had a plan about dengue: I would spray my clothes with DEET inside and out, strip twice a day and cover myself with DEET, and I would take refuge in my tent at sunset, before the mosquitoes came out, and not emerge until after sunrise.

In early January 2016, Chris Fisher and his team of archaeologists, Honduran and American, arrived at the site, set up a base camp, and flew in their supplies. They were working with the latest high-tech archaeological equipment, including tablet computers reinforced and cased to withstand the rigors of the jungle, state-of-the-art GPS units, and a portable lidar machine operated by Juan Carlos. Remarkably, neither

Juan Carlos nor anyone else who had been struck by disease on the original expedition was deterred from coming back, except Oscar Neil, who (for understandable reasons) informed the IHAH that he would not set foot in the jungle again.

Within a week, Fisher and his team were ready to begin work at the cache. Breaking ground in the lost city generated much excitement in the Honduran press, although so far, the location had successfully remained under wraps—a surprise, given how many people now knew about it. President Hernández announced to the country that he, personally, would fly in to the site to remove the first two artifacts and carry them to the new laboratory being built at the Aguacate airstrip. Aside from taking a deep personal interest in the project, the president wanted to put out some good news for the country.

As was perhaps to be expected, the flurry of news stories about the excavation revived the academic quarrel and also inflamed a segment of Honduras's indigenous community. The project's critics once again took to the blogs and complained to the press. The former head of the IHAH, Dario Euraque, told the website *Vice.com* that the archaeologists were taking credit for a discovery that was "not theirs" and that they had offended indigenous groups by engaging in "racist dialogue." He said that the publicity had left the ruins open to looting and that he was very sad to see Honduras turned "into a reality show." Some archaeologists and others accused President Hernández of exploiting the find to distract public attention from corruption, human rights abuses, and the murder of environmental activists. They condemned the expedition for cooperating with such a government.*

On January 13, a group of indigenous Honduran leaders, *los hijos de la Muskitia* or the Children of Mosquitia, wrote an open letter criticizing the government and claiming the excavation of T1 violated Indian treaties. The communiqué had a long list of demands, and it objected to the use of the term "Monkey God," which the writers considered "denigrating, discriminatory, and racist." The letter concluded, "We, the sons of the Indigenous Miskitu Community…demand the immediate return of all artifacts looted from our

---

* Corruption is a serious issue, and clearly there is an acute problem of human rights abuses in Honduras. While it is well beyond the scope of this book to investigate Honduran corruption, personally I saw no direct evidence of it in my own limited experience related to the current Hernández administration, nor in the military or at the IHAH. It must be said that, in general, if archaeologists refused on principle to work with governments known for corruption, most archaeology in the world would come to a halt; there could be no more archaeology in China, Russia, Egypt, Mexico, most of the Middle East, and many countries in Central and South America, Africa, and Southeast Asia. I present this not as a justification or an apology, but as an observation on the reality of doing archaeology in a difficult world.

sacred site called the White City." The letter included a map of Miskito territory that seemed to swallow the traditional lands of other indigenous Indian communities, such as the Pech and Tawahka, who are believed to be the actual descendants of the ancient people of Mosquitia. The issue of indigenous rights in Honduras is not simple; Honduras is a robust mestizo society in which most citizens, rich and poor, have a large proportion of Indian ancestry. The Miskito people are themselves of mixed Indian, African, Spanish, and English ancestry with roots not in the interior mountains where T1 is located, but along the coast.

When I asked Virgilio about the letter, he said the government was well aware of it, had long been expecting it, and would handle it. (As far as I could ascertain, the government handled it by ignoring it.)

John Hoopes organized a talk at his university on what he called "lost city hucksterism" entitled "The Lost City That Isn't." When I asked him what the talk would cover, he explained to me the discussion would be mostly aimed at helping students "think about how 'hot' issues such as those of colonialism, white supremacy, hypermasculinity, fantasy and imagination, [and] indigenous rights...intersect with the narratives that have been and are being spun about the White City."

In mid-January I flew to Tegucigalpa to reenter the jungle and report on the excavation for *National*

*Geographic.* I was curious to see how the president, his entourage, and the press were going to manage the snake- and disease-infested jungle. I also found myself stewing over the thought that the breathtaking perfection of the rainforest might have been ruined and the area degraded by human occupation, in which I had played a role.

My return trip to T1 began the morning of January 11, 2016, when a driver met me before dawn in Tegucigalpa for the long, overland trip to the airstrip, where an 8:00 a.m. military flight would take me into the valley. Virgilio had warned me to pack everything required for an overnight stay in the valley, including food and water, because helicopter transportation was uncertain and I would probably have to spend at least one night out there, maybe more. I tossed my over-stuffed backpack into the back of the old pickup truck with a cracked windshield and government logos emblazoned on the side. We took off at high speed, the truck zooming through the deserted, postapocalyptic streets of the capital. We were soon out of the city and roaring up and down dizzying mountain roads. An hour later, high in the mountains, we were enveloped in a dense fog. The yellow lights of the oncoming cars and trucks loomed ominously, flaring up like fireworks, and then thundered past, the tail-lights winking out in the inky dark. As the light of dawn crept up, tatters of fog clung to the hillsides and filled the lowlands with mist. The Honduran interior is spectacularly beautiful and rugged, one mountain chain after the other, separated by deep green valleys. As we went up and down, the enchanted names of the villages flashed past—El Mago, Guaimaca, Campamento, Lepaguare, Las Joyas. They were the same towns we had passed a year before, but this time, shrouded in early morning mist, they looked otherworldly and aroused in me a sense of the inscrutability and "cognitive dissonance" of Honduras today.

We arrived at the Aguacate airstrip well in time for the flight, which was delayed by many hours. I was surprised to see how quickly the shabby terminal building had been smartly renovated into an archaeological laboratory. Next to that stood a brand-new military barracks, pale yellow cinder blocks with a corrugated tin roof—quarters for the soldiers rotating in and out of the site.

The Honduran helicopter, an olive-green Bell UH-1, was waiting on the tarmac. We eventually took off and an hour later we cleared the notch, the magical vale of T1 once more unrolling before us, stippled in sunlight. But as we slowed into a hover above the camp, my fears seemed confirmed: From the air the area along the river was unrecognizable. A new and bigger landing zone had been hacked out of the dense vegetation on the opposite side of the river, with a dirt landing pad marked with a giant red X in plastic strips.

We landed and I hopped out with my backpack, the chopper soon thundering back into the sky. Everything was different. I picked my way across withered heaps of macheted vegetation and crossed the river on a set of single logs laid in a zigzag fashion. A massive flood had scoured the valley after the 2015 expedition, washing away the old landing zone and turning it into a rocky island in the middle of the river. The flood had also changed the river's course, carving a new channel closer to the embankment that led up to the camp. Luckily, the archaeological site, situated on the high terraces above the floodplain, had not been affected.

When I climbed the embankment, I was again shocked at the change to our former campsite. All the ground vegetation and small trees had been chopped down and cleared, leaving just the larger trees. It was sunny, open, hot, and trampled. The ineffable mystery of being immersed in the living, breathing rainforest was gone; the area felt shrunken and bedraggled. A year of continuous occupation had taken its toll. No longer were there individual tents and hammocks tucked here and there among the great gloomy trees, each camp hidden in its own glade. Instead, a tent city had been erected. The encampment of the Honduran soldiers stood naked and exposed in the hot sun, a series of green canvas huts and blue tarps erected on wooden poles, wreathed in the smoke of cooking fires. It was safer from snakes, but far less evocative. Walkways of cut bamboo and wooden pallets were laid over the muddy ground, and a generator blatted away. I felt distressed even as I understood these were unavoidable changes, the inevitable result of our expedition's exploration of the valley. Even the sounds of the jungle were different; the cries and calls were more distant, the wildlife having retreated into the forest.

But at the edge of the clearing, I was happy to see the virgin wall of jungle still rising up on all sides, dark, unfathomable, muttering with animal sounds. Our camp was still but a tiny puncture wound in the great wilderness. As I entered the camp, I greeted Spud, who was in the kitchen area making coffee. He was the logistics manager of this expedition, as Woody and Sully were off on other projects. Major improvements had been made; the sea of sucking mud that almost drowned us last time was now being dealt with by elevated pathways and decking made of wooden pallets topped with heavy rubber matting.

I tried to pitch my tent as far away from the tent city as possible, but as I scouted out an area at the edge of the clearing a polite young soldier on patrol stopped me and ushered me back with gestures. "No, no, señor," he said. "*Serpientes para allá*. Snakes over there."

Disgruntled, I set up my tent in an open spot in the midst of the tent city. I crawled inside, stripped, and smeared myself with 100 percent DEET for the second time that day. I sprayed my clothes and put them back on, the choking stench of bug spray filling the inside of the tent. I then grabbed my notebook and camera and hiked up to the lost city. A good trail had been cleared to it—no need for a machete-wielding escort and no possibility of getting lost. The day was lovely, the sky full of drifting cumulus.

I crossed the river via another single-log bridge and followed the trail. When I came to the steep slope below the pyramid, I found a gang of soldiers cutting a staircase in the earth, which they were shoring up with stakes and logs, for the president's visit. A nylon rope served as a handrail. As I climbed the stairs and reached the base of the pyramid, the trail narrowed and once again I was back in mostly intact jungle, thankful to see it the same, except for a sign that read, in Spanish, NO SMOKING FROM HERE ON.

The site of the cache was mostly unchanged. Only a minimal amount of clearing had been done, just enough to give Anna, Chris, and the other archaeologists elbow room. Chris had taken the greatest care to keep it as undisturbed as possible.

I greeted Chris and Anna, who were working on a single square meter of ground, which held the artifacts the president would remove the next day. Anna was carefully brushing earth off a spectacular ritual vessel carved with vulture heads. I met the new archaeologists working on the site, both Honduran and North American.

The cache area had been cordoned off with yellow tape and gridded with string into one-meter-square units. In the few days since work had commenced, three of those squares had been opened up. Two were densely packed with breathtaking artifacts. A third square had been cut into the ground off to one side, beyond the cache, to determine the natural stratigraphy of the site—how the layers of earth were laid down without artifacts—as a control.

I was happy to see Dave Yoder, once again festooned with camera equipment, taking photos. He was covering the excavation for *National Geographic*, and he looked vastly better than the last time I saw him. I asked Dave about his leish. The good news was that, even with only two infusions, his disease had healed quickly and there had been no need for additional treatment. But his recovery from the drug ordeal had been agonizing. "I felt exhausted and tired for months afterward," he told me. "I'm not sure I've really recovered yet, to be honest."

How did he feel about going back to the jungle? Was he worried about his safety?

"I'm a photographer," he said with a snort. "I don't come to places like this to be *safe*." And he wasn't safe: Later in the month on that assignment, Dave had several close calls. One night, on his way to the latrine, he ran into what he described as a "totally pissed-off" four-foot coral snake crawling down a bamboo stalk. It reached the ground and headed straight into camp, even as Dave tried flashing it with his headlamp and stomping on the ground to scare it off. The Honduran soldiers ran a "snake patrol" at night, and they arrived just in time to chop the snake up with a machete. ("I felt bad about it, but it's the middle of the night, you can't transport it, what do you do?" He added drily, "At least it saved the lives of countless rodents.")

Later that month, Dave and Spud, along with several of the archaeologists, were almost killed in a helicopter accident. They were flying out of the valley in the same chopper that had flown me in, an old Bell Huey gunship that had seen action in Vietnam and still had .50-caliber machine-gun door mounts. The door was open, a common practice so Dave could shoot photos unimpeded. But when Dave finished photographing and someone went to slide the door shut, it was sucked clear off the side of the helicopter. On its tumbling fall to the jungle it gouged holes in the fuselage and barely missed the tail rotor and stabilizing fins. If it had nicked either, there would have been eight body bags coming out of T1. Chris had been fanatical about trying to minimize the risk to his team, and he was extremely upset when he heard about the close call. The cause of the accident, I found out later, was that the doors on this kind of Bell Huey have to be shut in a specific way during flight to avoid creating a differential air pressure strong enough to blow a door off its hinges.

While Dave light-painted and photographed the artifacts, one of his assistants filmed the site from above using a drone, which buzzed about the jungle like some giant Cretaceous insect. Chris paced about the site, giving instructions on locking it down to protect it during the president's visit the next day. The work involved shoring up the edges of the excavation pit with pieces of plywood to reinforce them against trampling feet, as well as stringing police tape in an effort at crowd control. He did not want people walking among the artifacts. Chris had carefully choreographed the visit and had a clipboard with a list of the select few who would be allowed inside the yellow tape for the photo op.

He was not in a good mood. He had not been happy to learn that a curious soldier the previous month had innocently dug up a couple of artifacts, including the famous jaguar head, to see what they looked like underneath. (No looting, however, had taken place, contrary to Sully's prediction.) A perfectionist obsessed with his work, he did not welcome the potential threat to the integrity of the site even by the president of the country. On top of that, he was worried about his looming deadline. It was now clear to him that it would be impossible to finish excavating, stabilizing, and conserving the artifacts by February 1, when his grant ran out and he had to return to the States to resume teaching. The cache was huge—much bigger than could be seen on the surface.

On a professional level he was also distressed by a lack of support from his university. His participation in the identification and excavation of T1 had garnered significant media attention for Colorado State, with Chris being featured in both the *New Yorker* and *National Geographic* and highlighted in the CSU alumni magazine. His work at Angamuco was also well known and respected. For the 2015 expedition the university required Chris to "buy out one of his classes"—that is, he had to come up with the money himself to hire an adjunct to teach his classes while he was away in Honduras, with the other class being taught on an accelerated schedule. Steve Elkins had given the university an eight-thousand-dollar gift out of his own pocket to help make it possible.

During the 2016 excavation, the department required Chris to teach the first two weeks of his classes online—from the jungle—which often meant flying in a helicopter to Catacamas, where there was an Internet connection. The department chair asked him to confine his field research from then on to the summer months, when there are no classes. The summer, however, is the rainy season in Honduras and in Mexico, a period when it is difficult to do archaeological excavation.

Despite these frustrations, the difficulties of being an impecunious and underappreciated archaeologist were, for a long time, more than compensated by the chance to participate in a remarkable, once-in-a-lifetime discovery. From the beginning, Chris had been a driving force of energy and enthusiasm on the team, a devoted professional so eager to explore this untouched landscape that on our first trip into the ruins he had forged ahead, leaving me and Woody in the dust, snakes and jungle dangers be damned. Yet as reckless as he was with his own safety, he was fiercely protective of his team. When the near-miss helicopter accident that threatened his archaeologists was followed by several cases of leish after this second trip to the jungle, Chris concluded it was simply too dangerous to send any more people into T1. "The takeaway from this," he said, "is very clear—the risk of working at the site is simply too great." After this second month at the site, he would direct no more archaeology at T1.

As the group worked the site, my gaze drifted toward the earthen pyramid, whose jungled form loomed above the cache site. Three monstrous trees grew in a cluster just above the cache, and beyond that the actual form of the pyramid vanished in a mass of vegetation. I wondered if the pyramid remained the same. Past the worksite, I climbed past the great trees and soon found myself in the emerald twilight of virgin rainforest. I was glad to see it had remained untouched since the year before. At the top of the pyramid I halted, breathing in the fecund smell and trying to connect with the city as it may have been at its apex, before its abrupt and tragic end. The density of vegetation still shut out any hint of the city's layout or size. Even at the summit I was still buried in shaggy giants that towered a hundred feet or more above my head, draped with tree-killer vines and creepers. I could not see the archaeologists working below, but their voices filtered up through the leaves, distorted and unintelligible, sounding like the murmuring of ghosts.

I focused my attention on the ground at the summit. It was exactly as it had been a year ago when we first climbed up. There was one vague, rectangular depression and other lumps that must have been the remains of a small temple or structure. This would be another place to excavate, to try to understand the ancient rituals of this vanished people, but a part of me hoped it wouldn't happen, that this spot might never lose its mystery. I wondered what ceremonies had taken place here. The Maya and other Mesoamerican cultures engaged in human sacrifice, presenting the gods with that most sacred and precious nourishment—human blood. The priest would either decapitate the victim or split the breastbone and yank out the still-beating heart, offering it to the sky. These sacrifices were often conducted at the top of a pyramid in view of all. Did the Mosquitia people also conduct such rites? When the city at T1 was swept by epidemics, and the people felt they had been abandoned by their gods, I wondered what ceremonies they might have performed in a desperate effort to restore the cosmic order. Whatever they did, it failed; feeling cursed and rejected by the gods, they left the city, never to return.

With these sobering thoughts in mind, I descended from the hill and made my way back to camp as the setting sun filled the treetops. After dinner, when it got dark and the bugs came out, I forgot my promise to take refuge in my tent and instead lingered in the kitchen area with Chris, Dave, Anna, Spud, and the rest. We relaxed under the tarp, telling stories, listening to music, and drinking tea by the light of a softly hissing Coleman lantern. There is something irresistible about an evening in camp, when the temperature cools and the soft night air is filled with the sounds of wildlife, while everyone kicks back from the work of the day. Over at the soldiers' camp, a string of Christmas lights lit up and we heard the sounds of an action film echoing from the main tent.

The next morning, I was glad to hear the familiar roar of the howler monkeys at dawn, although they had by now retreated across the river. The morning mist filled the air. The soldiers were back at work, excited and nervous, putting the finishing touches on the staircase for the president's visit later that morning. Their boots were polished, weapons cleaned and oiled, uniforms as neat as possible in the steamy jungle environment.

The mist broke around midmorning and a brief rain fell in the weak sunlight. Then the sound of helicopters filled the air, distant at first, getting louder. Three landed in quick succession, disgorging press and Honduran officials—and Steve Elkins. The brass included the commanding general of the Honduran army; the minister of defense; Ramón Espinoza, the minister of science and technology; and Virgilio. Out of the third helicopter, emblazoned with Honduran flags, stepped the president of the country, Juan Orlando Hernández, accompanied by the American ambassador, James Nealon.

Chris Fisher greeted President Hernández on the landing pad with an urgent gift: a brand-new pair of snake gaiters to put on before he went any farther. We stood by while the president cheerfully wrapped them around his calves, chatting in English with Steve, Chris, and the ambassador. Dressed in a guayabera shirt and a Panama hat, Hernández was not a tall man; he had a friendly, boyish face, and carried himself without any of the stiffness or pomp one might expect from the country's leader. Indeed, I had noticed that when people entered the T1 valley, a place so completely cut off from the world, distinctions and hierarchical divisions seemed to fall away. I found myself, for example, rolling up my sleeve and comparing my leishmaniasis scars with those of Lt. Col. Oseguera.

I followed as the president and his entourage began the hike up to the site, toiling up the earthen staircase and piling into the cache area, hemmed in by jungle. Chris's police tape was soon ignored and everyone crowded into the excavated area, tromping about and posing for photographs. I could see Chris trying to maintain his cool, a nervous smile plastered on his face.

The president was energized. This was more than an official duty. The first object to be removed, the stone vessel with the vulture heads, had been left in situ, on a pedestal of earth—exactly as it had been set in place as an offering five hundred years before. The president knelt next to it, along with Chris Fisher, Steve, Ramón Espinoza, and Virgilio. Steve placed his hand on the jar and said a few words. "It's been a long twenty-three years for this moment—finally! And it will probably be another two hundred years to find what's here." Chris and President Hernández then grasped the lugs on the massive vessel as the cameras flashed, dislodged it from its bed of centuries, and lifted it from the shallow hole.

While the artifacts were being packed for their trip out, I interviewed Hernández, who spoke with enthusiasm about the discovery and what it would mean for Honduras. As a child he had heard legends of Ciudad Blanca and had been moved by the news in 2012, when he was president of the Honduran Congress, that our shot-in-the-dark lidar survey of Mosquitia had turned up not one but two lost cities. "This is an archaeological and historic event," he said. "This culture is fascinating, but we've got a lot to learn, and it's going to take some time." He added, proudly, "We are happy to share this knowledge with the world." I thought about Juan Carlos's observation that Hondurans lacked a strong national identity and a sense of their own history. Perhaps we all shared a hope that this discovery might change that.

When the artifact was packed and ready, the archaeologists and soldiers carried it down the narrow jungle trail, a person at each corner, mimicking the litter technique used by Howard Carter at King Tut's tomb. The two artifacts, the jar and the were-jaguar metate, were stored aboard a helicopter.

Though I had anticipated a slightly longer stay, as I watched these activities I was suddenly told my ticket out of the jungle was the third helicopter, departing within the minute. Once again I had to seize my pack and scramble out of T1 in a hurry, with little time to wax sentimental. Soon we were aloft, sweeping above the treetops, heading for Catacamas. It would be my last visit to the valley.

When we arrived at the airstrip, everything was set up for an important national ceremony. A tent was pitched behind the lab, with chairs, loudspeakers, wide-screen televisions, and food. The informality of the jungle vanished in a sea of military officers, dignitaries, ministers, and press. With pomp and fanfare the crates were taken out of the helicopters and carried down the tarmac, parade-style, between lines of Honduran press and distinguished guests. As a flat-panel screen played a stirring video, Chris and an assistant, wearing latex gloves, unpacked the two artifacts and arranged them in museum cases on the stage, specially built to receive them. The were-jaguar metate sat on one side and the vulture jar on the other. When they were fixed in their cases and the glass tops put back on, the audience applauded the artifacts.

Chris gave a short speech, talking about how important it was to preserve the site and the surrounding rainforest and warning about the grave threat of the encroaching clear-cutting. "For the first time," he told the audience, "we are able to study this culture systematically."

President Hernández then gave a brief but moving speech, and his words took on an almost religious feeling. "God has blessed us to be alive in this moment so special in the history of Honduras," he said, adding that everyone assembled there had "great expectations of what this will mean for Honduras and the world." The discovery of T1, he said, was important beyond the benefit to archaeology. He outlined a vision of what it meant to Hondurans: Not only would it encourage tourism and help train a new generation of Honduran archaeologists; it also spoke to the very identity of the country and its people. Later he would build a special room in the presidential palace to display some of the artifacts.

Honduras is a spectacularly interesting country, whose people have a bifurcating history that goes back to both the Old World and the New. While the Spanish history of Honduras is well known, its pre-Columbian history (beyond Copán) is still an enigma. People need history in order to know themselves, to build a sense of identity and pride, continuity, community, and hope for the future. That is why the legend of the White City runs so deep in the Honduran national psyche: It's a direct connection to a pre-Columbian past that was rich, complex, and worthy of remembrance. Five hundred years ago, the survivors of the catastrophe at T1 who walked out the city did not just disappear. Most of them lived on, and their descendants are still part of the vibrant mestizo culture of Honduras today.

Hernández closed out his speech with one final, dramatic proclamation. The city in T1 would henceforth be given a real name: *La Ciudad del Jaguar*, the City of the Jaguar.

## CHAPTER 27

## We became orphans, oh my sons!

When humans first walked into the Americas over the Bering Land Bridge fifteen to twenty thousand years ago,* our species existed everywhere as small, wandering bands of hunter-gatherers. There were no cities, no towns, no farming or animal husbandry. We were spread out and moving all the time, only rarely encountering other groups. The low population densities prevented most potential diseases from gaining a foothold. People suffered from parasites and infections, but they did not get most of the diseases so familiar in recent human history—measles, chicken pox, colds, the flu, smallpox, tuberculosis, yellow fever, and bubonic plague, to name only a few.

---

* The time frame and migration route of the initial peopling of the Americas are much disputed.

In the last ten thousand years, as human population densities increased, disease moved into center stage of human affairs. Pandemics changed the very arc of human history. Despite our dazzling technology, we are still very much at the mercy of pathogens, old and new.

In his groundbreaking book *Guns, Germs, and Steel*, biologist Jared Diamond poses the question: Why did Old World diseases devastate the New World and not the other way around? Why did disease move in only one direction?* The answer lies in how the lives of Old World and New World people diverged after that cross-continental migration more than fifteen thousand years ago.

Farming, which allowed people to settle into towns and villages, was independently invented in both the Old World and the New. The key difference was in animal husbandry. In the Old World, a great variety of animals were domesticated, starting with cattle about eight to ten thousand years ago and quickly moving on to pigs, chickens, ducks, goats, and sheep. New World farmers domesticated animals as well, notably llamas, guinea pigs, dogs, and turkeys. But in Europe (and Asia and Africa), the raising and breeding of livestock

---

* The one notable exception is syphilis, which Columbus's men likely brought back to the Old World on the first voyage's return.

became a central aspect of life, an essential activity in almost every household. For thousands of years, Europeans lived in close quarters with their livestock and were continuously exposed to their microbes and diseases. In the New World, perhaps because they had more space and fewer domesticated animals, people did not live cheek by fowl with their animals.

Humans do not usually catch infectious diseases from animals; pathogens tend to confine their nasty work to a single species or genus. (Leishmaniasis is a striking exception.) But microbes mutate all the time. Once in a while, an animal pathogen will change in such a way that it suddenly infects a person. When people in the Near East first domesticated cattle from a type of wild ox called an aurochs, a mutation in the cowpox virus allowed it to jump into humans—and smallpox was born. Rinderpest in cattle migrated to people and became measles. Tuberculosis probably originated in cattle, influenza in birds and pigs, whooping cough in pigs or dogs, and malaria in chickens and ducks. The same process goes on today: Ebola probably jumped to humans from bats, while HIV crashed into our species from monkeys and chimpanzees.

Alongside the domestication of animals, humans in the Old World began settling down in villages, towns, and cities. People lived together in much denser numbers than before. Cities, with their bustle, trade, filth, and close quarters, created a marvelous home for pathogens and an ideal staging ground for epidemics. So when diseases migrated from livestock to people, epidemics broke out. Those diseases found plenty of human fuel, racing from town to town and country to country and even crossing the oceans on board ships. Biologists call these "crowd diseases" because that's exactly what they need to propagate and evolve.

Epidemics periodically swept through European settlements, killing the susceptible and sparing the robust, culling the gene pool. As always, children were the majority of the victims. Almost no disease is 100 percent fatal: Some victims always survive. The survivors tended to have genes that helped them resist the disease a little better, and they passed that resistance on to their children. Over thousands of years and countless deaths, people in the Old World gradually built up a genetic resistance to many brutal epidemic diseases.

In the New World, on the other hand, no big-time diseases seem to have leapt from animals into the human population. While the Americas had cities as large as those in Europe, those cities were much newer at the time the Spanish arrived. People in the New World hadn't been living in close quarters long enough for crowd diseases to spring up and propagate. Native

Americans never had the opportunity to develop resistance to the myriad diseases that plagued Europeans.

This genetic resistance, by the way, should not be confused with acquired immunity. Acquired immunity is when a body gets rid of a pathogen and afterward maintains a state of high alert for that same microbe. It's why people don't normally get the same illness twice. Genetic resistance is something deeper and more mysterious. It is not acquired through exposure—you are born with it. Some people are born with greater resistance to certain diseases than others. The experience of our team in the valley of T1 is a textbook illustration. The doctors believe everyone on the expedition was bitten and exposed. Only half, however, came down with the disease. A few, like Juan Carlos, were able to fight it off without drugs. Others became seriously ill and some, even as I write this, are still struggling with the disease.

The genes that resist disease can only spread in a population through the pitiless lottery of natural selection. People with weaker immune systems (children especially) must die, while the stronger live, in order for a population to gain widespread resistance. A staggering amount of suffering and death over thousands of years went into building European (and African and Asian) resistance to crowd diseases. One biologist told me that what probably saved many indigenous

Indian cultures from complete extinction were the mass rapes of native women by European men; many of the babies from those rapes inherited European genetic resistance to disease. (The scientist, after telling me this horrifying theory, said, "For God's sake don't attach my name to that idea.")

In the New World, these many thousands of years of anguish and death were compressed into a window from 1494 to around 1650. The mass murder by pathogen happened in that one cruel century and a half, and it struck at precisely the worst moment, when the population of the New World had recently coalesced into big cities and reached the levels of density necessary for those epidemics to spread furiously. It was a perfect storm of infection.

We do not hear many of the voices of these victims. Only a handful of Native American eyewitness accounts of the cataclysm survive. One in particular stands out, a remarkable text called the *Annals of the Cakchiquels*, which describes an epidemic, probably smallpox or flu, that swept an area in Guatemala northwest of Mosquitia. This extraordinary manuscript, discovered in a remote convent in 1844, was written in a Mayan language called Cakchiquel by an Indian named Francisco Hernández Arana Xajilá. As a teenager, Arana Xajilá lived through the epidemic that destroyed his people.

It happened that during the twenty-fifth year [1520] the plague began, oh my sons! First they became ill of a cough, they suffered from nose-bleeds and illness of the bladder. It was truly terrible, the number of dead there were in that period. The prince Vakaki Ahmak died then. Little by little heavy shadows and black night enveloped our fathers and grandfathers and us also, oh my sons!... Great was the stench of the dead. After our fathers and grandfathers succumbed, half of the people fled to the fields. The dogs and the vultures devoured the bodies. The mortality was terrible... So it was that we became orphans, oh my sons! So we became when we were young. All of us were thus. We were born to die!

I would ask the reader to pause for a moment and ponder the statistics. Statistics are mere numbers; they need to be translated into human experience. What would a 90 percent mortality rate mean to the survivors and their society? The Black Death in Europe at its worst carried off 30 to 60 percent of the population. That was devastating enough. But the mortality rate wasn't high enough to destroy European civilization. A 90 percent mortality rate *is* high enough: It does not just kill people; it annihilates societies; it destroys languages, religions, histories, and cultures. It chokes off the transmission of knowledge from one generation to the next. The survivors are deprived of that vital human connection to their past; they are robbed of their stories, their music and dance, their spiritual practices and beliefs—they are stripped of their very identity.

The overall mortality rate in this wave of epidemics was indeed about 90 percent. To put that statistic into personal terms, make a list of the nineteen people closest to you: All but one will die. (This of course counts you also as a survivor.) Think what it would be like for you, as it was for the author of the Cakchiquel manuscript, to watch all these people die—your children, parents, grandparents, brothers and sisters, your friends, your community leaders and spiritual authorities. What would it do to you to see them perish in the most agonizing, humiliating, and terrifying ways possible? Imagine the breakdown of every pillar of your society; imagine the wasteland left behind, the towns and cities abandoned, the fields overgrown, the houses and streets strewn with the unburied dead; imagine the wealth rendered worthless, the stench, the flies, the scavenging animals, the loneliness and silence. Enlarge this scenario beyond towns and cities; enlarge it beyond kingdoms and civilizations; enlarge it beyond even continents—until it embraces half the planet. This inferno of contagion destroyed thousands of societies and millions of people, from Alaska to Tierra del Fuego, from California to New England, from the Amazon rainforest to the tundra of Hudson Bay. It is what destroyed T1, the City of the Jaguar, and the ancient people of Mosquitia.

This is the sort of thing that writers of postapocalyptic fiction put themselves to imagining, the stuff of our greatest news-cycle nightmares—but this very real Armageddon lies beyond reach of the darkest Hollywood movie fantasies. It was the greatest catastrophe ever to befall the human species.

Should sixteenth- and seventeenth-century Europeans be blamed? If one can blame the dead at all, they are answerable. The Spanish, English, and others contributed mightily to the death toll through cruelty, slavery, rape, abuse, starvation, war, and genocide. Europeans killed many native people directly without the assistance of disease. In some instances, they intentionally used disease as a biological weapon by, for example, giving Indians smallpox-infected blankets. And millions more Indians died of disease who might have survived, had European brutality not left them weakened and susceptible.

It is tempting to argue that if Europeans hadn't arrived in the New World, these deadly pandemics would not have happened. But the meeting of the Old World and the New was inevitable. If Europeans hadn't carried disease to the New World, Asians or Africans would have; or New World mariners would have eventually reached the Old. No matter what, disaster would have ensued. This was a monstrous geographic accident waiting to happen. This was a time bomb that had been ticking for fifteen thousand years—counting down to that fateful moment when a ship with sick passengers finally set sail across the wide ocean.

This is in no way an apologia for genocide. Still, the catastrophe was largely a natural event, a mindless biological imperative, a vast migration of dumb pathogens from one side of the planet to the other.

There is much irony in the story of our own disease. The strain of leishmaniasis that befell us is a rare example of a New World disease attacking (mostly) Old World people. While I obviously don't believe in curses, there is an inescapable sense of commination in the fact that a New World city destroyed by Old World disease wreaked havoc on its Old World rediscoverers with a New World disease. But this irony misses the modern lesson: This was a Third World disease attacking First World people. The world is now divided into Third and First, not Old and New. Pathogens once confined to the Third World are now making deadly inroads into the First. This is the future trajectory of disease on planet Earth. Pathogens have no boundaries; they are the ultimate travelers; they go wherever there's human fuel. We First Worlders have become far too complacent in the idea that disease, especially NTDs, can be quarantined to the Third World, and that we can live safely in our communities supposedly gated against pathogens, ignoring the suffering of the poor and sick in faraway lands.

The HIV medical crisis has already pushed leishmaniasis into new areas of the globe, especially southern Europe. HIV vastly increases the destructive power of leish and vice versa. A leishmania/HIV coinfection is a terrible combination, considered to be a "new" disease all of its own, almost impossible to treat and usually fatal. HIV and leishmania become locked in a vicious cycle of mutual reinforcement. If a person with leishmaniasis gets HIV, the leish accelerates the onset of full-blown AIDS while blocking the effectiveness of anti-HIV drugs. The reverse is also true: A person with HIV who lives where there's leishmaniasis is a hundred to a thousand times more likely than a healthy person to get the disease, due to a weakened immune system. People suffering from a leish/HIV coinfection are so teeming with the parasite that they become super-hosts, potent reservoirs accelerating its spread. And visceral leish, like HIV, has been shown to be transmitted by dirty needles among IV drug users; two studies in the late nineties found leish parasites on some 50 percent of dirty needles discarded by drug users in Madrid at two different locations several years apart. Sixty-eight percent of all visceral leishmaniasis cases in Spain were among IV drug users.

Leishmaniasis is a disease that thrives among the detritus of human misery and neglect: ramshackle housing, rats, overcrowded slums, garbage dumps, open sewers, feral dogs, malnutrition, addiction, lack of health care, poverty, war, and terrorism. Cutaneous leish is now running rampant in the areas of Iraq and Syria controlled by ISIS—so much so that families there are choosing to intentionally inoculate their young girls with leishmaniasis on a covered part of their body so that they will not get it on their faces, where it will leave a scar. (This type of leish is a mild variety that usually goes away on its own, leaving the person immune.)

Since 1993, the leishmania parasite has been spreading, not just because of HIV coinfection but also as people move from rural areas into cities. It is attacking people who venture into the rainforest for projects such as dam and road building, logging, and drug smuggling, as well as adventure tourism, photography, journalism, and archaeology. Strange tales abound. Almost everyone on a Costa Rican jungle yoga adventure was struck down by leish. A survival show contestant lost part of his ear to leish. A team of filmmakers shooting an adventure tourist video were stricken with leish.

Leish is now spreading in the United States. Over the course of the entire twentieth century, only twenty-nine cases of leish were reported in the United States, all of which occurred in Texas close to the Mexican border. But in 2004, a young man from a small town in southeastern Oklahoma, ten miles from the Arkansas border, visited his doctor complaining of a sore on his face that wouldn't heal. The doctor cut it off and sent it to a pathologist in Oklahoma City, who was stymied by what it might be and stored the frozen tissue. A year later, this same pathologist, by sheer chance, got another tissue sample from another patient living in the same small town. The pathologist immediately called the Oklahoma State Department of Health and reached Dr. Kristy Bradley, the state epidemiologist. She and her staff ordered the two tissue samples sent to the Centers for Disease Control in Atlanta. The diagnosis came back: cutaneous leishmaniasis, of a mild type that can usually be cured by surgically removing the ulcer. (Both patients were, in fact, cured this way.)

At the time that Dr. Bradley was investigating the disease in Oklahoma, an outbreak of cutaneous leishmaniasis occurred in northeastern Texas and in a string of suburbs in the Dallas–Fort Worth metro area; the dozen or so victims included a little girl who had lesions on her face, and in one case a cat and a human in the same household got the disease. Doctors in the health departments of Texas and Oklahoma joined forces to track the source. They were especially worried because none of the victims had traveled: They had gotten the disease in their own backyards.

Dr. Bradley led the investigation of the two cases in Oklahoma. She assembled a team that included an entomologist and a biologist. When the team visited the patients and surveyed their properties, they noted burrows of wood rats and populations of sand flies, which they concluded must have been the host and vector. The investigators trapped a number of rats and sand flies and tested them for leish. None had the disease, but by this time the mini-outbreak had died down.

I called Bradley and asked if the leish had really died out or if it was still around. "I'm sure it hasn't gone away," she said. "It's smoldering somewhere out there, quietly cycling in nature," waiting for the right combination of circumstances to break out again. When she and her team mapped leish cases in the United States over time, they revealed an inexorable spread northeastward across Texas and Oklahoma, aiming for other states in a northeasterly direction.

Why?

Her answer was immediate: "Climate change." As the United States becomes warmer, she said, the ranges of the sand fly and the wood rat are both creeping northward, the leish parasite tagging along. The sand fly genus known to spread this kind of leish has now been found in the United States five hundred miles northwest and two hundred miles northeast of its previously established range.

A recent study modeled the possible expansion of leishmaniasis across the United States over the next sixty-five years. Since it takes both vector and host to spread the disease, the scientists wanted to know where the sand fly/wood rat combination would migrate together. They looked at two future climate scenarios, best case and worst case. For each case, they extrapolated out to the years 2020, 2050, and 2080. Even under the best-case climate assumptions, they discovered that global warming would push leishmaniasis across the entire United States into southeastern Canada by 2080. Hundreds of millions of Americans could be exposed—and this is just by wood rats. Since many other species of mammals can host the leish parasite—including cats and dogs—we know the potential problem is far greater than what was described by this study.* A similar spread of the disease is expected in Europe and Asia.

---

* Recently there have been serious outbreaks of deadly visceral leishmaniasis in dog kennels across the United States, with the very real possibility of dog-to-human transmission.

It seems that leishmaniasis, a disease that has troubled the human race since time immemorial, has in the twenty-first century come into its own. Anthony Fauci, director of the National Institute of Allergy and Infectious Diseases at the NIH, told our team bluntly that, by going into the jungle and getting leishmaniasis, "You got a really cold jolt of what it's like for the bottom billion people on earth." We were, he said, confronted in a very dramatic way with what many people have to live with their entire lives. If there's a silver lining to our ordeal, he told us, "it's that you'll now be telling your story, calling attention to what is a very prevalent, very serious disease."

If leish continues to spread as predicted in the United States, by the end of the century it may no longer be confined to the "bottom billion" in faraway lands. It will be in our own backyards.

Global warming has opened the southern door of the United States not just to leish but to many other diseases. The big ones now entering our country include Zika, West Nile virus, chikungunya, and dengue fever. Even diseases like cholera, Ebola, Lyme, babesiosis, and bubonic plague will potentially infect more people as global warming accelerates.

Modern travel has given infectious disease new ways to spread. Bubonic plague in the fourteenth century traveled from Central Asia to the Levant and

Europe by horse, camel, and boat; the Zika virus in the twenty-first century jumped from Yap Island in Micronesia to French Polynesia, Brazil, the Caribbean, and Central America by 2015, all by plane. In the summer of 2016, Zika arrived in Miami, again on an airplane. The 2009 outbreak of deadly H1N1 swine flu in Mexico hitched rides on planes to strike as far away as Japan, New Zealand, Egypt, Canada, and Iceland. As Richard Preston noted in his terrifying book *The Hot Zone*, "A hot virus from the rain forest lives within a twenty-four-hour plane flight from every city on earth."

The world's last great pandemic was the Spanish flu outbreak in 1918 that killed a hundred million people—about 5 percent of the world's population. If a pandemic like that were to happen again, it would spread faster and might be impossible to contain. According to the Bill & Melinda Gates Foundation, in such a pandemic "the death toll could reach 360 million"—even with the full deployment of vaccines and powerful modern drugs. The Gates Foundation estimated that the pandemic would also devastate the world financially, precipitating a three-trillion-dollar economic collapse. This is not scaremongering: Most epidemiologists believe such a pandemic will eventually happen.

\* \* \*

Archaeology contains many cautionary tales for us to ponder in the twenty-first century, not just about disease but also about human success and failure. It teaches us lessons in environmental degradation, income inequality, war, violence, class division, exploitation, social upheaval, and religious fanaticism. But archaeology also teaches us how cultures have thrived and endured, overcoming the challenges of the environment and the darker side of human nature. It shows us how people adapted, lived their lives, and found fulfillment and meaning under fantastically diverse conditions. It tracks both the failures and the successes. It tells us how cultures faced difficulty and challenge, sometimes in successful ways and sometimes in ways that, while successful at first, sowed the seeds of eventual collapse. The Maya created a vibrant and brilliant society that, in the end, failed to adjust to a changing environment and the needs of its people; so did the Roman Empire and the ancient Khmer, to pluck civilizations randomly out of the hat. But the people of the City of the Jaguar *did* adapt to the challenges of the rainforest, and they continued to thrive in one of the harshest environments on the planet, transforming it into a beautiful garden—until their abrupt demise.

I can recall the very moment when we stumbled over the cache and I first saw that jaguar head coming out of the ground. Gleaming with rain, it rose up snarling, as if struggling to escape the earth. It was an image that spoke directly to me across the centuries—forging an immediate, emotive connection to these vanished people. What had been theoretical for me became real: This spirited image had been created by people who were confident, accomplished, and formidable. Standing in the gloom among the ancient mounds, I could almost feel the presence of the invisible dead. At its zenith, the people of the city of T1, the City of the Jaguar, must have felt nearly invulnerable in their valley redoubt ringed by mountains. What power could overthrow their mighty gods and potent rituals? But the unseen invader ghosted in and visited upon them a destruction that was as impossible to resist as it was to predict. Sometimes, a society can see its end approaching from afar and still not be able to adapt, like the Maya; at other times, the curtain drops without warning and the show is over.

No civilization has survived forever. All move toward dissolution, one after the other, like waves of the sea falling upon the shore. None, including ours, is exempt from the universal fate.

# Acknowledgments

In addition to the people featured in this book, I would like to thank many others not mentioned in the book who made this project possible.

I would like to express my deep appreciation for the cooperation, permission, and support of the Government of Honduras: in particular, President Porfirio Lobo Sosa; President Juan Orlando Hernández Alvarado; Secretary of the Interior and Population Áfrico Madrid Hart; Minister of Science and Technology Ramón Espinoza; Virgilio Paredes Trapero, Director of the Honduran Institute for Anthropology and History (IHAH); Oscar Neil Cruz, Chief of the Archaeology Division of IHAH; and archaeologists Ranferi Juárez Silva, Norman Martínez, and Santiago Escobar. I am grateful to Minister of Defense Samuel Reyes and the Armed Forces of Honduras under the command of Gen. Fredy Santiago Díaz Zelaya; Gen. Carlos Roberto Puerto; Lt. Col. Willy Joel Oseguera and the soldiers of TESON, Honduran Special Forces.

I also wish to thank my many fine editors: Millicent

Bennett and Melanie Gold at Grand Central Publishing; Alan Burdick and Dorothy Wickenden at the *New Yorker*; Jamie Shreeve and Susan Goldberg at *National Geographic*; and Jaime Levine. Special thanks also to Eric Simonoff, Raffaella De Angelis, and Alicia Gordon at William Morris Endeavor; Jeremy Sabloff, Santa Fe Institute; Michael Brown, School for Advanced Research; David Hurst Thomas, American Museum of Natural History; William Fash, Harvard University; the late Evon Z. Vogt, Harvard University; George Rossman, Caltech; Ann Ramenofsky, University of New Mexico; Timothy D. Maxwell, New Mexico Office of Archaeological Studies; Fredrik Hiebert, National Geographic Society; and Robert Crippen, NASA Jet Propulsion Laboratory.

I am as always and forever grateful to my friends and colleagues at Hachette Book Group: Michael Pietsch, Jamie Raab, Caitlin Mulrooney-Lyski, Brian McLendon, Deb Futter, Andrew Duncan, Beth de Guzman, Oscar Stern, Shelby Howick, Flamur Tonuzi, and Jessica Pierce. Additional sincere thanks to Barbara Peters, Poisoned Pen Bookstore; Devereux Chatillon; Garry Spire; Maggie Begley; Wendi Weger; Myles Elsing; Roberto Ysais; and Karen Copeland, who keeps it all going. And a very special thanks to my wife, Christine, and Selene, Josh, Aletheia, and Isaac, and my mother, Doffy.

Finally, I would like to express my great appreciation to the National Institutes of Health, which, through its extraordinarily valuable and effective medical research programs, has lifted the burden of sickness and misery from millions of people in America and across the world. I would note that in the past decade, because of ill-advised Congressional budget-cutting, the NIH has seen its financing slashed by over 20 percent, which has compromised and even shut down some of its most important research programs into health issues that affect all of us: infectious disease, cancer, diabetes, stroke, heart disease, arthritis, mental illness, addiction, and so much more. There may be no better use of taxpayer dollars than in funding the NIH; it is a shining example of something our government does extremely well, which because of financial and profit requirements cannot be accomplished by the private sector.

# Sources and Bibliography

The conversations reported in this book were either recorded on tape or written down at the time they occurred. The events were chronicled in real time, in contemporary notes or on video. No details, events, discoveries, or conversations have been reconstructed after the fact or imagined. To avoid confusion and unnecessary complexity, some quotations from interviews conducted on separate occasions have been combined in the same conversation.

Sources are listed in the approximate order they appear in each chapter.

Chapters with no sources listed are based on the author's personal experience only.

## Chapter 2: Somewhere in the Americas

Author interviews and correspondence with Ron Blom and Bob Crippen, Jet Propulsion Laboratory, August and September 1997.

Author interview with David Stuart, Harvard University, 1997.

Author interview with Gordon Willey, Harvard University, 1997.

Author interviews and correspondence with Steve Elkins, 1997.

### Chapter 3: The Devil Had Killed Him

*The Fifth Letter of Hernan Cortes to the Emperor Charles V*, translated from the original Spanish by Don Pascual de Gayangos. Originally published by the Hakluyt Society. New York: Lenox Hill Publishers (Burt Franklin), reprinted 1970. Retrieved from the website of the Library of the University of California.

Christopher Begley and Ellen Cox, "Reading and Writing the White City Legend: Allegories Past and Future." *Southwest Philosophy Review*, Vol. 23, No. 1, January 2007.

John L. Stephens, *Incidents of Travel in Central America, Chiapas and Yucatan*, Vols. 1 and 2. New York: Dover Publications, 1969.

Eduard Conzemius, "Los Indios Payas de Honduras: Estudio Geográfico, Histórico, Etnográfico y Lingüístico," *Journal de la Société des Américanistes*, Vol. 19, 1927. Retrieved from persee.fr.

William Duncan Strong, "1936 Strong Honduras Expedition," Vols. 1 and 2. Washington, DC: Smithsonian Institution. Unpublished journals.

William Duncan Strong, "Honduras Expedition Journal 1933." Washington, DC: Smithsonian Institution. Unpublished journal.

Ralph Solecki and Charles Wagley, "William Duncan Strong, 1899–1962." *American Anthropologist*, Vol. 65, No. 5, 1963. Retrieved pdf from Wiley Online Library.

### Chapter 4: A Land of Cruel Jungles

Christopher S. Stewart, *Jungleland*. New York: Harper-Collins, 2013 (e-book edition).

Lawrence M. Small, "A Passionate Collector." Washington, DC: *Smithsonian* magazine, November 2000.

"George Heye Dies; Museum Founder." *New York Times*, January 21, 1957.

Leona Raphael, "Explorer Seeks Fabled Lost City; Spurns Weaker Sex Companionship." *Calgary Daily Herald*, June 16, 1934.

"Frederick Mitchell-Hedges Dies; British Explorer and Author, 76." *New York Times*, June 13, 1959.

J. Eric S. Thompson, *Maya Archaeologist*. London: Robert Hale, 1963.

"Seek Cradle of Race in American Jungle." *New York Times*, January 24, 1931.

"Hold-Up of Explorer in England Proves Hoax." *New York Times*, January 17, 1927.

## Chapter 5: One of the Few Remaining Mysteries

" 'City of Monkey God' Is Believed Located." *New York Times*, July 12, 1940.

"Honduran Jungles Yield Indian Data." *New York Times*, August 2, 1940.

"TV Producer a Suicide." *New York Times*, June 28, 1954.

Christopher S. Stewart, *Jungleland*, op. cit.

National Museum of the American Indian, Smithsonian Institution. Fifty-two unpublished accession catalog cards and photographs from the Theodore Morde Third Honduran Expedition.

Theodore Morde, "In the Lost City of Ancient America's Monkey God." *Milwaukee Sentinel*, September 22, 1940.

"Seek Long Lost City of Monkey God." *Sunday Morning Star*, United Press, April 7, 1940.

"Theodore Ambrose Morde, 1911–1954." Unpublished, bound volume of original documents, letters, articles, photographs, and typescripts by or relating to Theodore Morde. In the possession of the Morde family.

Theodore Morde and Lawrence Brown, unpublished journals of the Third Honduran Expedition (3 vols.), 1940. In the possession of the Morde family.

E-mail from Christopher Begley, November 4, 2015, confirming Lancetillal as Morde's presumed city.

Correspondence with Derek Parent, 2015, 2016.

## Chapter 6: The Heart of Darkness

Author interviews and correspondence with Steve Elkins, 1997, 2010–2016.

Author interviews with Bruce Heinicke, 2012.

Steve Elkins interview with George Hasemann, 1994.

Author correspondence with the University of Pennsylvania and Penn State, 2015, 2016.

Bhupendra Jasani, "Remote Monitoring from Space: The Resolution Revolution." In *Verification Yearbook, 2000*. London: Vertic, 2000. Retrieved from www.vertic.org/media/Archived_Publications/Yearbooks/2000/VY00_Jasani.pdf.

Steve Elkins interview with Sam Glassmire, 1997.

Sam Glassmire, *The Bush*. Privately published book, 2002.

Sam Glassmire, "He Found a Lost City." *Denver Post Sunday Empire Magazine*, November 27 and December 4, 1960.

Sam Glassmire, hand-drawn map, dated February 2, 1960.

"Obituary for Glassmire." *Albuquerque Journal*, December 1, 2002.

Thomas H. Maugh II, "Ubar, Fabled Lost City, Found by L.A. Team." *Los Angeles Times*, February 5, 1992.

### *Chapter 7: The Fish That Swallowed the Whale*

Philip Sherwell, "Welcome to Honduras, the Most Dangerous Country on the Planet." *Telegraph*, November 16, 2013.

Rich Cohen, *The Fish That Ate the Whale*, New York: Farrar, Straus and Giroux, 2012.

Boston Fruit Company, Boston Fruit Company Records, 1891–1901. Baker Library, Harvard Business School. Retrieved from Online Archival Search Information System.

United Fruit Company, "Andrew W. Preston Biography." Retrieved from unitedfruit.org.

William Finnegan, "An Old-Fashioned Coup." *New Yorker*, November 30, 2009.

### *Chapter 8: Lasers in the Jungle*

"The Loot of Lima Treasure Story." Retrieved from aqvisions.com.

Arlen F. Chase, Diane Z. Chase, and John F. Weishampel, "Lasers in the Jungle." *Archaeology*, Vol. 63, No. 4, July/August 2010.

Arlen F. Chase et al., "Geospatial Revolution and Remote Sensing LiDAR in Mesoamerican Archaeology." *Proceedings of the National Academy of Sciences*, Vol. 109, No. 32, June 25, 2012. Retrieved from pnas.org.

Arlen F. Chase et al., "Airborne LiDAR, Archaeology, and the Ancient Maya Landscape at Caracol, Belize." *Journal of Archaeological Science*, Vol. 38, No. 2, February 2011.

Juan Carlos Fernández Díaz, "Lifting the Canopy Veil." *Imaging Notes*, Vol. 26, No. 2, Spring 2011.

### Chapter 9: Something That Nobody Had Done

Author interviews and correspondence with Bruce Heinicke, 2012, 2013.
Author interview with Mabel Heinicke, 2013.
Author interview with Ramesh Shrestha, 2013.
Author interview with William Carter, 2013.
Author interviews with Michael Sartori, 2012, 2013.
Author interviews with Steve Elkins, 2012–2016.
Author interview with President Porfirio Lobo and Minister Áfrico Madrid, 2013.

### Chapter 10: The Most Dangerous Place on the Planet

Author interviews with Bill Benenson, 2012, 2013, 2016.
Author interviews with Juan Carlos Fernández, 2012, 2013, 2016.
Author interview with Tom Weinberg, 2016.
Author interviews and correspondence with Bruce Heinicke, 2012, 2013.

## Chapter 11: Uncharted Territory

Author interviews with Chuck Gross, 2012, 2013.

Author interviews with Juan Carlos Fernández, 2012, 2015.

Author interview with Ramesh Shrestha, 2013.

Author interview with William Carter, 2013.

Author interviews with Michael Sartori, 2012, 2013.

Ramesh L. Shrestha and William E. Carter, "In Search of the 'Lost City' by Airborne Laser Swath Mapping in Honduras, Final Report." Houston: GSE Research Center, University of Houston, July 18, 2012. (Unpublished report.)


## Chapter 12: No Coincidences

Author interview with África Madrid, 2013.

"The Government of Honduras and UTL Scientific, LLC Announce Completion of First-Ever LiDAR Imaging Survey of La Mosquitia Region of Honduras." Press release, UTL Scientific, May 15, 2012.

"UH Research Team Uses Airborne LiDAR to Unveil Possible Honduran Archaeological Ruins." Press release, University of Houston, June 5, 2012.

Author interview with Rosemary Joyce, 2012.

"Mythical Ciudad Blanca," May 20, 2012. Retrieved from hondurasculturepolitics.blogspot.com. One of the unnamed authors of this blog post is Rosemary Joyce.

Rosemary Joyce, "Good Science, Big Hype, Bad Archaeology," June 7, 2012. Retrieved from the Berkeley Blog, blogs.berkeley.edu.

Author interviews with Chris Fisher, 2013, 2015, 2016.

Author interview with Alicia González, 2013.

### Chapter 19: Controversy

Interview with Trond Larsen, 2016.

Letter from Harrison Ford to President Hernández, April 22, 2016.

"Letter from International Scholars: Archaeological Finds in Honduras." Posted March 6, 2015. Retrieved from realhonduranarchaeology.wordpress.com.

"Who Signed the Letter from International Scholars?" Retrieved from realhonduranarchaeology.wordpress.com.

The list of signatories is: Christopher Begley, PhD, Transylvania University; Eva Martinez, PhD, Universidad Nacional Autónoma de Honduras; Rosemary Joyce, PhD, University of California–Berkeley; John Hoopes, PhD, University of Kansas; Warwick Bray, PhD, Emeritus Professor of Latin American Archaeology, University College London; Mark Bonta, PhD, Pennsylvania State University; Julia

Hendon, PhD, Gettysburg College; Pastor Gomez, PhD, Honduran archaeologist and historian; Alexander Geurds, PhD, University of Leiden and University of Colorado–Boulder; Carmen Julia Fajardo, Licda, Universidad Nacional Autónoma de Honduras; Gloria Lara Pinto, PhD, Universidad Nacional autónoma de honduras; Jorge G. Marcos, PhD, Centro de Estudios Arqueológicos y Antropológicos, Escuela Superior Politécnica del Litoral, Guayaquil, Ecuador; Geoff McCafferty, PhD, University of Calgary; Adam Benfer, MA, University of Calgary, PhD candidate; Ricardo Agurcia, MA, Asociación Copán; Karen Holmberg, PhD, New York University; Roberto Herrera, MA, Hunter College, City University of New York, PhD candidate, University of New Mexico; Christopher Fung, PhD, University of Massachusetts–Boston; Brent Metz, PhD, University of Kansas; Jeb Card, PhD, Miami University; Ronald Webb, PhD, Temple University; Karen O'Day, PhD, University of Wisconsin–Eau Claire; Antoinette Egitto, PhD, Haskell Indian Nations University; Grant Berning, BA, University of Kansas, MA candidate; Roos Vlaskamp, MA, Leiden University, PhD candidate; Silvia Gonzalez, MA, Universidad Nacional Autónoma de Honduras.

Charles C. Poling, "A Lost City Found?" *American Archaeology*, Vol. 19, No. 2, Summer 2015. (Some of the quoted passages came from correspondence with Poling and the editors of *American Archaeology* that were not published in the final article.)

Becca Clemens, "Transy Professor Gets Grant to Search for 'Lost City' in Honduras." *Lexington Herald Leader*, July 5, 2011. Retrieved from www.kentucky.com/news/local/counties/fayette -county/article44114496.html.

Chris Kenning, "Kentucky Professor a Real-Life Indiana Jones." *Louisville Courier-Journal*, June 10, 2016.

Sarah Larimer, "The Very Real Search for an Ancient City that Probably Doesn't Exist." *Washington Post*, January 11, 2016.

Chris Begley, "The Pech and Archaeology in the Mosquitia." Posted March 15, 2015. Retrieved from realhonduranarchaeology.wordpress.com.

Alan Yuhas, "Archaeologists Condemn National Geographic over Claims of Honduran 'Lost Cities.'" *Guardian*, March 11, 2015.

"Media FAQ: Under the LiDAR Expedition." February 2015. Retrieved from resilientworld.com.

Author interviews with Virgilio Paredes, 2015, 2016.

## Chapter 20: The Cave of the Glowing Skulls

Timothy Berg, "Digging 3,000 Years into the Past." Retrieved from old.planeta.com.

Author interview with James Brady, 2015.

James E. Brady, George Hasemann, and John H. Fogarty, "Buried Secrets, Luminous Find." *Americas*, Vol. 47, No. 4, July–August 1955.

John Noble Wilford, "Age of Burials In Honduras Stuns Scholars." *New York Times*, January 26, 1995.

Joel Skidmore, "Copan's Founder." Retrieved from mesoweb.com.

William L. Fash, *Scribes, Warriors and Kings: The City of Copán and the Ancient Maya*. New York: Thames & Hudson, 1991.

Ellen E. Bell, Marcello A. Canuto, and Robert J. Sharer, eds., *Understanding Early Classic Copan*. Philadelphia: University of Pennsylvania Museum of Archaeology and Anthropology, 2004.

B. L. Turner and Jeremy A. Sabloff, "Classic Period Collapse of the Central Maya Lowlands: Insights about Human–Environment Relationships for Sustainability." *PNAS*, Vol. 109, No. 35, August 2012. Retrieved from pnas.org/content/109/35/13908.

Marilyn A. Masson, "Maya Collapse Cycles," *PNAS*, Vol. 109, No. 45, November 2012. Retrieved from pnas.org/content/109/45/18237.

Simon Martin and Nikolai Grube, *Chronicle of the Maya Kings and Queens*, second edition. London: Thames & Hudson, 2008.

Zach Zorich, "The Man under the Jaguar Mountain." *Archaeology*, Vol. 62, No. 5, September/October 2009.

David Stuart, "The Arrival of Strangers." Extract of a paper presented at Princeton University, October 1996, revised February 1998. Retrieved from mesoweb.com.

Fray Diego Durán, *Book of the Gods and Rites and the Ancient Calendar*, translated and edited by Fernando Horcasitas and Doris Heyden. Norman, OK: University of Oklahoma Press, 1975.

M.R., "Palace Coop." *Economist*, March 14, 2014.

Jared Diamond, *Collapse*. New York: Penguin, 2011 (e-book edition).

Evon Z. Vogt, *Fieldwork among the Maya*. Albuquerque: University of New Mexico Press, 1994.

Author interview with John Hoopes, 2016.

Author interviews with Christopher Begley, 2012, 2015, 2016.

Christopher Taylor Begley, "Elite Power Strategies and External Connections in Ancient Eastern Honduras." Unpublished dissertation, University of Chicago, 1999.

Oscar Neil Cruz, *Informe Exploración en la Mosquitia*. Tegucigalpa: IHAH Archives, February 2015. Unpublished report.

Christopher T. Fisher et al., "Identifying Ancient Settlement Patterns through LiDAR in the Mosquitia

Region of Honduras." *PLOS/one*, Vol 11, No. 8, August 2016. Retrieved from journals.plos.org/plosone/article?id=10.1371%2Fjournal.pone.0159890.

Dealbook, "Blankfein Says He's Just Doing 'God's Work.'" *New York Times*, November 9, 2009.

David Grann, *The Lost City of Z*. New York: Doubleday, 2009.

Author interviews with Chris Fisher, 2015, 2016.

Author interview with Oscar Neil Cruz, 2015.

### Chapter 21: The Symbol of Death

George R. Rossman, "Studies on Rocks from the UTL Archeology Site in Honduras." Unpublished report, December 19, 2015.

Author interview with Chris Fisher, 2016.

Author interview with John Hoopes, 2016.

Author correspondence with Rosemary Joyce, 2016.

Anne Chapman, *Masters of Animals: Oral Traditions of the Tolupan Indians, Honduras*. Philadelphia: Gordon and Breach, 1992.

David E. Stuart, *Anasazi America: Seventeen Centuries on the Road from Center Place*. Albuquerque: University of New Mexico Press, 2014.

### Chapter 22: They Came to Wither the Flowers

Noble David Cook, *Born to Die: Disease and New*

*World Conquest, 1492–1650*. Cambridge, UK: Cambridge University Press, 1998.

Bartolomé de las Casas, *A Brief Account of the Destruction of the Indies*. London: Printed for R. Hewson at the Crown in Cornhill, 1689. Retrieved from Project Gutenberg. Also sourced is the original Spanish-language version, retrieved from Project Gutenberg.

William M. Denevan, ed., *The Native Population of the Americas in 1492*, second edition. Madison, WI: University of Wisconsin Press, 1992.

David Henige, *Numbers from Nowhere: The American Indian Contact Population Debate*. Norman, OK: University of Oklahoma Press, 1998.

Alfred W. Crosby Jr., *The Columbian Exchange: Biological and Cultural Consequences of 1492*, 30th anniversary edition. Westport, CT: Praeger Publishers, 2003.

Richard Preston, *The Demon in the Freezer: A True Story*. New York: Random House, 2002.

Hugh Thomas, *Conquest: Montezuma, Cortés, and the Fall of Old Mexico*. New York: Simon & Schuster, 1994.

Linda Newson, *The Cost of Conquest: Indian Decline in Honduras under the Spanish Rule*. Dellplain Latin American Studies No. 20. Boulder, CO: Westview Press, 1986.

Ann F. Ramenofsky, *Vectors of Death: The Archaeology of European Contact.* Albuquerque: University of New Mexico Press, 1988.

## Chapter 23: White Leprosy

G. Poinar Jr. and R. Poinar, "Evidence of Vector-Borne Disease of Early Cretaceous Reptiles." *Vector Borne Zoonotic Disease*, Vol. 4, No. 4, Winter 2004. Retrieved from ncbi.nlm.nih.gov/pubmed/15682513.

F. F. Tuon, V. A. Neto, and V. S. Amato, "Leishmania: Origin, Evolution and Future since the Precambrian." *FEMS Immunology and Medical Microbiology*, Vol. 54, No. 2, November 2008. Retrieved from ncbi.nlm.nih.gov/pubmed/18631183.

F. E. G. Cox, ed., *The Wellcome Trust Illustrated History of Tropical Diseases.* London: Trustees of the Wellcome Trust, 1996.

Centers for Disease Control and Prevention, "Leishmaniasis." Retrieved from cdc.gov.

Elizabeth Martinson et al., "Pathoecology of Chiribaya Parasitism." *Memórias do Instituto Oswaldo Cruz*, Vol. 98. Rio de Janeiro, January 2003. Retrieved from scielo.br.

Maria Antonietta Costa et al., "Ancient Leishmaniasis in a Highland Desert of Northern Chile." *PLOS/one*, Vol. 4, No. 9, September 2009. Retrieved from journals.plos.org.

Alun Salt, "Ancient Skulls Haunted by Their Past." September 28, 2009. Retrieved from alunsalt.com.

Author interview with James Kus, 2016.

Daniel W. Gade, *Nature and Culture in the Andes.* Madison: University of Wisconsin Press, 1999.

*Obituary Notices of Fellows Deceased*, Proceedings of the Royal Society of London, Series B, Containing Papers of a Biological Character, Vol. 102, No. 720, April 2, 1928. (Biography of William Leishman.)

## Chapter 24: The National Institutes of Health

Author interviews with Dr. Theodore Nash, 2015, 2016.

Author interview with Dr. Elise O'Connell, 2016.

Author interviews with Dave Yoder, 2015, 2016.

## Chapter 25: An Isolated Species

Author interviews with Dr. David Sacks, 2015.

Benenson Productions, taped interview with Dr. David Sacks, 2015.

Author interview with Dr. Michael Grigg, 2016.

## Chapter 26: La Ciudad del Jaguar

Author interview and correspondence with Juan Carlos Fernández, 2016.

Gabriela Gorbea, "Looters, Tourism, and Racism: Controversy Surrounds 'Discovery' of Lost City in

Honduras." Vice.com, March 31, 2016. Retrieved fromnews.vice.com/article/honduras-rainforest-con troversy-white-city-lost-civilization.

MASTA, "Comunicado Publico," retrieved from www .mastamiskitu.org/files/COMUNICADO _PUEBLO_MISKITU-CASO_CIUDAD _BLANCA.pdf. (Translation by author.)

Communication with John Hoopes, 2016.

Author interview with President Juan Orlando Hernández, 2016.

## Chapter 27: We Became Orphans

Jared Diamond, *Guns, Germs, and Steel: The Fates of Human Societies.* New York: W. W. Norton, 1999 (e-book edition).

Adrián Recinos and Delia Goetz, translators. *The Annals of the Cakchiquels.* Norman, OK: University of Oklahoma Press, 1953.

R. Molina, L. Gradoni, and J. Alvar, "HIV and the Transmission of Leishmania." *Annals of Tropical Medicine and Parasitology*, Vol. 97, Supp. 1, May 2003. Retrieved from www.who.int/leishmaniasis/ burden/hiv_coinfection/ATMP3.pdf.

World Health Organization, "Leishmaniasis and HIV Coinfection." Retrieved from the World Health Organization website, who.int.

Author interview with Dr. Kristy Bradley, 2016.

Carmen F. Clarke et al., "Emergence of Autochthonous Cutaneous Leishmaniasis in Northeastern Texas and Southeastern Oklahoma." *American Journal of Tropical Medicine and Hygiene*, Vol. 88, No. 1, January 2013. Retrieved from ncbi.nlm.nih.gov/pmc/articles/PMC3541728/.

Christine A. Petersen and Stephen C. Barr, "Canine Leishmaniasis in North America: Emerging or Newly Recognized?" *Veterinary Clinics of North America: Small Animal Practice*, Vol. 39, No. 6, November 2009. Retrieved from ncbi.nlm.nih.gov/pmc/articles/PMC2824922/.

Bill & Melinda Gates Foundation, "Preparing for Pandemics." July 10, 2016. Retrieved from paidpost.nytimes.com/gates-foundation/preparing-for-pandemics.html.

Camila González et al. "Climate Change and Risk of Leishmaniasis in North America: Predictions from Ecological Niche Models of Vector and Reservoir Hosts." *PLOS/Neglected Tropical Diseases*, Vol. 4, No. 1, January 2010. Retrieved from ncbi.nlm.nih.gov/pmc/articles/PMC2799657/.

Benenson Productions, taped interview with Dr. Anthony Fauci, 2015.

# About the Author

DOUGLAS PRESTON worked as a writer and editor for the American Museum of Natural History and taught writing at Princeton University. He has written for the *New Yorker, Natural History, National Geographic, Harper's, Smithsonian*, and the *Atlantic*. The author of several acclaimed nonfiction books—including *Cities of Gold* and *The Monster of Florence*—Preston is also the coauthor with Lincoln Child of the bestselling series of novels featuring FBI agent Pendergast.

# Photo Credits

All photos used with permission.

**page 10** (top and bottom) Photographs by Douglas Preston

**page 11** (top and bottom) Photographs by Douglas Preston

**page 12** (top) UTL,LLC/BENENSON PRODUCTIONS, frame grab of video shot by Lucian Read; (bottom) Photograph by Dave Yoder/National Geographic Magazine

**page 13** (top and bottom) Photographs by Douglas Preston

**page 14** (top) Photograph by Douglas Preston; (bottom) Photograph by Dave Yoder/National Geographic Magazine

**page 15** (top and bottom) Photographs by Dave Yoder/National Geographic Magazine

**page 16** (top) Photograph by Dave Yoder/National Geographic Magazine; (bottom) Photograph by Douglas Preston

Sketch Map
of
Honduras
Expedition
(Jan.– July, 1933.)

Guatemala

Brit. Honduras

Quirigua

S Hov

Guatemala ⊙ City

Copan

Salvador

Tegue

Pacific
Ocean

Gulf of Fouseca